Experiences with Stopping Inflation

Experiences
with
Stopping Inflation

Leland B. Yeager
and associates

American Enterprise Institute for Public Policy Research
Washington and London

Leland B. Yeager is Paul Goodloe McIntire Professor of Economics at the University of Virginia.

Professor Yeager and his associates undertook this study while he was director of the James Madison Center of the American Enterprise Institute for Public Policy Research in Charlottesville, Virginia. The James Madison Center was established as a research office of AEI by the late Professor G. Warren Nutter, and it carried on for one year after his death in January 1979. Marie-Christine MacAndrew and Anne Hobbs assisted with the study. Janneke van Beusekom, Matthew Cushing, Kelfala Kallon, and Charles Perdue may be regarded as coauthors.

Library of Congress Cataloging in Publication Data

Yeager, Leland B.
  Experiences with stopping inflation.

  (AEI studies ; 320)
  1. Inflation (Finance)—History.   I. Title.
II. Series.
HG229.Y4   332.4'1   81-4643
ISBN 0-8447-3438-1   AACR2
ISBN 0-8442-3439-X (pbk.)

AEI Studies 320

Printed in the United States of America

Contents

1
Questions and Concepts

The James Madison Center was assigned the task of surveying historical episodes in which inflation was stopped or almost stopped. (Some efforts that ultimately failed also drew our attention.) For each successful episode, we ask how the trick was accomplished. What had been the nature and origin of the inflation? How severe were the side effects, in the form of recession and unemployment, of taking the cure? What lessons emerge from comparing the episodes? For example, how does the degree of credibility of a switch to a policy of stabilization affect the severity of the side effects?

Our method was to cast our net widely, dipping into the vast historical material already available rather than intensively working over the statistics of only one or a few episodes. We were especially anxious to find a clear-cut example of stabilization after the sort of inflation that the United States is experiencing, inflation long persisting (and fluctuating) at rates intermediate between a creep and a gallop. Ideally, we sought a stabilization achieved despite the lack of special favorable conditions that the United States also lacks. After several months of search, we cannot be positive that no such cases exist in the historical record, but any that may exist must be few and obscure. The elusiveness of such a case is significant. The inflation that the United States is suffering does seem to be of just the kind that is hardest to stop. Both mild, brief inflations and extreme inflations present an easier challenge than an entrenched intermediate inflation.

Reasons for this judgment will emerge in the pages that follow. These reasons involve the theoretical concepts that we needed, along with some hypotheses or questions, to give direction to our search for facts and figures and to help in organizing our findings. This first section of our study lays out these strands of theory. They include, for example, the concept of the momentum of inflation (related to the popular notion of a "basic" or "underlying" rate of inflation), as well as consideration of how a slowdown in the growth of the money supply and nominal spending or nominal income has its impact split between slowdowns in real economic activity and in the rise of prices. Our presentation of these ideas is conditioned partly by the historical experiences summarized in the sections that follow; the ideas are not pure preconceptions.

Costs of Inflation

Our study was premised on the idea that inflation is harmful and that stopping it is desirable (though not at any cost whatsoever). Only a sketchy reminder of the costs of inflation is necessary here. These costs include those of otherwise unnecessary efforts to economize on holding cash balances. If one takes seriously the idea that the business cash balances are a factor of production, then one should be concerned that their holders' reactions to inflation reduce the amount of this factor in real terms. Both capital and labor are deprived of part of this complementary factor and suffer productivity losses.[1]

Similar points hold for trade credit. A business firm typically is holding some non-interest-bearing claims on its customers as part of a regular customer-supplier relation that both find advantageous. When money rates of interest come to reflect substantial rates of inflation, the loss of interest involved in holding trade debt, as in holding money, becomes more serious. It becomes worthwhile to take more trouble in collecting debts promptly, exerting otherwise unadvisable pressure on debtors. Such efforts consume labor and other resources. Since debtors have similar incentives to delay payment, the loss can be considerable.[2]

Several other costs of inflations, although almost impossible to quantify, are nevertheless real. Business and personal habits (like the allocation of a family's housekeeping money) have been on the assumption of stable prices and are not easily broken; yet leaving them unbroken in the face of severe inflation creates obvious distortions. Accounting and tax systems, and even the general legal system, have also been based on the assumption of stable money. Rapid change in

---

[1] Robert Mundell, "Comment," in Emil Claassen and Pascal Salin, eds., *Stabilization Policies in Interdependent Economies* (New York: American Elsevier, 1972), p. 62. On the notion of cash balances as a factor of production, also see Reuben Kessel and Armen A. Alchian, "Effects of Inflation," *Journal of Political Economy*, vol. 70 (December 1962), pp. 521–537.

[2] John Hicks, "Expected Inflation," in his *Economic Perspective: Further Essays on Money and Growth* (Oxford: Clarendon Press, 1977), pp. 116–117 (an extract from an article in *Three Banks Review*, September 1970).

money's value twists them out of shape. Legislation may put these things right again (for a time) but only by reopening closed issues and consuming time and energy in political discussions. Notions of fairness are also involved. Prices and wages are "made" in most markets, not just impersonally "determined" by supply and demand. It helps set prices and wages in a way that seems fair to the parties concerned if one can appeal to precedent, presuming that what was acceptable before will be acceptable again. A rapidly changing price level invalidates this approach.

It is sometimes said that mild inflation may facilitate changing relative wage rates as efficiency may require. This advantage, if real at all, can be significant only at low rates of inflation, for it itself depends on some confidence in the value of money. Inflation at a substantial rate entails loss of time and temper in continually revising institutional and quasi-institutional arrangements, as well as in labor unrest. Such considerations are important not only in the labor market. Any system of prices (say, a system of railway fares) should satisfy hard-to-reconcile canons of both economic efficiency and fairness. A system works more easily if it is allowed to acquire some sanction by custom—if it is not frequently being torn up by the roots. Considerations like these form the principal reason why, in the judgment of J. R. Hicks, any inflation should be held to a modest rate.[3]

Inflation at an extreme rate, although not at a merely intermediate rate, significantly increases the costs of transactions as people try to get rid of money soon after receiving it. An observer of the Austrian scene in the early 1920s noted the costs of constant shopping and queuing and the sacrifice of family time together because of frenetic shopping expeditions. Such costs fell mainly on the humbler elements of society, since servants could be assigned the task of shopping in upper-class households.[4]

Inflation sabotages the transmission of information by prices. Ideally, each price conveys information to the prospective buyer of a

---

[3] Ibid., pp. 114–116. On the role of notions of equity in setting prices and especially wages, also see Arthur M. Okun, "An Efficient Strategy to Combat Inflation," The Brookings Bulletin, vol. 15, no. 4 (Spring 1979), pp. 1–5.

[4] Charles S. Maier, "The Politics of Inflation in the Twentieth Century," in Fred Hirsch and John H. Goldthorpe, eds., The Political Economy of Inflation (Cambridge: Harvard University Press, 1978), p. 71n., citing Ilse Arlt, "Der Einzelhaushalt," in Julius Bunzel, ed., Geldentwertung und Stabilisierung in ihren Einflüssen auf die soziale Entwicklung in Österreich, Schriften des Vereins für Sozialpolitik, vol. 169, 1925. Twenty years later, Maier notes, Michael Kalecki would emphasize this aspect of inequality as an argument for rationing in wartime Britain (Kalecki, "Three Ways to Full Employment," in Oxford University Institute of Statistics, Studies in War Economics [Oxford: Blackwell, 1947]).

good about how much sacrifice of other goods its purchase would entail, as well as information about how attractive an offer each prospective seller is making in comparison with his rivals' offers. Inflation renders such information obsolete or unreliable more quickly. Prices and interest rates are also distorted by the particular ways or channels in which inflationary amounts of new money are injected into the economy. For institutional reasons, some prices are less promptly flexible than others, so that inflation further distorts relative prices. Inflation simply cannot be uniform and predictable. Incorrect price signals and incentives lead to patterns of resource allocation different from those that would otherwise occur. The price system becomes less efficient in responding to consumers' tastes and to objective circumstances and in coordinating economic activity. Even if inflation does not shrink the overall real volume of economic activity, however supposedly measured, it may well reduce the ultimate human satisfactions derived from that total because of changes in its composition.

To mention one obvious, though presumably unimportant, example, resources are diverted into books and periodicals on financial survival in inflation and into expensive investment consultations and seminars. More generally, inflation alters the mix of real economic activity. It reduces the relative rewards of sober activity devoted to improving products or cutting the costs of producing or distributing them; it increases the relative rewards of being a crafty operator—of predicting prices and policies, of cleverly wheeling and dealing, of sizing up the intellects and moral characters of potential trading partners and associates. It also puts a relative premium on trying to protect oneself through political activities, broadly conceived, in contrast with more market-oriented activities.[5]

We have already noted that inflation hampers comparing the offers being made by rival potential trading partners. The German inflation of the 1920s, according to a keen observer, suspended the process of selection of the fittest firms.[6] When people are so anxious to part with their melting money that they do not shop around as carefully as they otherwise would, even sellers of shoddy and overpriced goods will find some customers. Although this erosion of the competitive process of rewarding efficiency and punishing inefficiency is

---

[5] Some of these points are developed in Axel Leijonhufvud, "Costs and Consequences of Inflation," in G. C. Harcourt, ed., *The Microfoundations of Macroeconomics* (Boulder: Westview Press, 1977), pp. 265–312. As Milton Friedman says, prudent behavior becomes reckless and reckless behavior, prudent. "Inflation and Unemployment" (Nobel lecture, November 29, 1976), p. 20 of typescript.

[6] Costantino Bresciani-Turroni, *The Economics of Inflation* (London: Allen & Unwin, 1937), pp. 391–392.

4

most clearly evident in hyperinflations, it presumably occurs in more moderate degree in more moderate inflations.

Another cost that becomes more evident in extreme inflations, when financial assets have ceased to serve as stores of wealth, involves a resort to commodities, foreign exchange, and real estate instead. The unloading of commodity inventories and foreign-exchange holdings when stabilization comes is evidence of the hoarding during the inflation. An example appeared during the credit squeeze imposed in Germany in the spring of 1924 by way of consolidating the recently achieved stabilization. (The period shortly after stabilization provides relevant evidence because the inventory holdings were a hangover from the inflation period and, furthermore, were being maintained partly from fear that the stabilization might come undone.)

The time and effort devoted to coping with inflation, as well as the uncertainty and sheer anxiety it causes, should count negatively in a comprehensive assessment. Seeking to protect their savings, savers must look beyond the familiar financial intermediaries and beyond the stock market. Wise stock-market investment, never easy, becomes all the harder when inflation interacts with conventional accounting and with the tax laws to erode profitability or at least to make it more difficult to assess. Alternatives, including real estate, art objects, and all sorts of "collectibles," are touted as inflation hedges. Placement of savings becomes a less impersonal matter than it is when money is stable. Wise investment in nonstandard assets requires detailed knowledge, including, for some of them, personal contacts and personal knowledge of the abilities and moral characters of specific persons. Savers themselves must grope amateurishly for the expertise that they could leave to financial intermediaries in calmer times. The relevant information, being more specific and heterogenous than information about the conventional outlets for savings, is more subject to obsolescence.

The diversion of savings into unconventional forms presumably interferes with the process of conveying command over real resources not devoted to current consumption into the hands of those who will use those resources for real capital formation (or for its likewise productive counterparts, such as research and training).[7] People's pro-

---

[7] For eloquent remarks about the sidetracking of savings from capital formation into gold, jewels, foreign money and foreign securities, luxury cars, furniture, real estate, and so forth; about the appearance of easy gains; about the separation created between activities that are privately and those that are socially most profitable; and about social tensions bred by inflation, see G. A. Costanzo, *Programas de estabilización económica en América Latina* (Mexico City: Centro de Estudios Monetarios Latinoamericanos, 1961), pp. 130–135.

pensity to accumulate wealth, which in more stable times is satisfied by accumulation of real capital goods or of financial assets corresponding to real capital formation, is now satisfied partly by accumulation of assets whose rising values constitute rising wealth more from the narrow personal point of view than from the social point of view. (In technical terms, the rising values of such assets exert a Pigou or wealth effect that makes the economywide propensity to save lower than it would otherwise be and so restricts the allocation of resources into real capital formation.) Economic growth suffers.

The older textbooks of money and banking emphasize the many ways in which the use of money helps make production efficient and responsive to people's wants. It does so by facilitating all of the following: exchange and the fine-grained division of labor, credit operations, financial markets, and real capital formation, and economic calculation and informed choice through comparisons of revenues and costs, of prospective profits in different lines of production, of satisfactions prospectively obtained and forgone, and of the offers of rival potential trading partners. If we take these services seriously, then we should recognize how erosion and instability of money's purchasing power impair the smooth performance of its functions.

Some observers make a still more general argument. Inflation frustrates much personal planning, whether for retirement, travel, or education of one's children. By causing disillusionment and breeding discontent, it excites doubts among people about themselves, about the competence of government, and about the free-enterprise system. Those who have lived through severe inflations have noted the erosion of the work ethic and of other established values, and not merely of the value of money, as the hard-working and thrifty middle class suffers undeserved impoverishment and as inflation profiteers flaunt their conspicuous consumption. Attitudes toward crime change as people find themselves driven, for self-preservation, to evading various economic controls.[8]

Sources of Inflation

Understanding the cause of a disorder is likely to be helpful in its treatment. Some persons would have us believe that inflation is a kind of plague or invasion striking from outside and that the role of government is to fight it. Arthur Burns, for example, says that

---

[8] Arthur F. Burns, *Inflation Must Be Stopped*, Reprint, no. 99 (Washington, D.C.: American Enterprise Institute, June 1979), pp. 1–2. Professor Leo Grebler has emphasized (in a personal letter) the sorts of cost that amount to abrasion of the entire fabric of society.

There are many causes of inflation. Some arise from within a country, as when demands for goods and services exceed the available supply, or when workers press for increases in wages that exceed improvements in productivity, or when businessmen seek to enlarge their profit margins through higher prices. International factors play a role, as when oil-exporting countries raise the price of oil. It is nevertheless the duty of our federal government under existing law to serve as the balance wheel of the economy, and that involves an obligation to restrain or to offset upward pressures on the general price level that arise in the private economy. Our government has performed this function badly in recent times; and it is therefore basically responsible for the persistent and unprecedentedly rapid inflation that has occurred in our country since the mid-1960s.[9]

Harry Johnson commented on an economist friend working for an international organization:

One of the responsibilities of a job like that is to claim that inflation is something that happens and no one is really to blame. An irresistible political and social set of forces obliges the politicians to abandon their responsibilities of serving the social good, and along with that goes the idea that somehow the public should be cajoled or persuaded or forced to do the politicians' job for them. . . . [S]ervants of governments like to put forward [that interpretation] to persuade the public that the politicians really are better than they are in fact. . . . [Actually,] it is a politician's job to control inflation, it is not the responsibility of every individual citizen to behave in a non-inflationary way, and to ask them to do so is an abnegation of political responsibility.[10]

Inflations of significant degree and duration always involve monetary expansion. By now, or so one hopes, the reasoning and evidence for this proposition no longer need repeating. Historically, several kinds of situation have given rise to inflationary money creation. Perhaps the most readily understandable case is creation of money to cover government deficit spending. The link between deficits and money issue can range from the direct and obvious, as in rolling the printing presses to pay for a war, to the quite roundabout and loose, as in the United States nowadays. Creating money to cover the losses of government-owned enterprises is also a familiar story, particularly

---

[9] Ibid., pp. 2–3.
[10] Harry Johnson, "Panel Discussion on World Inflation," in Claassen and Salin, *Stabilization Policies*, p. 312.

in Latin America. So is creation of money to provide credit to the private sector.[11]

At least two types of vicious circle have been observed in inflations centering around a government deficit. First, if taxes and the prices charged by government enterprises are adjusted only with delays or if income taxes are collected on the basis of incomes earned several months or a year earlier, then inflation itself tends to increase government expenditures ahead of revenues, widening the deficit and occasioning still bigger issues of money. (This particular kind of interaction is likely to be absent or outweighed in pay-as-you-go tax systems or in systems in which progressive rates and inflation interact to raise the effective average tax rate, or both.)[12]

A second type of vicious circle hinges on the fact that the size of government deficit as a proportion of national income that can be financed by money issue without causing inflation is inversely related to the country's income velocity of money. A rise in the inflation rate not only magnifies money's effect on prices by raising its income velocity but also, once velocity has risen, decreases the relative size of the government deficit that could be financed by money issue without raising prices.[13] In other words, an inflation-motivated rise in velocity increases the inflationary impact of issuing money to finance a government deficit amounting to a given proportion of national income. This is the other side of the coin of the phenomenon sometimes observed at times of successful stabilization, when the decline in velocity due to belief that inflation has stopped facilitates the financing of a temporarily continuing government deficit during the period of transition to a balanced budget.

The early 1970s provide many examples, although hardly history's earliest examples, of imported inflation. Our discussion of the German and Swiss experiences will explore this in some detail. Trying to keep the exchange rate of the home currency fixed in the face of balance-of-payments surpluses expands the home money supply. An intertwining aspect of imported inflation at a fixed exchange rate is that price inflation in the outside world tends to raise prices at home in a direct, mechanical way, particularly prices of import and export

---

[11] Early-twentieth-century Chile provides an example. A conservative government dominated by a landowner class with heavy mortgage indebtedness pursued deliberately inflationary policies. See Frank Whitson Fetter, *Monetary Inflation in Chile* (Princeton: Princeton University Press, 1931).

[12] Felipe Pazos, *Chronic Inflation in Latin America* (New York: Praeger, 1972), pp. 97–98.

[13] Antonio Gómez Oliver and Valeriano García, "Experiencia inflacionaria reciente en América Latina," *Monetaria*, vol. 1, no. 1 (January-March 1978), p. 27.

goods. Although the local authorities may not think of their choice in just this way, they may act to expand the local money supply so that the rising prices do not erode its total purchasing power in real terms or so that money creation is not left entirely to the process already mentioned, which would leave more of any benefit to foreigners than to the domestic authorities. Massive oil price increases, particularly in countries heavily dependent on imported oil, would spell a mechanical increase of perhaps several percent in the country's price level; and in order not to let this increase erode the purchasing power of the total money supply and exert a contractionary effect on production and employment, the authorities feel some pressure to take steps to expand the money supply. This, in other words, would be monetary ratification of a cost push, with the push happening to come from abroad rather than from labor unions (or from business firms with discretionary pricing power).

Once a momentum of interacting wage and price increases has become established, regardless of just how, the authorities have to face the question whether to "ratify" those increases by money-supply expansion. (Having to make this choice is near the heart of the problem of stopping inflation and will occupy us at length later.) That much can be said in favor of the theory that blames inflation on cost push or a wage-price spiral. But if we recognize that the wage-price momentum got established in the first place by excessive money creation and demand pull rather than by entirely autonomous wage and price increases, we drop any notion that we have found a nonmonetary explanation of inflation.

Monetary inflation originating in a way that combines some features of imported inflation and the financing of government deficits, namely, inflation from foreign-exchange losses, has sometimes been observed in Latin America. Under multiple-exchange-rate systems, political pressures tend toward the central bank's buying foreign exchange at a higher price in local currency, by and large, than its selling price. Its purchases of foreign exchange thus inject more domestic money into circulation than its sales withdraw. In this respect, the process resembles the monetary expansion that occurs when a central bank holds a unitary exchange rate fixed in the face of a balance-of-payments surplus. Insofar as official losses are involved, the process resembles inflationary covering of the deficits of state enterprises. As G. A. Costanzo says, these exchange losses generate a net creation of credit.[14] In other words, the central bank's cheaper sales than purchases of foreign exchange constitute gifts of newly

---

[14] Costanzo, *Programas*, pp. 41–42, 48–51.

created domestic money to the economy, much as if money were being printed to confer subsidies (as in cases in which food subsidies, in particular, have contributed to government deficits and money creation). (The process also bears an analogy with the way that undervaluation of the home currency on the foreign exchanges can cause imported inflation, even though the inflation is not being exported from anywhere else.) The phenomenon of inflation from foreign exchange losses helps explain the logic of movement toward a unified and relatively free exchange-rate system as part of a stabilization program.

Cost push has been mentioned as one potential aspect of the inflationary process. To some extent, but not entirely, the oil price increases since 1973 had an exogenous political cause. F. Leutwiler, president of the Swiss National Bank, is one observer who sees reason to suppose that the inflation already under way in consequence of the last-ditch defense of the Bretton Woods System helped prod the Organization of Petroleum Exporting Countries (OPEC) into action. As he says,

> This particular climate of inflation and exuberant expansion not only prepared the ground, in the autumn of 1973, for the massive increase in the price of petroleum but even made it possible. The sudden rise in price of by far the most important energy product accentuated the upward pressure on the already high rates of inflation in most of the industrialized countries.[15]

Without denying that inflation is a monetary phenomenon, keen observers have also diagnosed it as a political problem. Fritz Machlup mentions episodes when inflation was stopped by strong-willed men with political influence—Monsignor Seipel in Austria in 1922, Dr. Schacht in Germany in 1923–1924, and Raymond Poincaré in France in 1926. The fact that inflation can be stopped with a change in the political situation suggests that condoning and making inflation in the first place are also largely political problems.

> We then have to ask what are the motivations of those who control the manufacture of money, the motivations that keep them adding to the stock of money.
> The first and strongest motivation is not to be shot and the second motivation is not to be fired.[16]

---

[15] Remarks at the stockholders' meeting of April 24, 1975, printed at the end of the Swiss National Bank, *Bulletin Mensuel*, May 1975, separate pages 1–6, quotation from p. 1.

[16] Fritz Machlup, "Panel Discussion," in Claassen and Salin, *Stabilization Policies*, p. 300.

Broadly speaking, inflation results from preoccupation with the short run and failure to take a long-run view. In episodes of imported inflation, for example, the politicians and central bankers of the victim countries delayed adjusting their exchange rates or floating them upward. Such action would have been unpopular with strong interests, notably import-competing and export producers, and something might have turned up to make such action unnecessary. For another example, consider the United States during and after the Vietnam war. It seemed expedient to delay tax increases or to avoid cuts in nonwar expenditures and to continue running up debt. It seemed convenient for the Federal Reserve System to concern itself with interest rates rather than with the money supply. When inflationary momentum became entrenched, it seemed convenient to the Federal Reserve—as it often seems to national monetary and fiscal authorities generally—to accommodate the rising prices and wages with monetary expansion rather than risk a business slump. If they do happen to blunder into a slump, it seems expedient for the authorities to try to stimulate the economy out of it, even at the risk of reigniting inflation. Briefly, both getting into inflation and then having trouble getting out of it are often political problems associated with the fragmentation of governmental decision making and with the short time-horizons of the decision makers.

Political and what might be called "sociological" impediments to noninflationary monetary policy often intertwine. Richard Cooper aptly said, "I have never been able to understand the impasse between the monetarist and the sociological explanations of inflation. I have always assumed the money supply to be sociologically determined."[17] Erich Streissler may have been right in tracing present-day inflation fundamentally to efforts by economic interest groups to enlist the political process in improving their relative income positions, even if this amounts to trying to divide up total income into shares totaling more than 100 percent.[18] This struggle does or could operate in several channels: directly through the government budget and the financing of deficits, through credit allocation and subsidies, and through protectionist, regulatory, and other measures tending to create upward pressures and downward rigidities in wages and prices and appearing to call, in turn, for monetary accommodation. This

---

[17] Quoted in editors' prologue, Hirsch and Goldthorpe, *Political Economy*, p. 1.

[18] "Personal Income Distribution and Inflation," in Helmut Frisch, ed., *Inflation in Small Countries* (Berlin, Heidelberg, and New York: Springer, 1976), pp. 343–356. What follows in the text is more embroidery on than a summary of what Streissler actually said.

struggle creates an inflation-prone economy in which "accidents" can play a significant role.

The struggle to divide up a whole into more than 100 percent of itself is self-defeating, of course (especially if we set aside minor and temporary exceptions hinging on capital consumption or deficits in foreign trade), while the very struggle is likely to impair the size of the whole. Even so, no group with meaningful political influence has reason to withdraw from the struggle, for doing so would impair its income share even more. The self-interest of the individual politician likewise requires him to respond to political realities that he might regret but is individually powerless to remedy. Here we have an example of tension between individual or sectional rationality and collective rationality. In other words, a decent restraint in clamoring for government action to redistribute income from others to oneself is a public, not a private, good.

If this diagnosis is correct, then merely to recite the standard monetarist prescription for curing inflation amounts to advocating that the problem be solved, somehow, but without probing deeply enough into the nature of the problem or into what would constitute a solution. The same diagnosis suggests why it is difficult to get a sound antiinflation program adopted and maintained. Yet the durability and credibility of such a policy have much to do with the expectations of the public and, in turn, with whether its recessionary side effects will be mild or severe.

These sweeping judgments are admittedly difficult to confirm or reject. Yet the historical survey to follow has some bearing on them.

The sources of inflation have included fallacious ideas. One of them centers around the failure to distinguish firmly enough between the nominal and real quantities of money—numbers of money units and purchasing power of the money supply. In Germany in 1923, for example, eminent financiers and politicians argued that there was neither monetary nor credit inflation: although the nominal value of the paper money supply was enormous, its real value or gold value was much lower than that of the prewar money supply. This doctrine overlooks the obvious reason why the real money stock had become so small: People were economizing drastically on holding wealth in the form of money precisely because inflation was so extreme.

Perhaps the most authoritative supporter of this fallacy in Germany, who expounded it in June 1923 before a committee of enquiry into the causes of the fall in the mark, adding that the gold in the Reichsbank amounted to a considerably higher proportion of the gold value of the paper money in circulation in 1923 than before the war, was Karl Helfferich, celebrated economist and former finance minister.

Rudolf Havenstein, president of the Reichsbank, expounded a related fallacy before the same committee—the doctrine that currency depreciation is due to an unfavorable balance of payments. This fallacy dates at least as far back as discussions of "the high price of bullion" in Great Britain during the Napoleonic wars, when the Bank of England had temporarily been relieved of the restraint on banknote issue posed by the gold redeemability requirement. In Germany, the balance-of-payments theorists commonly pointed to the country's heavy reparations payments. In August 1923, Havenstein denied that credit expansion had been feeding inflation in Germany. He argued that the loan and investment portfolio of the Reichsbank was worth well under half of its prewar value in gold marks.[19]

Variants of the "real-bills doctrine" are sometimes found at work in inflationary processes. Although demolished as long ago as 1802 by Henry Thornton,[20] the doctrine keeps being rediscovered as if it were a profound and original truth. In essence—but variations on this theme do occur—the doctrine holds that new money is not inflationary if issued to finance productive activities, since it will soon be matched by additional goods on which it can be spent. Briefly, the fallacy consists in believing that what happens to the price level depends not so much on the quantity of money as on the particular way in which new money is initially put into circulation. The doctrine fails to realize that creating new money to finance particular activities ordinarily does less to increase total production than to bid productive resources from other activities into the favored ones, while, at the same time, the intensified bidding for productive resources raises costs and prices.[21]

Related to the real-bills fallacy, and in particular to its supposition that the quantity of money is less important than its quality or the nature of its issue, is the notion that money cannot be inflationary if it is solidly backed. Proponents of issuing the assignats during the French Revolution argued, for example, that the issues would be harmless, indeed beneficial, because they were backed by nationalized lands. A preoccupation with backing has sometimes made the authorities passive in the face of imported inflation; creation of money to buy up gold and foreign exchange was supposedly acceptable

---

[19] Bresciani-Turroni, *Economics*, pp. 155–156. Bresciani-Turroni goes on to cite other authorities who held substantially the same fallacious ideas.

[20] Henry Thornton, *An Enquiry into the Nature and Effects of the Paper Credit of Great Britain*, ed. with an introduction by F. A. v. Hayek (New York: Rinehart, 1939). The doctrine was so called because it held that money issues were sound if connected with the banks' discounting of "real bills," that is, lending on bills of exchange associated with the production or marketing of actual goods.

[21] For further discussion, see Thornton, *Paper Credit*, or Lloyd W. Mints, *A History of Banking Theory* (Chicago: University of Chicago Press, 1945).

because, after all, the new money was being backed by the additional reserves acquired in the process.

One last fallacy to mention is the idea often encountered that the monetary authorities are not responsible for what happens to the quantity of money because it is passively responding to developments in income or prices. Indeed it may be, but only if the authorities are subordinating control of the money supply to some other objective, such as low interest rates or a fixed exchange rate. (Having institutions that made the money supply behave passively in some such way would count as an action of the monetary authorities, interpreted broadly to include the legislators or constitution makers.) Or the authorities might be passively creating new money to accommodate an established uptrend in prices and wages as they tried to postpone the painful adjustments expected to accompany an attempt at stabilization.

Classification of Inflations

Inflations may be classified in several ways besides source or origin: by severity or rate (mild, trotting, or galloping), by how long they have persisted, by whether they have been continuous or intermittent, by remedial measures taken, if any, and by the results of those measures. An explanation of why these distinctions can be important for the seriousness or the curability of an inflation will take some points for granted that are developed later in the section on momentum of inflation.

Other things being equal, a brief inflation is easier to stop than one of long duration because people have had less time to become accustomed to it, to develop expectations of its continuation, and to make the sorts of arrangements that, though wise from their private points of view, do contribute to its momentum. A wartime inflation is a prime example. The exceptional increases in the money supply have occurred over a few years at most; people recognize the occasion for them as atypical; and the end of wartime money issues signals a return to price stability, if not indeed to price reversals. The wartime inflation, if not actually reversed, can be regarded as a brief transition to a higher price level rather than as a continuing process. From a medium- or long-run perspective, a wartime inflation is a discrete episode of an increase in the money supply bringing a once-and-for-all rise in the price level. Being so recognized, wartime inflations need not go on reinforcing themselves by way of expectations. In earlier times, price levels and not just inflation rates were expected to come down after a war.

For similar reasons, creeping inflation is less serious if intermittent than if continuous. A persistent creeping inflation will tend to worsen if it is not halted, or so Gottfried Haberler has argued.[22] As it continues, more and more people take steps, through labor contracts and otherwise, to protect themselves against expected further price increases. Intermissions in inflation, by contrast, provide opportunities for confidence in the value of money to revive.[23]

It would be misleading to say, just because the Civil War and subsequent wars brought successively higher price peaks, that the United States has managed to live comfortably with chronic inflation for well over a century. Deep valleys with long flat bottoms separated those peaks on the long-term price curve, even though each valley was higher than the one before it. Inflations were intermittent—wartime or business-cycle episodes or upward phases of mild long waves. Only from World War II on did the price curve come to look like a flight of stairs, showing no substantial price declines. Not until then did the American people start becoming highly sensitive to inflation.[24]

The most significant change in the climate of expectations may have come even more recently, in the 1960s or 1970s. Several bouts of monetary restraint after World War II, bringing recessions and unemployment, finally (if temporarily) conquered inflation toward the end of the Eisenhower administration. Following the price increases during the Korean War and in the business boom of 1955–1956, balance-of-payments deterioration and continuing gold losses after 1957 had argued for returning to price stability. From 1958 through 1964, the wholesale price index remained nearly stable, while consumer price increases averaged only 1.2 percent a year. Then, as another recession was becoming evident during the 1960 presidential

---

[22] This is not to say that every creeping inflation inexorably becomes trotting and then galloping. Rather, "an expected and anticipated inflation loses its stimulating power unless it is allowed to accelerate beyond the expected rate and . . . , at a later stage, slowing down the rate of inflation has the same depressing effect on economic activity as stopping it altogether would have had earlier. This is . . . the real meaning of stagflation. . . . If we do not act now to curb inflation we merely postpone the day of reckoning." Gottfried Haberler, in Karl Brunner and Allan Meltzer, eds., *Institutional Arrangements and the Inflation Problem* (Amsterdam, New York, and Oxford: North-Holland Publishing Company, 1976), pp. 150–151.

[23] Gottfried Haberler, *Inflation, Its Causes and Cures*, rev. ed. (Washington, D.C.: American Enterprise Institute, July 1966), pp. 93–94. Haberler was ahead of most economists in rejecting the now discredited notion of a dependable tradeoff between unemployment and inflation. After a while, the inflation would be allowed to accelerate as efforts to resist unemployment intensified, or, if inflation were held to a creep, the unemployment would emerge that the creeping inflation was supposed to forestall.

[24] Ibid., pp. 56, 94, 97.

campaign, candidate John Kennedy promised "to get this country moving again."[25] The Vietnam war contributed its inflationary pressures a few years later. Haberler, writing in 1966, could say that the United States was then experiencing an inflation unique in its history.[26]

In the 1970s, the situation departed still further from earlier American experience. Arthur Okun called it unprecedented. "[T]he chronic inflation of the seventies is a new and different phenomenon that cannot be diagnosed correctly with old theories or treated effectively with old prescriptions." Before then, inflation rates rarely averaged above 2 percent for any sustained peacetime period. Price and wage decisions relied on the dollar as a basis for planning and budgeting. Labor and management had notions of appropriate wage increases and were willing to sign three-year contracts. Firms set their prices according to actual costs rather than projected replacement costs. Catalog prices were subject to change only infrequently, and salesmen accepted orders for future deliveries at firm prices. Regulatory commissions needed to review utility rates only occasionally. Then, in the mid-1960s, what Okun called a new era of inflation got under way. Every year since 1968 saw a higher inflation rate than any year between 1952 and 1967. During the 1970s, adjustments to persistent inflation altered wage- and price-setting practices. The notion of appropriate wage increases was revised upward, and escalator clauses spread in labor contracts. Business pricing came to reflect a growing gap between replacement costs and historical costs. Price increases came more often, and many firms stopped taking orders at fixed prices. Such adaptations to chronic inflation speeded up the interaction between prices and wages and other costs.[27]

While unprecedented for the United States, this situation is not wholly unprecedented, nor, despite Okun, does its diagnosis defy old theories. With particular reference to Latin America, Felipe Pazos has explained why wages and prices interact more closely in rapid inflations than in mild ones. He found it not surprising that wages and consumer prices were more tightly correlated over the period 1949–1970 in Argentina and Chile than in the United States. Workers are less alert to cost-of-living increases of 1 or 2 percent than to those of 30 percent or more; business firms are less influenced by wage increases of 3 to 5 percent than by increases ten or more times as large. In slow inflations, the increases in the cost of living are a factor of

---

[25] Philip Cagan in Cagan et al., *Economic Policy and Inflation in the Sixties* (Washington, D.C.: American Enterprise Institute, 1972), p. 90.

[26] Ibid., p. 97.

[27] Okun, "An Efficient Strategy," pp. 1–3.

lesser importance in wage negotiations than are the supply and demand for labor, the level of profits, the strength of the labor movement, and the attitude of labor leaders. In intermediate inflations, cost-of-living increases are the major factor in labor negotiations; in hyperinflations, they are essentially the only factor. Rises in the cost of living seem to play an increasingly important role in wage negotiations when inflation rises from 1 or 2 percent a year to 4 or 5 percent or higher. This probably explains, to a large extent, the continuation of wage increases in the United States after 1970 despite the increase in unemployment[28]—but more remains to be said about inflationary momentum.

The Analogy between Levels and Trends of Prices

Brief inflations have been easier to stop than inflations of long duration because they were changes in the level of prices rather than entrenched ongoing processes. This thought brings to mind an analogy between the inertia of an established price and wage *level* and the inertia of an established *trend*. Something like Newton's first law of motion is at work in both cases: Just as a body resists being set in motion or having the speed or direction of its motion changed, so prices on the average resist changes in their level or their trend, particularly cuts in their level or moderation of their uptrend.[29] The analogy suggests that experience with attempts to reverse wartime increases in the price level, as after the Napoleonic wars, the U.S. Civil War, and World War I, may be relevant to today's less ambitious goal of merely leveling off an established uptrend in prices and wages.

The analogy between deflating a price level and bringing down a price trend centers on the concept of stickiness. People tend to think of money as having a fairly definite value or rate of change of value, and they make their price and wage demands and decisions accordingly. But this expectational factor is not the only element of stickiness. Cost-price interrelations make it difficult to adjust prices downward without some assurance that costs will adjust downward too.

In an elementary textbook already in its fifth edition fifty years ago, Harry Gunnison Brown considered a case in which restriction of money and credit will cause a business depression unless prices and wages fall sufficiently to maintain the real money stock. In fact, they will not fall steeply and promptly enough.

> . . . there are various customary notions of what are reasonable prices for various goods and reasonable wages for labor

---

[28] Pazos, *Chronic Inflation*, p. 70.

[29] Ibid., pp. 88–89.

of various kinds and, furthermore, each person hopes to be able to get the old price or the old wage for what he has to sell and does not want to reduce until sure that his expenses will also be reduced. And so there is a general hesitancy, a holding off for standard prices, wages, and so on, to the inevitable slowing down of business.[30]

When a change in the volume or growth rate of money and spending has changed what *would be* the equilibrium level or trend of prices, this new equilibrium is not reached immediately. One view of what happens focuses on market conditions determining the millions of distinct prices whose average level or trend happens to be of interest. Another view of the same process is also instructive: The purchasing power of the money unit and its rate of erosion are being determined; but, instead of occurring on one particular market and impinging on one particular price, this process is diffused over millions of individual but interconnecting markets. Precisely because money does not have a specific market and price of its own, adjustment of the level or trend of its value is long drawn out; and the long-drawn-out character of this process contributes to the persistence of price inflation even after its monetary basis may have been stopped. Production and employment suffer because price trends do not fully absorb the impact of the deceleration of money and spending.

This unfavorable split between price and output responses could be avoided or mitigated if people saw truly convincing reasons to believe that the inflation was, in fact, being stopped. Unfortunately, no policy maker and no individual seller can confidently guess when prices might decelerate in response to monetary restraint. The individual seller knows only that this does not depend on his own sale and price decisions.[31] The action that would be in the interest of price setters and wage negotiators if they were acting collectively is not necessarily in the interest of each one acting separately. Instead of going first in moderating the rate of rise in the particular price or wage that he sets or negotiates, each one has reason to wait to see whether such restraint on the part of others, intensifying the competition that he faces or moderating the rise in his production costs or cost of living, as the case may be, will make it advantageous for him to *follow* with restraint of his own. This hesitation, though rational

[30] Harry Gunnison Brown, *Economic Science and the Common Welfare*, 5th ed. (Columbia, Missouri: Lucas Brothers, 1931), pp. 88–89, cf. pp. 84–86, 93, 111–117. Brown goes on to explain in some detail how this difficulty of prompt downward adjustments is largely due to the way that various prices and costs intertwine.

[31] William Fellner, in *Towards a Reconstruction of Macroeconomics*, excerpted in David C. Colander, ed., *Solutions to Inflation* (New York: Harcourt Brace Jovanovich, 1979), p. 91.

for each one, poses what might be called an Alphonse-and-Gaston problem for the collectivity.

Individual price setters and wage negotiators have reason for reluctance to go first in reducing a level of prices and wages that is too high for the nominal quantity of money; they have similar reason for reluctance to go first in breaking an established uptrend. Suppose that policy blunders have made the existing nominal quantity of money too small for the existing price level; money is in full-employment excess demand in the sense that actual cash balances add up to less than would be demanded at full employment, with the result that a depressed level of economic activity is what holds the demand for money down to the existing amount. Barring reversal of the policy blunder, it would be collectively rational for transactors to reduce the general level of prices and wages and other costs enough to make the money stock adequate in real terms for a full-employment volume of transactions. In view of the piecemeal way in which this general level is actually determined and adjusted, however, the individual agent may not find it rational promptly to cut the particular price or wage for which he is responsible, even though it is above the general-equilibrium level. Being first to move would change relative prices, perhaps to his disadvantage. Instead of going first, he may rationally wait to see what others do. Taking the lead in downward price and wage adjustments is more in the nature of public than a private good, and private incentives to supply public goods are notoriously weak. What is individually rational and what is collectively rational may well diverge, as the well-known example of the prisoners' dilemma illustrates. Taking the lead in restraining a price and wage uptrend is a similar case in point.

Noneconomic examples will help make this point still clearer.[32] Most members of a lecture audience might want to avoid sitting in the first few occupied rows, so those arriving early take seats toward the middle or rear. Those arriving later take seats behind the people already seated, leaving the front of the auditorium nearly empty. Most people wind up sitting further back than they really desire. Individually they do not want to move forward, but they wish that the audience as a whole would somehow move forward, leaving its members' relative positions unchanged. Most of the drivers waiting in a gasoline line, for another example, might wish that the line would form later in the morning (or wish that there were no panicky tank topping in the first place); but since each one is powerless to change the behavior of the others, he adjusts to it by joining the line early.

---

[32] See Thomas C. Schelling, *Micro Motives and Macro Behavior* (New York: Norton, 1978).

Similarly, money-supply contractions or decelerations create situations in which it is nevertheless individually rational for people to persist in setting prices and wages as before, even though a decision to reduce or restrain prices and wages would be rational if it could be made collectively. Individual and collective rationality might be reconciled in this context if everyone came firmly to believe that inflation was being stopped quickly. How such a belief might be created is close to the central question.

The analogy between levels and trends also holds regarding the split of a change in nominal spending between a change in production and employment on the one hand and a change in prices on the other. With the most favorable split conceivable, a deflation or slowdown of money and spending would have its entire impact on bringing down the price level or the price trend, as the case might be, with no damage at all to real activity. With the most unfavorable split, deflation of money and spending—either absolute or relative to the existing trend—would exert its entire impact on real activity, with no reduction in the level or uptrend of prices. In reality, of course, the impact falls partly on real activity and partly on the price level or trend. The factors tending to make the split relatively favorable or relatively unfavorable are obviously relevant to the ease or difficulty of stopping an inflation.

The analogy holds between accomplishing mild or extreme price-level reductions and stopping mild or extreme inflations. As Henry Thornton already recognized in 1811, it is a reasonable objective to "restore the standard of the country" after the money has suffered a mild loss of purchasing power and of foreign-exchange value but not to reverse an extreme depreciation.[33] Similarly, stopping a mild inflation does not require as much of a cutback in money-supply growth and as much of a threat to production and employment as trying to stop a more severe inflation. (Some qualifications regarding extreme inflation, however, will be noted later.)

The analogy also holds on several other points. One concerns disappointment of expectations. Just as getting a price level down will disappoint debtors, so will stopping an inflationary trend that they had expected to persist; inflation creates vested interests in its continuation. Another point concerns the Phillips curve, or something like it. In epochs when the price and wage level undergoes discrete changes from time to time but sustained inflations and deflations are unknown, we would find low (that is, reduced but incompletely re-

---

[33] Speech in Parliament. Thornton, *Paper Credit*, app. III.

duced) price and wage levels associated with relatively heavy unemployment and high levels with slight unemployment. The apparent causation, though, would be spurious. Unemployment would be affected not by the price and wage level as such but by the unexpected monetary change that had also been lowering or raising that level. Something similar holds true of Phillips curves of the more familiar kind, which until recently were interpreted as associating heavy or slight unemployment with low or high wage and price inflation. Actually, heavy or slight unemployment was associated instead with decelerations or accelerations of money growth and spending that had not been fully expected and allowed for.

The analogy also holds with regard to policy laxness. If we think that maintaining a particular price level—today's—does not really matter, then we tend to become complacent about changes in it and about inflation. Similarly, if we think that what particular inflation rate we have does not matter much, then we become complacent about accelerating inflation.

Just as we can find analogies between levels and trends of prices, so we could probably find analogies between trends and accelerations. Policy makers could conceivably blunder into a state of affairs in which these more sophisticated analogies became relevant to understanding what is happening. People might become more or less adjusted not merely to continuing inflation but to its continuing acceleration. If so, a monetary change that would tend to reduce—but not stop—the price acceleration might disappoint expectations, transitionally worsen the impairment of economic coordination, and impinge on real activity. (If this remark is not clear, the ensuing discussion of stagflation may help clear it up.)

The analogy between levels and trends does not hold in all respects. (Analogies are, after all, just that, not total correspondences.) The velocity of money is not (permanently) affected by a once-and-for-all change in the price level due to a money-supply change, yet it is affected (once and for all) by a change in the inflation rate. A continuous change in velocity, so far as it depends on the rate of price inflation, presupposes a continuous change in that rate. Similarly, the particular price level does not, in principle, affect the size of real money balances demanded, but the inflation rate does. Because of general interdependence, affecting real money balances means, in principle, affecting all real magnitudes. Money can be "neutral," then, so far as only its quantity but not its growth rate is concerned. (Money could conceivably be neutral even with regard to its growth rate only if the new money were injected by equiproportionate additions to all individual holdings.)

Inflationary Momentum and the Side Effects
of Trying to Stop Inflation

The aspect of the analogy most pertinent to our purposes is that the reasons for sluggishness in reducing a disequilibrium price level carry over to sluggish deceleration of an entrenched price uptrend. Even if a solution to underlying difficulties (such as government deficit spending) does permit stopping the inflationary creation of money, prices and wages will continue rising for months, even years, with a momentum of their own. With nominal money growth slowed, the stock of real money balances shrinks, contributing to monetary disequilibrium and thus to a slowdown in production and employment. Just as a shrinkage that makes the *quantity* of money inadequate to sustain the prevailing *level* of prices contracts real economic activity, so a reduction that makes the money *growth rate* inadequate to sustain an entrenched *uptrend* in prices causes a real contraction or at least restricts real growth. In a sense, stagflation is the consequence of too little current monetary growth against a background of too much growth earlier. The earlier excessive growth established the uptrend still eroding the real purchasing power of the money supply and spending stream. On many such occasions, the unwanted real side effects have apparently made the authorities lose their nerve and switch back to a policy of "growth." (The very prospect of side effects may block a determined antiinflationary policy in the first place.) Yet from a longer-term perspective than the authorities may feel politically able to adopt, no conclusion follows in favor of accelerating monetary growth again, since doing so would make the stagflation dilemma worse later on.

Reference to the withdrawal pangs of trying to end inflation returns us to our question of how the impact of restraint on money and spending is split between prices and real activity. How unfavorable or favorable the split is depends on the circumstances, considered in this section, that govern how persistent inflationary momentum is. It is a familiar but inexact remark that slow real economic growth or actual recession tends to restrain inflation (and, conversely, that rapid real growth is inflationary). The reverse accords better with the equation of exchange, $MV = PQ$, where Q refers to some measure of real activity or total production. Presumably underlying the common remark is the idea that slowed real growth is one consequence of and serves as a measure or indicator of a slowdown in nominal income and the money supply. If this is what is meant, however, the standard formulation is unfortunate. Imagine—trying to gauge the antiinflationary intensity of monetary policy by an unwanted side effect of that policy, namely, a real slowdown, especially since, as $MV = PQ$ shows, the side effect competes with the desired price deceleration!

The diagnosis of stagflation that focuses on how the momentum of price and wage increases erodes real money balances and the flow of real spending is of course incomplete. Inflation impairs the information-transmitting and coordinating properties of the price mechanism and distorts relative prices, frustrating some exchanges. Just how inflationary quantities of money enter the economy can be relevant, and interest rates may figure among the prices that are distorted. Inflation distorts the pattern of production and resource allocation—in favor, for example, of supposed "inflation hedges." If a policy of trying to reduce inflation seems to be working or to have some chance of success, then people will tend to shift production and resource allocation back toward more normal patterns, giving rise to frictional losses of production and employment.

As an example of distortions during the Brazilian inflation of the 1960s, Alexandre Kafka mentions the hoarding of goods, particularly durable consumer goods. Stabilization would perhaps bring dishoarding of the kinds of durable goods bought by firms and would weaken incentives to accumulate durable consumer goods, so that the industries producing them would suffer recession. Kafka mentions the paradoxical result that at times, in the midst of a stabilization program, the authorities felt obliged to stimulate consumer credit to prevent a real stabilization crisis.[34]

Part of the purpose of ending inflation is to reverse inflationary distortions of resource allocation. Similarly, if stabilization reinstates the competitive process of selecting the fittest firms, then some firms that were being kept afloat by the peculiarities of the inflationary situation will go bankrupt. Their plants and equipment and employees will have to shift into the hands of better management or into more desired lines of production. The shifting will involve frictions, and real activity will suffer for a while.

These considerations reinforce the judgment that stabilization with a pure price impact and no unfavorable real side effects is practically impossible. They also argue that delay makes stopping inflation all the more painful by letting distortions worsen in the meantime.

The distinction between credit-intensive and non-credit-intensive businesses and products is relevant to the side effects of monetary

---

[34] Alexandre Kafka, "The Brazilian Stabilization Program, 1964–66," *Journal of Political Economy*, vol. 75 (August 1967), part 2, p. 608. The German inflation of 1922–23 likewise caused real distortions of resource allocation that later had to be undone, including impairment of competition and of the selection of the fittest firms; see the section on that episode below.

slowdown. In our type of money and banking system, a slowdown in money-supply growth will transitionally tighten credit. This is only a transitional effect, of course, since, in comparison of alternative equilibriums, the real cost or availability of credit does not depend on the quantity of money. But during the transition, the particular burdening of credit-intensive firms can be a further source of resource reallocation and frictions.[35]

Yet these additional characteristics of stagflation should not draw attention away from price and wage momentum. This momentum has two main aspects, "catching up" and "expectations." Both involve complex interrelations and time lags. Prices and wages and other costs are determined in piecemeal and decentralized ways; some firms' selling prices are other firms' costs. Except for coming close to doing so in hyperinflations, not all prices and wage rates rise in step with each other, month by month and week by week. Only the prices of securities and standardized commodities traded on organized exchanges respond to supply and demand from hour to hour and minute to minute. Most individual prices and wages are adjusted only from time to time. As a result, the structure of relative prices is constantly undergoing distortions and corrections. At any time, many prices and wages are temporarily lagging behind others in the inflationary procession. While some workers will have just received wage increases, others will have received their latest increases perhaps eleven months before and be in line for another increase soon.

> A price increase in one sector pushes up costs in others, and each increase then works its way through the price structure. At the stage of final goods and services, price increases add to the cost of living, feeding back on wages and costs in the earlier stages of production, then to work forward again.

Not even large nominal gains always "put union wages ahead *in real terms*. Such settlements can represent a catching up with past real losses due to cost-of-living increases. . . ." Union power, without being the actual cause of inflation, can contribute to its persistence. "The whipsaw process of each handsome settlement giving rise to militant demands by other unions for equal or better treatment has created the alarming prospect of a very slow cooling of the rampant inflationary psychology."[36]

Revision of expiring contracts is not the only way that catching up, broadly interpreted, works. Some existing contracts, with the parties' intention of keeping abreast of the general trend of money's

---

[35] Cf. Colander, *Solutions*, p. 105n.
[36] Cagan, *Economic Policy*, pp. 141–142.

ceive. In adjusting their own prices or wage demands, they
ll allow for this erosion already experienced since their last
but also may well include an allowance for further ero-
ensuing months. Strong anticipations of inflation can
direct influence of demand on prices (and also of prices on
demanded). Cost increases are more readily and fully
g despite weakness in demand if that weakness is viewed
y and prices are expected to continue in an uptrend. Costs
ush each other up with less friction.[41] As buyers become
to repeatedly paying increased prices and find it increas-
lt to keep abreast of and compare the prices asked by rival
become less sensitive to price competition. Sellers become
to passing actual and even expected cost increases on to
ners without meeting too much buyer resistance.

seller of some product or type of labor for which demand
deficient—a businessman dissatisfied with his sales or a
r dissatisfied with his members' employment—may well
g or may even increase his money price anyway. He can
real or relative price in order to attract buyers simply by
nominal increase smaller than the general inflation rate.[42]
s and wages are generally rising, to join in the procession
ssarily to push for an increased price in real terms but
void an unnecessarily large markdown. Why take less than
will bear? Why sacrifice to the advantage of others? Even
hould experience some drop or lag in sales attributable to
e nominal price increase, he could expect the continuing
ation of costs and prices to make his price soon competi-
ceptable after all. Why reverse a slightly premature price
at customers will soon be willing to pay?

nse, the ordinary nominal money unit loses its character as
which price and wage demands and offers and decisions
. Instead, some sort of vaguely conceived purchasing-
replaces it. Money illusion of the ordinary sort, predicated
of the purchasing power of the nominal unit, breaks down
vay to an illusion—if indeed it is an illusion—of continu-
sing-power erosion. Attunement to a perceived trend re-
presumption of a stable money unit.

nomic Policy, p. 143.

hufvud made this point orally in a conference at Rutgers University,
April 1979 and in "Stagflation," mimeographed (lecture at Nihon
okyo, January 19, 1980), pp. 10–11. The point accords well with what
nic Inflation, p. 70 and passim) reports about inflationary Latin
at the overwhelmingly dominant consideration in wage negotiations
ng adjustments.

depreciation, have already scheduled future price or wage increases. If
the monetary authority does somehow succeed in getting price inflation
down below the rate that had been expected, then nominal wage increases scheduled in view of earlier expectations will result in higher
real wage rates than intended, contributing to unemployment.[37]

To notice cost-price interactions is not to adopt a cost-push
theory of inflation. In some stages of the inflation process, costs may
seem to rise first, with prices following later; yet this sequence can be
spurious as evidence of causation. A micro view helps show why. A
firm's standard response to strengthened demand for its products is
to try to increase quantities available for sale. A retailer will order
more goods. A manufacturer will order more materials, seek more
labor, and perhaps try to expand his plant and equipment. Each individual businessman might think that, given time, he could meet the
increased demand for his product without raising prices. Yet as businessmen transmit the increased demands for final products back to the
factors of production, competing for materials, labor, and plants and
equipment, they bid up these cost elements. To the individual businessman, then, the chief factor justifying and requiring a rise in his
selling prices is the rise in his costs. From his standpoint, the inflation
may look like a cost-push process, even though costs are in fact rising
as inflationary demands for final products are transmitted back to
factors of production.

For these and other reasons, a change in monetary policy and in
the flow of spending on final goods and services has its impact spread
over many months, even years. If monetary policy were to be
tightened and an inflationary expansion of demand checked, much of
the adjustment of prices to the earlier demand inflation would remain
to be completed. In summary, prices would continue rising for at
least three reasons. First, contractual prices and wages would be re-
negotiated as contracts expired. Second, costs and prices would interact in sequences complicated by the fact that some firms' prices are
other firms' costs. Third—a point still to be developed—buyers and
sellers would be acting on expectations formed during the period of
active monetary inflation.

A study by Joel Popkin sheds light on cost-price interaction and
catching up. Popkin distinguishes between primary-goods and
finished-goods industries. For the most part, prices respond directly

[37] Herbert Giersch uses this point as an argument for indexing to help avoid
unintended spurts in real wage rates when price inflation decelerates. Herbert
Giersch, "Index Clauses and the Fight against Inflation," in Giersch et al.,
Essays on Inflation and Indexation (Washington, D.C.: American Enterprise Institute, 1974), p. 6.

to demand conditions only in the former. Prices of finished goods sold to consumers and other final users, however, are less sensitive to a drop in sales. These prices are based on costs, which include the prices of purchased materials and services. Unresponsive pricing of finished goods means that restraints on total spending can bring inflation down only in a roundabout way. Instead of depressing prices directly, a fall in spending on final goods depresses output. Their producers cut back their orders for raw materials, whose prices do decline in response. Lower costs of materials finally show up in a slowing of price increases for finished goods. Unfortunately, this effect is likely to be minor, since materials figure less heavily than wages in the costs of most finished goods; and wage increases are particularly slow to respond to a slowdown of price inflation. In most industries, Popkin found, unemployment or excess capacity has less influence in wage bargaining than increases in consumer prices and in wages in other industries. The wage-setting process is dominated by past increases in the cost of living and by workers' desire to catch up with wage increases achieved elsewhere. The responsiveness of prices to demand in industries producing basic materials but not in most industries producing finished goods is awkward for macroeconomic policy; yet this differential responsiveness is readily understandable. If the reverse pattern somehow prevailed, stabilization policies would have better prospects of success.[38]

Outside of sectors whose products are traded in organized competitive markets, notions of fairness condition interactions among prices and wages and other costs. Concerned about maintaining their market shares over the long run, sellers try to keep their customers loyal by treating them reasonably in good times and bad, charging prices based on costs and fairly stable percentage markups. Employers and skilled workers, similarly, have a common interest in maintaining their relations over the long run. Employers have invested in a trained and loyal work force as well as in plant and equipment. They recognize that slashing wages in a slump would make resentful workers quit the next time jobs were abundant. Even during recessions and with plenty of job applicants, firms may have reason to raise wages in step with the wages of other workers in similar situations. Although

[38] Joel Popkin, "Price Behavior in the Manufacturing Sector for Sixteen Industries Classified by Stage-of-Process," National Bureau of Economic Research, Working Paper, no. 238 (Washington, D.C., March 1978). Compare a summary and commentary in "Why the Odds Are Against the Inflation Fighters," *Business Week*, June 5, 1978, pp. 83–85. Several discussions of Latin American inflation, as well as Jerome L. Stein, "Inside the Monetarist Black Box," chap. 3 in Stein, ed., *Monetarism* (Amsterdam and New York: North-Holland Publishing Company, 1976), emphasize the catching-up aspects of inflationary momentum.

such price and wage strategies help customers and suppliers and workers the sensitivity of prices and wages t As a result, prices and wages are slov of nominal spending. Similarly, an abate when the growth of nominal sp the early response consists partly of

Because costs and prices interac with time lags, many prices and wag after monetary expansion is checked. somehow would leave them stuck aw and the distorted structure of relative with some transactions and so with p abstract theory, these distortions cou some prices and wages that averaged Actually, the difficulties that obstruct trends obstruct all the more powerfull and wages. Thus, catching up does inflation.

These considerations, reinforced by shall review, suggest a silver lining to persists and becomes faster and more f the intervals between price and wage a of higher wages and other costs into prices into higher wages occurs more lags means that antiinflation policy wou prolonged catching up with which to co be easier to stop an extreme inflation tha

Expectations form the second aspec (Actually, the two aspects overlap and guished, and the interaction of various both.) When prices and wages have been several years, people recognize what is h tinue, and make their own pricing decisi cordingly. (They do so, anyway, unless circumstances provides a reason for doing the sort presented here, however, even i does support expectations that trends will being made not every day but only from ti account of the erosion of the purchasing p

[39] Okun, "An Efficient Strategy," p. 2.
[40] Ibid., p. 3.

that they not only adjustme sion in t reduce th quantitie passed al as tempo and price accuston ingly dif sellers, t accustor their cu

Ev is curre union l forgo c reduce keeping When is not simply the ma if a se an exc genera tive a increas

the u are f powe on st and ing place

[41] Ca
[42] Ax
Newa
Univ
Pazo
Ame
is co

Again our levels-and-trends analogy proves helpful. Just as the distinction between individual and collective rationality helps explain the difficulty of reducing a price level, so it helps explain the difficulty of slowing an uptrend. Expectations figure in this difficulty. The less successfully monetary restraint decelerates prices, as we recall, the worse are its recessionary side effects.

Suppose that I, an individual businessman, perceive that a newly introduced policy of monetary restraint ought to stop inflation. (The effect that a policy "ought" to have is the one that it is designed to have in the light of correct economic theory, or the one that it would have if people quite generally understood it and modified their behavior accordingly.) Even so, how can I count on *others'* having the same perceptions and modifying their behavior accordingly? How can I be confident that my workers will restrain their wage demands and my suppliers and competitors their prices? I have good reason, as already argued, to postpone changes in my own pricing policy until I get a better reading on what the situation is, including, in particular, on how other people may be modifying their price and wage policies. (My policy, like theirs, had been to keep marking up my selling prices in line with the entrenched general trend unless faced with definite conditions of costs and competition that recommend doing otherwise.) Of course, if I and all other price setters and wage negotiators were to make our decisions collectively and simultaneously, then it would be in our collective interest to avoid the side effects of the new policy of monetary restraint by practicing appropriate price and wage restraint. In fact, though, we make our price and wage decisions piecemeal, opening the way for the previously mentioned divergence between collective and individual rationality.

This divergence is not a defect of the market system but rather the inevitable consequence of the circumstances with which it must cope. One of its great virtues is that it does not require or impose collective decisions. This fact becomes less of a virtue when the problem of stopping inflation arises, but we can hardly expect a world whose features are all desirable in all respects and under all circumstances. The dispersion of knowledge and the fact that it can be effectively used only through decentralized decisions and in a market-coordinated way is one of the hard facts of reality. It forms part of the reason why monetary disturbances can be so pervasively disruptive: They overtax the knowledge-mobilizing and signaling processes of the market. None of this amounts to a recommendation to give up and let an entrenched inflation keep rolling. Far from being a solution, that would make the attempted cure all the more painful when belatedly undertaken.

The expectational aspect of inflationary momentum makes the *credibility* of an antiinflation policy of great importance to how severe the withdrawal pangs will be.[43] If a program of monetary restraint is not credible—if price setters and wage negotiators think that the authorities will lose their nerve and switch gears at the first sign of recessionary side effects—then those parties will expect the inflation to continue and will make their price and wage decisions accordingly. The unintended consequence will be an unfavorable split between the price and quantity responses to monetary restriction. If, on the contrary, people are convinced that the authorities will persist in monetary restriction indefinitely no matter how bad the side effects, so that the price and wage inflation is bound to abate, then everyone should realize that, if he nevertheless persists in price or wage increases at the same old pace, he will find himself ahead of the stalled inflationary procession and will lose customers or jobs. People will moderate their price and wage demands, making the split less unfavorable to continued production and employment.

It is only superficially paradoxical, then, that in two alternative situations with objectively the same degree of monetary restriction, the recessionary side effects will actually be milder when the authorities are believed ready to tolerate such effects than when the authorities are suspected of irresoluteness. How, though, could a resolute policy be made convincing from the start? Unfortunately, the required declarations and actions are unlikely under our sort of political system. If, however, the necessary declarations and actions could somehow occur and did succeed in making practically everyone believe that inflation was being stopped quickly, then the monetary slowdown would damage production and employment only mildly.

While a resolute and credible antiinflation program could thus conceivably turn expectations around almost at once, the catch-up aspect of inflationary momentum appears less tractable. Still, if the turnaround in inflationary expectations were quick and complete enough, relative prices could conceivably be restored to an approximate equilibrium pattern through declines in previously leading prices that averaged out catch-up increases in previously lagging prices. This is just an extreme benchmark case, of course, and not a practical possibility; but it figures in an explanation of why it is important, in com-

[43] William Fellner has long insisted on points like these. See, for example, his *Towards a Reconstruction*, especially pp. 2–3, 12–15, 116–118, and "The Core of the Controversy about Reducing Inflation: An Introductory Analysis," in William Fellner, project director, *Contemporary Economic Problems 1978* (Washington, D.C.: American Enterprise Institute, 1978), pp. 1–12.
Carried to an extreme, the view expounded here becomes the currently fashionable doctrine of rational expectations.

paring historical episodes, to pay attention to how definite and credible the antiinflation programs were.

Next we note the policy aspect of momentum. Some people do succeed in adjusting to inflation and would suffer if their adjustments were rendered inappropriate. Perhaps the most vivid example concerns young couples who buy more expensive houses than they would otherwise think prudent, incurring almost crushing burdens of mortgage payments in relation to income. They do so because they expect their incomes to rise with inflation, making mortgage payments smaller and smaller relatively. An end to inflation would penalize such people in a double-barreled way. First, the mortgage payments would remain a crushing burden unless they sold the house. Second, prices would probably drop because the exceptional demand for real estate as inflation hedges would have vanished. More generally, taking inflation and the inflation premium out of interest rates would have an impact on property values, benefiting some persons and firms and victimizing others.[44] Still more generally, certain activities—examples have been mentioned—flourish more in an inflationary than in a stable environment. Their shriveling would hurt people who had devoted their money and careers to them. As inflation continues and becomes more deeply ingrained, more and more people get into such a position. Political pressures from them, even if only unorganized pressures, work to keep inflation going.

A probably more important reason for continuing money-supply expansion is that the authorities fear the side effects of discontinuing the monetary accommodation of the entrenched price-and-wage uptrend. (Again the analogy between inflation and an addictive drug comes to mind.) The argument was commonly heard in Germany in the early 1920s that the printing presses had to keep rolling to satisfy the "needs of trade" at constantly rising prices and wages. The same argument has been heeded in the United States in recent years, even though to a less spectacular extent. The Federal Reserve has been expanding the money supply at a rate greater than would be compatible with price stability for fear of the side effects of failing to do so. For some such reason, even a majority of monetarists, apparently, call for stopping inflation only gradually by a merely gradual withdrawal of its monetary accommodation.

Conditions Favorable and Unfavorable for Stopping Inflation

Gottfried Haberler has noted "cases where an inflation has been stopped without any prolonged recession," notably those of Germany

---

[44] Clark Warburton, "How to Stop Inflation and Reduce Interest Rates, Now and Permanently," mimeographed (September 1974), p. 15.

and France after World Wars I and II. The hyperinflation that climaxed in Germany in 1923 "was an uncontrolled profit inflation, prices running ahead of wages." Germany after World War II had a repressed inflation: Its symptoms were suppressed by tight controls, which also strangled economic activity. Not only was the money overhang removed by currency reform in 1948, but controls were abolished at one stroke, setting the stage for sustained economic expansion. Recent inflation in the United States has been of a different nature and much less amenable to a relatively painless cure.[45]

At least two considerations suggest that stopping a hyperinflation should be easier than stopping a moderate inflation. First, monetary disorder has become so extreme that conditions simply cannot be left to continue as they are, and this perception invites a rapid change of expectations. People are so desperate for a usable money that they are ready and eager to believe in a clear break with past policy. A switch in policy can be more credible. (A new money unit, if adopted, contributes to the perception that policy has entirely changed.) A second reason is brought to mind by the observed fact that in extreme inflation, the rate of price increases varies widely from month to month. This free oscillation of price changes reflects the replacement of long-term contracts and price-setting for substantial periods by contracting and wage- and price-setting from day to day. Lumpy adjustments of lagging wages and prices are no longer occurring; inflationary pressures, instead of being partly accumulated and carried over to the following month or year, express themselves as they are generated; the catch-up element of inflationary momentum has disappeared.[46] Furthermore, the disappearance of substantial leads and lags in the inflationary procession means that no important interest group stands to gain or lose according to just when the inflation is stopped; in particular, none has reason to urge delay until after its next round of wage or price adjustments.

Not so paradoxically, then, inflation that practically destroys the old money unit creates a relatively favorable opportunity. Success depends, as ever, on getting money-supply growth under control; but *additional* difficulties—adverse side effects—are relatively slight at the climax of a hyperinflation.

At the other extreme, also, it should be easier to stop a mild infla-

---

[45] Haberler in Brunner and Meltzer, *Institutional Arrangements*, p. 152n.

As the German banker Hermann Abs once said, the German hyperinflation of 1923 was an abscess that could be lanced (whereas the Brazilian inflation of the 1960s was a less easily treatable case of blood poisoning). Kafka, "Brazilian Stabilization," pp. 630–631.

[46] Pazos, *Chronic Inflation*, especially pp. 19, 93.

tion than one of an intermediate degree. Mildness keeps inflationary expectations from becoming keen and deeply entrenched. Although prices and wages are adjusted only piecemeal over time, the resulting distortion of relative prices and the catch-up aspect of inflationary momentum are slight. Stopping a mild inflation requires only slight change in money-supply growth and the price-level trend, so production and employment are threatened and expectations disappointed only slightly. To invoke our earlier analogy, the difficulty of stopping a merely mild price inflation is slight for the same sort of reason as why the difficulty is slight of reversing a merely small wartime increase in the price level.

Intermediate inflation exhibits neither the slightness of the required monetary change and of the associated threat to production and employment required to stop a mild inflation nor the amenability to a quick fix that hyperinflation may offer. An intermediate inflation lacks the opportunities offered by either extreme and combines the catch-up and expectational elements of inflationary momentum at their worst.

The foregoing considerations suggest that, in an inflation such as the United States is experiencing, things may have to get worse before they can get better. We may have to reach a panicky state before taking the cure. This is not to say that it is downright impossible to wind down an inflation of our present type, but extreme practical difficulties do obstruct a direct move back to monetary stability.

The principle that things have to get worse before they can get better was apparently illustrated in France in July 1926, when the danger of degeneration into hyperinflation motivated a dramatic turn in policy. Italy provided another example in the summer of 1947. Even the United States experienced a mild illustration of the principle on November 1, 1978. On October 24, President Carter had announced an antiinflation program that was regarded as unconvincing, including wage and price controls as it did (so-called voluntary controls). The ensuing deterioration of the price situation and particularly of the dollar's exchange rate prodded the administration to announce further measures on November 1, including gestures of orthodox antiinflationary monetary policy. These brought recovery of the dollar on the exchanges and a temporary drop in the price of gold. To motivate a resolute and enduring antiinflation policy, however, the panic over money may have to become worse than in the autumn of 1978.

In some cases, conditions relatively favorable to stopping inflation may hinge on its nature or source. If the process of importing inflation at a fixed exchange rate has been at work, as in Germany and

Switzerland in the early 1970s, then floating the exchange rate represents a clear and obvious shift in policy and so should be conducive to turning expectations around. If, furthermore, the monetary authorities responsible for such a currency seize the opportunity provided by floating to pursue a less expansionary policy, a virtuous circle can result. The home currency's upward float on the foreign-exchange market lowers the home-currency prices of imported goods and perhaps of import-competing and export goods also, which is helpful in breaking the momentum of inflation in both its catch-up and expectational aspects. This facilitation of noninflationary money-supply policy further tends to strengthen the currency on the exchanges and so on. (The historical sections will have more to say about this virtuous circle.)

Because its current inflation has for the most part not been imported, the United States lacks the opportunity for a dramatic change of the kind just mentioned. Even so, some aspects of the virtuous circle could operate if the United States could somehow first make progress in winding down its inflation rate. Perception of this progress would help strengthen the dollar on the exchanges. In fact, the historically based greater usefulness of the dollar than of other currencies in international transactions provides plenty of scope for demand to turn in its favor if the inflation cost of holding dollar assets is seen to be abating. On the other hand, the virtuous circle working through import and export prices could not be as important as it was for Switzerland and Germany because of the smaller share of foreign trade in the American economy.

Decontrol

It could count as a favorable condition for stopping inflation that the inflationary difficulties were being compounded by price and wage and exchange controls, for the increased efficiency resulting from their removal—the increased output or real availability of goods—could help absorb inflationary demands. This remark seems applicable to stabilization programs in Argentina, Bolivia, Paraguay, and possibly Burma and other countries, whether or not the authorities took full advantage of the opportunity mentioned.

Controls have contributed on some occasions to the catch-up aspect of inflationary momentum, reinforcing market practices whereby only some prices rise almost continuously while others climb staircases, as it were, with steps of different lengths and heights. Governments, notably in Latin America, have often delayed adjustments in pegged exchange rates and in public-utility rates and have put price ceilings on foodstuffs, raw materials, and fuel. While temporarily containing cost pressures, the controls have discouraged production of the affected goods and services or have required government spending on subsidies. The economy is exposed, furthermore, to periodic large cost and price readjustments instead of to smaller and more nearly continuous adjustments.[47]

Chile has furnished an apparent example of controls aggravating inflation. Inflation tended to worsen the slow growth of agricultural output because governments tried to repress it with food price ceilings and with exchange-rate policies that also caused agricultural prices to lag behind the rise of other prices. Even after the authorities allowed agricultural prices to catch up, the discouragement to production would sometimes continue because producers expected the catch up to prove only temporary and the relation between agricultural and industrial prices to keep changing erratically. The resulting deficiency of growth in agricultural output would raise food prices in the long run and so contribute to wage increases or would contribute to foreign-exchange shortages by reducing exports or expanding imports.[48]

Controls

When controls have been working in this way, their removal can understandably assist an antiinflation program. Just as the removal of controls might be an antiinflationary factor, so, paradoxically, might their imposition. Their scope and importance as an antiinflation device, however, is narrowly limited. Perhaps the most nearly economically respectable argument for wage and price controls is that they can dramatize a policy shift and so help break the expectations that had been contributing to the momentum of inflation.[49] Some such hope underlay the controls instituted by President Nixon in August 1971.[50]

---

[47] Ibid., pp. 21, 26.

[48] Ibid., pp. 40–41.

[49] "Only when the public sees that the inflation has stopped, will it stop expecting the inflation to continue." Abba Lerner and David C. Colander, "MAP: A Cure for Inflation," in Colander, Solutions, p. 212. MAP is the authors' market antiinflation plan, a variant of tax-based incomes policy. A related argument is that controls could be a synchronizing mechanism and in effect impose a coordinated decision to stop raising prices and wages. The usual piecemeal method of setting prices and wages, under which everyone has reason to wait for everyone else to go first in practicing restraint, would be temporarily set aside. See Robert R. Keller, "Inflation, Monetarism, and Price Controls," Nebraska Journal of Economics and Business, vol. 19 (Winter 1980), pp. 30–40.

[50] William Fellner in Cagan, Economic Policy, p. 256.

Using temporary controls during a period of economic slack to break the inflationary spiral carried over from earlier conditions must be clearly distinguished from trying permanently to suppress the pressure of excess demand on prices. While the case for temporary controls to hasten the transition warranted by monetary and fiscal restraint is much more nearly respectable than the case for permanent controls, it is far from conclusive. The control policy of 1971 could devise only arbitrary criteria for regulating *relative* wages and prices while the general rate of inflation was being reduced.[51] Because controls lock relative prices into what is or soon becomes a disequilibrium pattern, success with their use probably must come quickly if it is to come at all. Even when adopted as part of a comprehensive program for stopping monetary expansion, controls are less likely to work successfully if recent experience with their inappropriate use has discredited them with the public. The Argentine antiinflation program that began in 1967 had an apparent brief success with wage and price controls while the exchange rate previously kept fixed at an unrealistic level was adjusted. Monetary expansion resumed, however, and the stabilization collapsed.

Ideally, controls would somehow serve to break the momentum of inflation without being so rigid as to sabotage the price mechanism. The search for such an ideal gives rise to proposals for tax-based incomes policies and wage-increase-permit plans.[52]

Exchange Stabilization

Exchange-rate stabilization resembles a wage-and-price freeze in being an attempt to break into the inflation spiral by fixing *something*. Rapid inflation involves either almost continuous exchange depreciation or at least frequent devaluation of the currency. In such a vicious circle, monetary expansion is not unmistakably the driving force. It is partly the *result* of spiraling prices. The government's expenditures may be rising apace with the price level, while its revenues come from taxes based on the lower prices and nominal incomes of several months before. In a rapid inflation, this lag between the public's incurring taxes and paying them can be a major cause of a government budget deficit covered by the printing press. Some of the extreme European inflations after World War I provide examples. In some

---

[51] Ibid., p. 256.

[52] Some of these are reviewed in Colander, *Solutions*.

episodes, the central bank had been granting commercial credits (and creating money) to satisfy the "needs of trade" at rising prices.

Recognizing these passive aspects of monetary expansion in no way contradicts the quantity theory. Of course, stabilization requires getting monetary expansion under control, but breaking into the vicious circle can be a way of doing just that. The exchange rate may be the point where the break-in can be accomplished with the quickest and most evident results, including a shift of expectations, especially if the exchange rate had come to be regarded as the main indicator of what was happening to the value of money. The Austrian government adopted this approach in 1922. Foreign loan commitments and government pledges of financial probity helped make exchange-rate pegging stick. With confidence returning, the demand to hold purchasing power in the form of Austrian crowns revived. To prevent this slump in velocity from causing severe deflation, the National Bank was able to issue additional crowns while buying foreign exchange. The Bolivian stabilization program of 1956 also focused on exchange-rate stabilization, supported by U.S. aid to cover budget deficits.

The cases mentioned were those of small countries whose domestic currencies were only a minor factor on the world foreign-exchange market and could be pegged to some dominant foreign currency. The United States could hardly do anything similar. The dollar is a bigger factor on foreign-exchange markets than any other single currency. Furthermore, pegging the dollar to one foreign currency would not mean pegging it to foreign currencies in general as long as the foreign currencies were fluctuating among themselves. An attempt by the United States to peg onto some particular foreign currency by borrowing and selling it—and the very mention of borrowing it indicates that the cooperation of the country whose currency was being used would be required—would tend more to depress that particular foreign currency than to stabilize the dollar against foreign currencies in general.

Alternatively, could the United States try to stabilize the dollar against gold? Since gold is not an actual currency in which goods and services are priced, pegging the dollar to it would not do much directly to stabilize prices, not even the prices of imports and exports.

This is not to deny the possibility of a virtuous circle. If the United States could somehow get its inflation under control, then the dollar would tend to strengthen on the foreign exchange market, restraining import and export prices. But this would be the consequence of domestic measures to control the inflation and not a case of exchange-rate stabilization initiating the virtuous circle.

Gradualism or a Quick Fix?

One leading question about historical episodes of ending inflation concerns whether stabilization was sought and achieved gradually or quickly. Almost all of the successes that have come to our attention involved stopping or drastically slowing price inflation within a few months. This fact may have some implications. Anyway, we want to ask what circumstances recommend gradualism and which recommend a quick fix.

The broadest, most intuitive, and least analytical argument for gradualism is that one should tackle a difficult task in small, manageable stages rather than try to accomplish it in one backbreaking effort. One more nearly specific argument is that a stabilization slump results not merely from the erosion of real money and spending by price-and-wage momentum but also from frictions in reversing an inflation-distorted allocation of resources; a gradual reallocation could at least hold down those frictions. Related considerations argue, on the other hand, that gradualness—delay—allows inflation-hedging allocations of resources to become all the more significant, requiring all the larger readjustments later. This consideration is reinforced by the point that a gradual program—that is, an undertaking to get inflation under control eventually—may lack the credibility of a program seen to be vigorous and to have early results.

Alexandre Kafka's preference for gradualism in dealing with Brazilian inflation in the mid-1960s apparently hinges on particular features of the local scene. Government wages and salaries had recently been increased, making government jobs exceptionally attractive, even though government payrolls seemed overloaded already. Furthermore, the minimum wage had recently been increased to a probably excessive level. Since wages and salaries could hardly be reduced in money terms, it was necessary to let inflation continue for a while, Kafka apparently felt, in order to whittle them down in real terms.[53] This condition is really part of the catch-up aspect of inflationary momentum, since to whittle down leading wages or prices relatively is to let the lagging ones catch up.

The Federal Reserve Bank of Minneapolis has argued for a steady and credible but also gradual antiinflation policy. Its reasons are largely psychological or political. Having observed stop and go and many surprises in macroeconomic policy, many persons would doubt the government's will to reform itself and to persist in a sequence of announced gradual steps toward price stability. To those persons, an

---

[53] Kafka, "Brazilian Stabilization," p. 609.

actual change of that kind, including of course a slowdown in monetary growth, would come as a surprise. This surprise would leave the momentum of prices and wages intact. Recessionary side effects would occur and, as in the past, could lead to abandonment of the antiinflation program.

Because it would take time for the government to demonstrate its resolve to persist in a program of slowing down the growth of total spending, the initial steps must be small. Once it has demonstrated its determination, however, and as measures of monetary restraint no longer come as surprises, then even large steps would no longer bring severe side effects. (The Bank recognized that if people were not committed by existing contracts and if they somehow did firmly believe that the government would persist in its antiinflation measures—which, however, is unlikely—then even large initial steps would not cause a recession.)[54]

This argument for gradualness amounts to saying that confidence in a resolute antiinflation policy simply cannot be achieved quickly; the policy shift is bound to come as a surprise. The strategy, therefore, is to keep the spending restraint mild at first in order to avoid serious side effects but to persist in restraint so that the public comes to perceive the resoluteness of the new policy. As this resoluteness increasingly commands confidence, the policy could even be intensified without severe side effects. The argument does not deny that even a sudden dramatic policy change could bring only mild side effects provided that complete trust in its resoluteness prevailed from the start. Doubt would in fact prevail, however, according to the argument. It takes time to achieve the degree of credibility necessary for avoiding severe side effects.

Juan de Pablo's argument for gradualness likewise hinges on the slowness of any change in perceptions and expectations. Experience with Argentina's stabilization program adopted in 1967 suggested that, when a country has been suffering an inflationary process for a long time, an antiinflationary strategy based on a sudden reduction in the inflation rate stands at a disadvantage because individuals will not "recognize" that reduction and will continue making their decisions in nominal terms. Around the end of 1967, real rates of interest in Argentina rose considerably as nominal interest rates were reduced less than the rate of inflation. In principle, this rise in real rates should have curtailed the volume of credit demanded, but in fact an expansion occurred. Another variable affected by money illusion was the real wage rate. Not fully recognizing the slowdown of price inflation,

---

[54] Federal Reserve Bank of Minneapolis, *1978 Annual Report*, especially pp. 6–7.

workers tended to demand nominal wages that implied increases in real wages. If businessmen increase their indebtedness despite the rise in the real rate of interest and if workers demand nominal wage increases incompatible with overall productivity growth and price stability, then the only way of "solving" the incompatibilities is to abandon the stabilization program and let prices rise.[55]

In saying that money illusion bars quick success against inflation, Pablo was evidently referring to a distinctive kind of money illusion that develops in inflationary times. Ordinarily, money illusion means persistence in thinking and acting as if the monetary unit were stable even when it is not. Pablo was referring, however, to persistence in a habit of adjusting to a continuous rise in the price level even when that price trend is being broken.

Another argument for only gradual stabilization is that a sudden end to inflation would hurt many people. Assets, such as houses, bought at prices reflecting intensified demand for them as supposed inflation hedges would fall in value if the expected further inflation did not occur. A quick stabilization would be hard on debtors who had borrowed, and at high interest rates, in the expectation of paying off their debts in depreciated dollars. Workers with long-term contracts stipulating periodic future wage increases in line with expected inflation would benefit from rapid stabilization (provided that they kept their jobs), while workers whose contracts came up for revision shortly afterwards would stand at a relative disadvantage. Even if a careful weighing of the economic pros and cons should definitely favor a quick stabilization, a gradual approach might be dictated by the political considerations, including resistance from those who consider all quick measures dangerous.[56]

The very authors who report these arguments for gradualism recognize that they are not conclusive. One might argue, on the contrary, that a gradual slowing of inflation only spreads the withdrawal pangs over a longer time period, while partially continuing the pains of the inflation itself. Furthermore, gradualism lacks the signs of a dramatic change of course that would be helpful in turning expectations around. The American people would be skeptical after their

---

[55] Juan Carlos de Pablo, *Política antiinflacionaria en la Argentina, 1967–1970* (Buenos Aires: Amorrortu Editores, 1970), pp. 112–113. Pablo's points about money illusion and wage rates, phrased differently, enter into Milton Friedman's argument for indexing as a way of helping facilitate an end to inflation.

[56] Lerner and Colander, "MAP," pp. 219–220. These authors are reviewing the arguments mentioned in the context of their proposal for a market antiinflation plan.

repeated experience with vague and gradual antiinflation programs that were abandoned. Furthermore, even if a gradual program really were succeeding, its success could be obscured—and a turnaround in expectations blocked—by upward jumps in the price level due to all sorts of unforeseeable temporary disturbances on the domestic or world scene. The program might be abandoned as a failure before the disturbance ran its course. Gradualism is thus dangerous. A dramatic demonstration may be necessary to break inflationary expectations.[57]

Alexandre Kafka, though judging that gradualism was the only course for Brazil in the mid-1960s, nevertheless recognized some risks. Gradualism dissipates the unique opportunity provided by establishment of a new government, if one has been established. Energetic measures might be acceptable at such a time but be resented later. The task of planning correctly during a period of announced decline in inflation, but decline at an unspecified rate, is almost as hard for businessmen as the task of planning under continuing inflation, and harder than planning under monetary stability.[58] Gradual stabilization perpetuates uncertainty about the purchasing power of the money unit over a long period, whereas quick stabilization cuts short this period of uncertainty.

Kafka distinguishes between the speed of stopping inflation and the speed of removing price repressions in the form of controls, subsidies, and the like. It might even help to save some of the decontrol until later, after that step had become less likely to rekindle inflationary expectations.[59]

If controls, and in particular a wage and price freeze, form part of a stabilization program, they are the focus of still another argument for aiming at quick rather than gradual success. A frozen pattern of relative prices and wages will become increasingly wrong and unfair, eroding the acceptability of the controls, as time goes on and as the underlying determinants of supply and demand change. Hence the importance of severe monetary action capable of soon replacing the direct controls.[60]

With regard to political acceptability, Ernest Sturc drew a lesson from the stabilization programs of Austria, Turkey, and Finland in the 1950s: "The period of readjustment and the necessary transfer of resources must not be too long. For the failure to achieve tangible

---

[57] Ibid., p. 220; and Lerner, in Colander, *Solutions*, p. 196.
[58] Kafka, "Brazilian Stabilization," p. 610.
[59] Ibid., especially p. 607.
[60] This is one major theme of Pablo, *Política*.

results within a reasonable period is very likely to weaken the political consensus that favors stabilization policies."[61]

The architect of the Bolivian stabilization program of 1956–1957, George Jackson Eder, answers the argument for gradualism by quoting Graeme S. Dorrance to the effect that "a gradual approach is fraught with more danger than sudden stabilization." Ending a hyperinflation is bound to produce serious imbalances, tensions, and hardships, which are more pronounced the longer the inflation had lasted and the more exaggerated the distortions it had caused. No nation can be expected to endure a lengthy period of painful readjustment, whereas a sharp break from hyperinflation has an almost anesthetic effect. No nation, so far as Eder recalled, had ever successfully ended a rampant inflation gradually. In Bolivia, such an attempt simply would not have worked.[62]

Irving S. Friedman distinguishes between gradualism in the success of a stabilization program and gradualism in taking the necessary measures. Bottlenecks or disturbances that cannot be eliminated at once may make instant price stability impossible. Wishful thinking and promises of quick success may lead to disappointment, with an adverse effect on expectations. Slogans about gradualism, however, may serve as an excuse for inadequate measures, and "gradualism in changing expectations or trends is self-defeating." The public must quickly be given reason to expect ever smaller price increases or even price declines.[63]

The architect of Bolivian stabilization noted the objection that the Bolivian experience might have little relevance for other Latin American countries, where inflation had been less extreme and presumably required less drastic and sudden remedies. His answer was that, wherever inflation has gotten out of control, as in Brazil, Argentina, Chile, and Colombia, a surgical operation and not a palliative was demanded. He could recall no case of uncontrolled inflation that had been cured gradually, as by reducing the annual rate from 100 to 50 to 20 percent and finally to 0. The maladjustments produced during a long inflation and the difficulties and distortions of readjustment are so great that one cannot expect the authorities and the public to suffer

---

[61] Ernest Sturc, "Stabilization Policies: Experience of Some European Countries in the 1950's," International Monetary Fund Staff Papers, vol. 15, no. 2 (July 1968), p. 216.

[62] George Jackson Eder, Inflation and Development in Latin America: A Case History of Inflation and Stabilization in Bolivia (Ann Arbor: Bureau of Business Research, University of Michigan, 1968), p. 277. Dorrance's words are quoted from "The Effect of Inflation on Economic Development," International Monetary Fund Staff Papers, vol. 10, no. 1 (March 1963), p. 29.

[63] "Comment," Journal of Political Economy, vol. 75 (August 1967), part 2, pp. 651–652.

patiently for two or three years while the monetary advisor assures them that all will turn out well in the end if they follow his advice. In stabilization above all, "Twere well it were done quickly."[64]

As implied by some of the points already reviewed, the relative strengths of the arguments for gradual and for quick stabilization depend on the particular circumstances of the case. If all prices, wages, salaries, rents, contractual values, rates, and tariffs are being adjusted at frequent intervals and are being kept nearly in line with each other, that circumstance would argue for quick stabilization. In the opposite case of infrequent adjustments at staggered times, suddenly applying the brakes to both demands and costs would create a pattern that would touch off complaints of injustice. If the brakes were applied to demand only, while costs and prices went on being pushed up as contracts of the lagging groups successively reached their renewal dates, recession would ensue.[65] The distinction between these cases is obviously related to the point made earlier that stopping an extreme inflation is in some respects easier than stopping a moderate inflation.

A case relatively amenable to sudden stabilization is one in which a flight from the domestic currency has raised prices, including the price of foreign exchange, to a higher level than the quantity of money, apart from psychological factors, warrants. This was apparently the situation in France in mid-1926. In Germany in November 1923, similarly, the price of foreign exchange and of the new Rentenmark in terms of the old paper marks had been pushed up, in this case by stabilization measures themselves, to above the level previously prevailing on the market. Like devaluing a weak currency with a margin to spare in order to facilitate its subsequent exchange stabilization, this was an example of *reculer pour mieux sauter*.

In an inflationary situation of the current U.S. type, the processes of cost-price interaction and catch-up prevent an instant stabilization of the price level. Yet this circumstance does not rule out sudden stabilization in the sense of a turnaround of expectations. Two situations are quite different: (1) expecting inflation to continue on its established course, and (2) perceiving a clampdown on money-supply growth and expecting no further price increases except by way of catch-up. If policy makers and the public could understand the catch-up process and why it did not demonstrate a failure of monetary restraint, then a sudden stabilization could be achieved as far as both monetary fundamentals and expectations were concerned.

---

[64] Eder, *Inflation and Development*, pp. xi–xii.
[65] Pazos, *Chronic Inflation*, p. 7.

Alfred Zanker, chief European economic correspondent of *U.S. News and World Report*, recommends some such approach for U.S. inflation. So far, fears of a bad recession have kept governments in the United States and abroad from acting long and forcefully enough against inflation. At least four times in twenty years, the United States has abandoned the remedy too soon, allowing inflation to resurge from a higher plateau. Policy makers now face a deep credibility gap. Zanker recommends stopping monetary expansion long enough to achieve a basic change in price expectations. A credit crunch and sweeping moves toward a balanced government budget would help restore confidence in the dollar. A publicity campaign would explain why so drastic a cure was needed and how it would succeed.

Historical experience suggested to Zanker that the side effects— layoffs, bankruptcies, and the like—would not be catastrophic and would reach their climax within six to twelve months. Business firms would respond with efforts to hold the line on costs and prices. Soon, with inflation receding fast and government finance looking healthier, interest rates would fall sharply, encouraging capital formation and renewed business expansion. The shock treatment would strengthen the dollar on the exchange markets, would encourage and facilitate antiinflation programs abroad, and would work toward moderation in the pricing of oil. Such shock treatment is no miracle weapon, no substitute for prudent policies and good management and hard work; but it is more attractive than tolerating a prolonged stagflation.[66]

We now turn to historical episodes.

---

[66] Alfred Zanker, "Shock Treatment for Inflation: Can It Work?" *U.S. News and World Report*, August 27, 1979, pp. 67–68.

2
Ending Hyperinflations

Austria in 1922

Austria in 1922 provides an example of a sudden end to extreme inflation. The Austro-Hungarian Monarchy had fallen apart at the end of World War I. The successor states embargoed the export of food to Austria. Even people in the surrounding countryside were inclined to restrict shipments to Vienna, where 1918 and 1919 brought famine. The Viennese bureaucracy, large even for the old empire, was swollen by return of administrators from the successor states. Those states were reluctant to share in the Monarchy's debts. The Allied powers, far from being eager to extend aid, expected reparations; and the Reparation Commission asserted a blanket lien against all Austrian property. The budget situation was chaotic. Major categories of expenditure included civil service salaries, unemployment doles, and pensions; the largest item (half of the expenditure in December 1921) was food subsidies. The ministries received extraordinary credits after spending their budget appropriations. Collapse of the industrial base and of personal incomes impaired tax revenues, and war-profits taxes were not collected. Fresh note issues covered government deficits.[1]

At the end of 1918, the note circulation of Austria-Hungary had been about 14 times as large and the price level about 25 times as high as before the war.[2] By the beginning of 1920, the Austrian price

---

[1] Leo Pasvolsky, *The Economic Nationalism of the Danubian States* (New York: Macmillan, 1928), pp. 96–98, 103; K. W. Rothschild, *Austria's Economic Development between the Two Wars* (London: Muller, 1947), pp. 16–17; David F. Strong, *Austria (October 1918–March 1919)* (New York: Columbia University Press, 1939), p. 203.

[2] Charts in J. van Walré de Bordes, *The Austrian Crown* (London: King, 1924), pp. 146–147.

The Austrian statistics are imprecise. Price indexes, in particular, were crudely constructed and were distorted by price and rent controls and subsidies. Indexes

level was about 49 times and the exchange rate on the U.S. dollar about 35 times as high as before the war. In January 1921, these figures were 92 for the price level and 134 for the dollar rate; in January 1922, they were 830 and 1164, respectively. At their respective peaks in September and August 1922, the price level and the exchange rate stood 14,153 and 16,877 times as high as before the war. In the last year of the inflation, between September 1921 and September 1922, the price level was multiplied by approximately 94. Its annual rate of rise reached 64,553 percent between mid-May and mid-June 1922, 6,304 percent between June and July, 627,192 percent between July and August, and 231,070 percent between August and September.[3]

The deterioration of money reached the stage at which exchange depreciation appeared to be pushing up prices within the country. After late 1920, and especially in the second half of 1921 and in the summer of 1922, the price of foreign exchange appeared to lead the rise of the exchange rate and of the bank-note circulation. Rising prices of imported materials boosted domestic production costs. Producers and retailers began estimating costs in foreign currency, adding a markup, and translating the result into Austrian crowns at the latest exchange rate. Foreign currencies were not only thus used as units of account but even gained some use as media of exchange. The printing presses rolled to cover government budget deficits, which from 1919 through 1922 amounted to half or two-thirds of government expenditures. Government spending, including costly food subsidies until their belated abolition late in 1921, rose roughly in step with the price level. Specific taxes and the prices of goods sold by the state (such as rail transportation and tobacco) lagged, and much of the real value of income taxes vanished in the lag between assessment and collection. The superficial view that exchange depreciation *caused* the price increases, deficits, and money issues gained apparent support from the fact that exchange stabilization preceded price stabilization.[4]

Actually, episodes of monetary expansion apparently lagging behind price spurts and exchange depreciation prove little about fundamental causation. Such a sequence typically reflects anticipations of a continuing process of rapid inflation. Money does not lose value at one stroke or at a uniform pace against all goods and services. Some

---

with different coverages or constructed by different authorities diverge notably. Still, these inexactnesses are insignificant in relation to the extreme inflation that all the figures show.

[3] From and calculated from Walré de Bordes, *Austrian Crown*, various tables and charts. Because of rent controls, the cost of living index with housing excluded has been used here.

[4] Walré de Bordes, *Austrian Crown*, passim.

prices are "stickier" than others. A floating exchange rate is among the least sticky of prices and can respond especially promptly to actual and anticipated changes in price levels and monetary conditions. This is not the same as its one-directionally determining prices and the quantity of money.

When its currency has reached a rate of deterioration so rapid as to be unserviceable as a unit for assessing and collecting taxes, then, as a League of Nations report observed, a country has two courses open to it. It can achieve a unit suitable for taxation and fiscal accounting either by adopting a foreign currency or gold or some other commodity or else by stabilizing the national currency by some initial means other than balancing the budget. Austria (and later Hungary) took the second course. First, it managed to stabilize the crown, thanks largely to a return of confidence under the influence of a scheme of financial reconstruction still being worked out under the auspices of the League of Nations; then this provisional stabilization made possible an increase in real tax revenues sufficient to balance the budget.[5]

Political change apparently played an important role in the reconstruction program. It was prerequisite to the grant of special powers that removed the government's financial measures from parliamentary scrutiny for two years and subjected them to League of Nations supervision. Against a background of political instability, Monsignor Ignaz Seipel, a Jesuit, become chancellor in May 1922 after organizing the nonsocialist parties into a bloc that would command a firm majority in Parliament. Seipel was a powerful and cogent speaker who impressed the Western powers as financially reliable. He knew how to use Austria's economic distress as a negotiating weapon and how to exploit Western fears that his country would be absorbed by Germany or would become an Italian vassal state. Eventually he persuaded the British, French, Czechosolvak, and Italian governments to guarantee a loan to Austria of 650 million gold crowns.[6]

It is noteworthy that the initial stabilization of the crown was achieved, in August 1922, before the foreign loans were actually received and even before the negotiations to obtain them were complete. Apparently the prospect of international assistance and intenational supervision of financial reform had a supportive psycho-

[5] League of Nations, *The Course and Control of Inflation* (Princeton, 1946), especially pp. 18, 61n., 69, 131.

[6] Charles S. Maier, "The Politics of Inflation in the Twentieth Century," in Fred Hirsch and John H. Goldthorpe, *The Political Economy of Inflation* (Cambridge: Harvard University Press, 1978), pp. 51–52; Walré de Bordes, *Austrian Crown*, p. 16; Elisabeth Barker, *Austria 1918–1972* (London: Macmillan, 1973), pp. 52–53; Karl R. Stadler, *Austria* (New York and Washington, D.C.: Praeger, 1971), pp. 121–123.

logical effect.[7] The stabilization action was preceded in July and August 1922 by a tightening of exchange controls, apparently with a beneficial direct effect but adverse psychological effect on the balance between supply of and demand for foreign currencies. The Austrian part of the Austro-Hungarian Bank tightened credit to make the speculative holding of foreign exchange more costly.[8] Then, on August 25, the foreign-exchange office began intervening to keep the price of the dollar from exceeding the rate reached on that day, 83,600 crowns (up from 50,875 on August 2, implying exchange depreciation of the crown at a 99.96 percent annual rate in those final three weeks). (Actually, the Swiss franc was chosen first as the basis of pegging, but a shift to a dollar peg was made a few months later.)[9] Thereafter, the dollar rate drifted unsteadily downward to as low as 70,025 on December 29; thus, the crown appreciated by 19.2 percent from its lowest point. The drift was not allowed to continue; in 1923, the crown was stabilized at around 71,000 per dollar, or at 0.14 of a cent per 100 crowns. It now took 14,400 paper crowns to equal 1 prewar crown in gold value.[10] At this depreciated level, the crown became one of the most stable currencies in Europe, earning the nickname of "the Alpine dollar."

Why wasn't the recovery of the crown on the foreign-exchange market allowed to continue? By the end of 1922, the authorities expected a considerable supply of foreign exchange on the market from government borrowing in foreign currencies and from repatriation of Austrian capital. They thought that a continuing rise would accelerate this repatriation and make the crown an object of bullish international speculation. (Something like that had happened to the Czechoslovak crown in 1921.) If it had kept on rising in 1923, the crown would have appeared more attractive than dollars, pounds, or Swiss francs to Germans trying to shelter their funds from the fall of the mark. A sharp and prolonged rise of the crown would have sorely burdened Austria industry. The authorities therefore decided to stabilize the exchange rate by buying up any excess supplies of foreign exchange.[11]

Prices leveled off dramatically soon after exchange depreciation was stopped on August 25. Merchants no longer considered it as necessary as before, in calculating their selling prices, to add an allowance for expected future depreciation. The public, having stocked

---

[7] League of Nations, *Course*, pp. 69, 131.

[8] Walré de Bordes, *Austrian Crown*, pp. 202–203.

[9] Ibid., p. 219.

[10] This figure is calculated from the gold contents of the relevant prewar and poststabilization coins.

[11] Walré de Bordes, *Austrian Crown*, pp. 217–218.

up on goods during its flight from the crown, was in a position to postpone some further purchases to see whether the stabilization would succeed; and its hesitation also prodded merchants to shave prices. The cost-of-living index, compiled as of the middle of each month, peaked in September, then sagged downward for the rest of 1922, the December index (housing excluded) being 22.5 percent below the peak. It then fluctuated gradually upward, reaching approximately the level of the earlier peak around the turn of the year 1923–1924.[12]

Meanwhile, steps were going forward to implement the financial measures whose mere prospect had brought such a dramatic change. Chancellor Seipel laid the Austrian question before the council of the League of Nations on September 5, 1922. A plan was worked out with the purpose, among others, of clearing away political clouds so as to improve Austria's ability to borrow private funds. Three protocols were signed in Geneva on October 4. The first reaffirmed Austria's political and economic independence. The second concerned the already mentioned guarantee of loans by four foreign governments; their purpose was to finance exchange-rate stabilization and to cover the government's budget deficit in a noninflationary way during a transition period. In the third protocol, the Austrian government pledged to submit a program of financial reforms to Parliament, to seek extraordinary powers to carry them out, to cease borrowing from the central bank, and to create a new and independent central bank. The League of Nations was to appoint a commissioner-general, without whose approval the Austrian government could spend none of the money provided by the loans.[13]

In November and December, the Austrian Parliament ratified the Geneva protocols, adopted the financial reform program, and granted the requested extraordinary powers to the government. The Austrian banks and public subscribed to the full amount of an internal short-term loan of 50 million gold crowns. In December, having been preceded in October by a provisional delegation of the League of Nations, the League's commissioner-general took up his duties in Vienna. In October, the Reparation Commission and, in December, individual foreign governments agreed to waive their liens on Austrian state assets that were to serve as security for the projected foreign loans.

[12] Ibid., pp. 83, 209, 211, and calculations from figures given there; see also the charts on pp. 150–151. League of Nations, *International Statistics Year-Book 1926* (Geneva, 1927), pp. 170, 174, shows prices drifting up a bit further in 1924.
[13] Walré de Bordes, *Austrian Crown*, pp. 28–29; Ivan T. Berend and György Ranki, *Economic Development in East-Central Europe in the 19th and 20th Centuries* (New York: Columbia University Press, 1974), p. 214.

The securities of the Austrian government's guaranteed foreign loans were successfully placed abroad in 1923, the short-term bills in February and the long-term bonds in the summer. These provided the government with enough funds (in foreign currencies) to cover its deficit until it could balance its budget.[14] Indirect taxes were increased, almost 85,000 public employees were dismissed, and pensions and similar benefits were kept from fully reflecting the depreciation of the currency.[15] The restoration of a stable currency unit in which taxes could be assessed and collected was instrumental in balancing the budget. Only a part of the foreign loans was actually used for covering budget deficits.[16]

During the first three months after stopping the crown's depreciation, the government continued its old habit of covering its deficit by borrowing newly printed paper money from the central bank. Then, in late November, as it began receiving the proceeds of its new domestic loans, the government discontinued its resort to the printing press. This step proved important in consolidating confidence. The old source of expansion of the money supply gave way to a new one: creation of domestic money as the authorities brought up heavy supplies of foreign exchange to resist an unwanted appreciation of the stabilized crown. The public's offerings of foreign exchange were especially large in December because of the exchange rates specified for subscriptions to the new internal loans and because of certain tax exemptions. This condition of the foreign-exchange market became temporarily reversed early in 1923 as delay in the floating of the first foreign loan, together with the government's difficulties in finding funds to meet its obligations, weakened confidence in the crown. The foreign short-term loan was floated at the end of February; however, negotiations for the long-term loan were proceeding well, the government's deficit was perceived to be shrinking, and the foreign-exchange position of the newly established Austrian National Bank began growing stronger week by week.[17]

In the ways just mentioned, the Austrian banknote circulation continued expanding. It grew by 17.9 percent in the last eight days of August 1922 and by 426.5 percent in the succeeding sixteen months, that is, at an annual rate of 247.6 percent. Even so, this represents a considerable slowdown in the rate of increase, which had amounted to an annual rate of 1753 percent from the beginning of 1922 to

---

[14] Walré de Bordes, *Austrian Crown*, pp. 30–31, 213–214.

[15] Stadler, *Austria*, p. 123.

[16] League of Nations, *Course*, pp. 61n, 69.

[17] Walré de Bordes, *Austrian Crown*, pp. 32, 205–206.

August 23.[18] That this continued though reduced monetary growth did not prove inflationary must be attributed to a strong recovery in the demand for domestic real cash balances, the latter being due in turn to belief that effective steps were being taken to save the crown. If the central bank had somehow held the money supply constant in the face of this strongly recovering demand, an extreme deflation would have resulted. (This same phenomenon of monetary expansion continuing after exchange stabilization would later be observed in Yugoslavia, Germany, Hungary, Poland, and other countries.)[19]

Walré de Bordes, writing early in 1924, worried that the continued creation of money against acquisitions of foreign exchange would rekindle Austrian inflation.[20] Some signs of this had already appeared in 1923 (as mentioned a few pages earlier, the cost-of-living index had regained its peak level after an initial dip). Furthermore, indexes compiled by the League of Nations do show wholesale and retail prices rising in the following couple of years. This movement was much milder and of a different character, however, than the one stopped in 1922. It constitutes a different story and does not alter the conclusion that Austrian inflation was essentially stopped cold.

One immediate side effect of stabilization was a business crisis. Some reallocations of resources were unavoidable and indeed appropriate; speculative businesses, for example, that had lived off the decline of the crown had to be liquidated. Unemployment rose, partly reflecting the government's discharge of surplus employees.[21] Conditions cannot have been entirely bleak, however, for the Austrian stock market, which had not kept pace with the inflation, boomed in 1923. An index of the share of prices of Austrian companies—prices in terms of a now approximately stable money—rose over 400 percent between September 1922 and September 1923. This boom is said to have contributed to the repatriation of Austrian capital and an inflow of foreign capital and thus to growth of the country's foreign-exchange reserves.[22]

Adoption of a new currency unit near the end of 1924 symbolically completed the stabilization program. The schilling replaced the

---

[18] Calculated from Walré de Bordes, *Austrian Crown*, tables on pp. 49–50.

[19] League of Nations, *Course*, p. 62; Costantino Bresciani-Turroni, *The Economics of Inflation* (London: Allen & Unwin, 1937), p. 338. Walré de Bordes suggests that the gradual disappearance of foreign banknotes from circulation also helped counterbalance the growth of the Austrian money supply; *Austrian Crown*, p. 210.

[20] Walré de Bordes, *Austrian Crown*, pp. 223–225.

[21] Ibid., pp. 218, 225; League of Nations, *The Financial Reconstruction of Austria* (Geneva, 1926), pp. 241–242.

[22] Walré de Bordes, *Austrian Crown*, pp. 215–217.

crown at the rate of 1 to 10,000. (In gold content, 1.44 schillings equaled 1 prewar crown.)

Summary and Comment. This switch to a new unit could not have had even a psychological effect in stopping inflation, since stabilization of the old unit had been achieved two years before. Stabilization came *suddenly*, after inflation had reached an intolerably extreme stage. (It is true that Austria did not generate such astronomical numbers as Germany generated a year later, but in both countries the currency unit was all but wiped out. What real difference does it make whether money holders and creditors lose all but 1/14,400 or all but one one-trillionth of the value of their monetary assets?) In Austria, a dramatic turnaround of expectations apparently hinged on political developments, broadly conceived. These included cabinet changes and prospects of a stabilization program involving foreign loans and international supervision of Austrian government finances.

Hungary in 1924

Hungary experienced about the same degree of inflation as Austria—that is, stabilized at nearly the same degree of depreciation from the currency's prewar gold value—and achieved stabilization in a similar manner, with the aid of loans and supervision provided under League of Nations auspices.[23] The stabilization, however, was delayed almost two years longer in Hungary.

Both countries shared the same background of wartime inflation. Both suffered dismemberment at the end of the war, but Hungary did not share the problems left over from having been the center of a now dismembered empire. As a predominantly agricultural country, Hungary did not face famine. It suffered other disorders, including initial attempts to resist dismemberment of the country, four and one-half months of a Communist regime, war with Czechoslovakia and Rumania, and, in 1921, two attempts by King Charles to regain his lost throne.

Hungary, unlike Austria, did not evoke much sympathy from the rest of the world. Her neighbors remained hostile. While it was recognized early that reparations could not be collected from Austria, Hungary was still held liable for them. (Thus, Hungary's objective strengths spelled political weakness.) The Reparation Commission

---

[23] The chief sources for this section are Pasvolsky, *Economic Nationalism*; League of Nations, *The Financial Reconstruction of Hungary* (Geneva, 1926); and Lowell L. Ecker, "The Hungarian Thrift Crown," *American Economic Review*, September 1933, pp. 471–474.

held a lien of indefinite amount and duration on the country's assets; it might be compared to a potential marginal tax rate of 100 percent. Economic success would entail paying reparations, while distress might bring aid. These circumstances made borrowing abroad substantially impossible; and they weakened the authorities' incentives to make stabilization efforts, since the Reparation Commission might take any revenues or loan proceeds that might be raised.

The tale of budget deficits is much the same as for other East European countries at the time. State enterprises ran at a loss, flour was sold to the urban population at subsidized prices, civil servants' salaries and pensions weighed heavily, debt service payments were burdensome until rapid inflation eroded them, freshly printed banknotes covered the deficits, and the exchange rate plummeted.

Under Dr. Roland Hegedüs, who became finance minister with almost dictatorial authority for one year, a comprehensive attempt at stabilization was made in 1921. Hegedüs introduced and increased a large number of taxes, including a 20 percent capital levy. His program apparently did restore confidence in the future of the currency for a while. It stemmed the flight from the crown and enabled the government to stop the printing presses in March 1921. The exchange rate expressed in paper crowns per prewar gold crown improved from 2,100 in January to 2,030 in February and to 880 in May.

By August and September, however, the rate worsened again to 1,410 and then 2,100. Dr. Hegedüs resigned in September, and the reform failed. Actually collecting the new taxes had proved hard to organize. The political situation, as already mentioned, remained unstable. The program was viewed as too ambitious, since it aimed not merely at stabilizing but at appreciating the currency (which it briefly did). Although Hegedüs wanted to raise foreign loans to cover the budget deficit, the blanket lien held by the Reparation Commission thwarted putting up the required collateral.

In April 1923, the Hungarian government asked the Reparation Commission to lift the lien on its assets so that they might serve as security for an external loan. The commission agreed to do so only for specific loans and on condition that part of the proceeds go for reparations. The government was unable to negotiate any loans on these terms, and the crown sank further on the exchanges.

In return for a Hungarian pledge not to disturb the political order in Central Europe, Czechoslovakia, Rumania, and Yugoslavia agreed in July 1923 not to stand in the way of international assistance to Hungary. Removing this obstacle paved the way for the League of Nations application to Hungary of essentially the same program that had proved successful in Austria.

Meanwhile, the government attempted to stem the inflation by introducing a "savings crown" in February 1924. This new and supposedly stable unit of account was defined in terms of foreign-exchange rates and security prices but lacked any direct tie to internal prices. It was supposed to regularize debtor-creditor relations, promote saving, and form the basis for tax collections. It was not popular, partly because of its complexity, and survived only four and one-half months.

Another event of February 1924 was the Reparation Commission's lifting of its lien on Hungarian assets. That step was contingent on implementation of the League of Nations plan for financial reconstruction. Reparations payments were not to begin until after the reconstruction period, and the burden was light, with per capital payments much smaller than those imposed on Germany.

Progress then came rapidly. Protocols setting forth the reconstruction plan were signed in Geneva in March 1924. The League of Nations appointed a delegation to work out fiscal and currency reforms in collaboration with the Hungarian government and appointed a commissioner-general to supervise the reform and allocate the proceeds of the loans being provided. The reform was sweeping, not piecemeal. Government expenditures were cut, taxes raised, and state enterprises put on a self-supporting basis. Stabilization of exchange rates and prices, artificial at first, was to be part of the effort of getting government expenditures under control. A new central bank, the Hungarian National Bank, was established in April 1924 and began operations in June. It was forbidden to make advances to the government. It obtained a 4-million-pound loan from the Bank of England to help finance stabilizing the crown against the pound sterling.

The Hungarian currency reached its low point on the exchanges in June 1924, and the price inflation essentially came to an end shortly thereafter. Earlier that year, between January and February, it had reached an annual rate of over 109,000 percent as measured by the wholesale price index and of nearly 60,000 percent as measured by the retail index. The wholesale index peaked in July at 22,945 times the level of 1913 and, after an intermediate sag, peaked again in December at 23,466 (representing a modest 5.5 percent annual rate of increase from the July level). Wholesale prices then definitely declined—at a 17.4 percent annual rate from December 1924 to June 1926. The retail price index peaked in July 1924 at 22,018 times the level of ten years before and sagged thereafter (the annual rate of decline amounted to 13.1 percent between July 1924 and June 1926). Thus, inflation, when it ended, ended suddenly.

Government revenues turned out larger than expected and budget balance was achieved sooner—in fact, during the first few months of League of Nations supervision. League control of both Hungarian and Austrian finances ended on the same date, June 30, 1926, having lasted one and a half years longer in Austria.

Hungary completed its currency reform in 1925 by introducing a new unit, the pengö, valued at 12,500 paper crowns and with the same gold content as 17½ U.S. cents. Thus, while the paper crown was ultimately stabilized at about the same level in Hungary as in Austria, Hungary adopted the larger new unit. In neither country, and in contrast with what happened in Germany, was introduction of a new unit an integral part of the stabilization process. Instead, the already stabilized old unit was replaced with a new one of more convenient size.

Summary. The Hungarian stabilization was achieved rapidly but after earlier false starts. Action was taken simultaneously on the budgetary and money-supply fundamentals and on the exchange rate. Political change in the form of international assistance and supervision seems to have been a key element in success.

Germany, 1923–1924

Germany's rapid stabilization and the conditions that made it possible offer instructive contrasts with attempts to stabilize from inflation running at a moderate rate. Germany's inflation lagged behind Austria's chronologically in generating numbers of any given size, but it lasted longer and finally produced much bigger numbers. The prewar mint par had been 4.2 marks per dollar. The quotation averaged 6 marks in 1918 and stood at 14 in June 1919, 39 in June 1920, 69 in June 1921, 317 in June 1922, nearly 18,000 in January 1923, and around 100,000 in June 1923. The end-of-year wholesale price index stood at 2.6 times the prewar level in 1918, 8 times in 1919, 14 in 1920, 35 in 1921, and 1,475 in 1922. The mark was finally stabilized at 1 trillion times as many marks per dollar as before World War I. At the end of 1923, the wholesale and cost-of-living indexes stood about 1.3 and 1.4 trillion times as high, respectively, as before the war. Between June and December 1923, wholesale prices were rising at an average annual rate of 536 quadrillion percent and the cost of living at an average annual rate of 3.45 quintillion percent.[24]

---

[24] The words "billion," "trillion," and so on are used here in the American (and French) meaning, not in the German (and British) meaning. The rates of rise mentioned were calculated from League of Nations, *International Statistical Year-Book, 1926*, pp. 170, 174.

In such conditions, it is doubtful that some prices were lagging for many months, weeks, or even days behind others; the catch-up element in inflationary momentum must have been almost wiped out. Furthermore, since it was intolerable and almost inconceivable for such a situation to continue much longer and since the authorities were bound to change course somehow or other, expectations must have been ripe for a turnaround.

Political circumstances were contributing to the government's budget deficit and its being covered by the printing press. The Versailles Treaty had saddled Germany with an acknowledgment of guilt for the war and an obligation to compensate the victims. At times, as in Austria, exchange depreciation of the currency ran ahead of and superficially appeared to be causing the rise of prices and of the banknote circulation; this was notably true at the time of heavy reparations transfers in September 1921 and August 1922. Government expenditures rose with prices, while revenues lagged because specific taxes and nontax revenues were adjusted tardily and because income taxes collected in a given year were based on incomes of the year before, when nominal prices and incomes had been much lower. In January 1923, French and Belgian troops occupied the industrial Ruhr valley to prod the defaulting Germans into fuller and more prompt reparations payments. The Germans responded with "passive resistance," including deliberate absenteeism from industrial jobs. Government support of the resisting workers further burdened the budget. By the end of October 1923, the government's ordinary receipts were covering only about 0.8 percent of expenditures; the government was raising money almost exclusively by borrowing at the Reichsbank, which simply rolled the printing presses.

New money also poured out on loan to private businessmen, who eagerly borrowed with the prospect of repaying some weeks or months later in marks that would have depreciated much further in the meanwhile. Charging interest at rates that came nowhere near to fully reflecting the extreme inflation, the Reichsbank was practically giving money away. Its president, Rudolf Havenstein, adhered to the real-bills or needs-of-trade fallacy and considered it his duty to supply the growing amounts of money needed to conduct transactions at the ever higher price level. At one point, he seriously expressed hope that installation of new high-speed currency printing presses would overcome the supposed shortage of money.[25]

---

[25] For insight into Havenstein's thinking, see League of Nations, *Course*, pp. 16–17, 31, and Havenstein's address to the executive committee of the Reichsbank, August 25, 1923, reprinted in Fritz K. Ringer, ed., *The German Inflation of 1923* (New York: Oxford University Press, 1969), pp. 93–96.

In August 1923, the cabinet of Chancellor Wilhelm Cuno, which had waged the Ruhr struggle, resigned. A new coalition government headed by Gustav Stresemann succeeded it on August 15 and ordered an end to passive resistance. Payments to resisting workers and officials stopped. In November, the occupying authorities and representatives of industry, with the German government concurring, signed agreements under which the companies were to pay taxes and deliver products directly to the Allies. It seems to be no mere coincidence that the Ruhr conflict and the great inflation ended at the same time.[26] Meanwhile, Stresemann's new finance minister, Hans Luther, who took office early in October, worked energetically for budget stabilization.

The eventual replacement of the inflated mark by a new stable money was foreshadowed by several experiments with alternative moneys. Rye and other commodities and even kilowatt hours of electricity were used as units of value in some privately issued bonds. As in the last phases of some other extreme inflations, the legal paper money partially came to be replaced not only as a store and standard of value but even as a means of payment. Little by little, foreign money or the old national metallic money (which had been hoarded) or money created by private firms entered circulation. In the summer of 1922, important industries began expressing prices in foreign money or gold marks, even though paper marks remained the predominant medium of exchange. In the summer of 1923, when rapid shrinkage of the total real value of the paper money supply made the shortage of means of payment acute at times, emergency issues proliferated. By the autumn, 2,000 different kinds were said to be in circulation. Some were denominated in depreciating paper marks, others in units of supposedly stable value. Under a law of August 14, 1923, the government began issuing bonds and notes denominated in gold. For the first time, it officially introduced the concept of a gold mark having the traditional exchange rate of 4.20 per dollar. Although the new securities had no backing and no guarantee of stability beyond vague words, the public eagerly adopted those of small denominations (which ranged to as small as one-tenth of a dollar, forty-two pfennigs) as means of payment. Furthermore, the government encouraged the piggybacking onto its gold loan of stable-value emergency moneys issued principally by states, towns, and chambers of commerce. These issues were to be backed by the deposit of equivalent amounts of gold-loan securities or of special gold

---

[26] Gustav Stolper, *The German Economy 1870 to the Present* (1967), passages reprinted in Ringer, *German Inflation*, pp. 75–76.

treasury bonds created for the purpose. The railway administration was authorized to issue constant-value emergency money similarly backed.[27]

The reform plan ultimately adopted emerged from discussions of earlier proposals. The economist Karl Helfferich proposed what would have been an official application of private experiments with using commodities as units of account. A new bank financed by agriculture, trade, and industry would issue marks valued in rye. Three months after its establishment, the bank would pay the government 300 million gold marks worth of rye mark notes, with which the government would pay off its short-term debt to the Reichsbank. Thereafter, the government would be barred from financing its budget deficits at the Reichsbank. Helfferich's rye notes would have constituted a purely internal currency, but industrialists wanted an internationally usable one. The government prepared two bills, one instituting a rye mark and the other a new mark defined in gold. After discussion of these bills by a committee of experts early in September 1923, the government submitted a revised bill to the Reichstag on October 1. It provided for a new gold mark to be issued by a new bank. It was considered important to separate the new money from the government and the Reichsbank; because of the latter's role in the inflation, not much trust would have been placed in its promise to stop covering the budget deficit after granting the government one last credit.[28]

Under a law passed two days before, Finance Minister Luther issued a decree on October 15 for establishment of the German Rentenbank. Its capital would come from agricultural, industrial, commercial, and banking enterprises; and it would hold a kind of mortgage claim on German agricultural and forest land and business enterprises. Against each 500 gold marks of this rather fictitious asset, it could issue 500 units of a new currency, the Rentenmark, and holders could convert each 500 Rentenmarks into a bond having a nominal value of 500 gold marks. (The names of the bank and currency, suggestive of this arrangement, are attributable to Luther.) The link of the Rentenmark to gold was thus indirect and not particularly operational, but it was significant, especially since the concept of a gold mark worth 4.2 to the dollar had already been adopted in the government's gold loan of August 1923. Government offices

[27] Costantino Bresciani-Turroni, *The Economics of Inflation* (London: Allen & Unwin, 1937), pp. 314–344; Rolf E. Lüke, *Von der Stabilisierung zur Krise* (Zürich: Polygraphischer Verlag, 1958), p. 9.

[28] Lüke, *Stabilisierung*, pp. 10–16.

would accept payments in the new currency, but it would not be legal tender.[29]

The decree scheduled the opening of the new bank and launching of the Rentenmark for one month later, November 15. After that date, further discounting of treasury bills at the Reichsbank would be forbidden (but, in the intervening month, the government could persist in its inflationary financing, and did so heavily). The Rentenbank was required to grant the government an interest-free loan of 300 million Rentenmarks, which the government would use to pay off debts to the Reichsbank. The Rentenbank was also obliged to make additional credits available to the government, but with their total amount strictly limited to 1,200 million Rentenmarks.

On November 12, at the request of Finance Minister Luther, Dr. Hjalmar Schacht, a banker from the private sector, became currency commissioner in charge of the stabilization program. It would have been natural to give this responsibility to the president of the Reichsbank, but he and the government had long disagreed on currency questions. The difficulty posed by the separation of the two offices was removed by the death on November 20 of Rudolf Havenstein, whom Schacht succeeded as Reichsbank president the following month.[30] That date, November 20, also happened to be the date of fixing what finally proved to be the definitive exchange rate of the old paper mark in terms of the new mark, gold, and foreign exchange.

Rentenmark notes were put into circulation in three ways: The government paid some salaries and other expenses in new notes borrowed from the Rentenbank; the Reichsbank paid out some of its new loans in Rentenmarks; and the Reichsbank publicly offered to exchange old marks into Rentenmarks. A strike by Berlin printers contributed to a shortage of the new notes at first; and expectations of a further decline in the real value of the old mark—expectations that proved correct between November 15 and November 20—motivated people to stand in long lines at the counters of the Reichsbank.[31]

From the time of its introduction, the Rentenmark's exchange rate with the gold mark and the dollar was implicitly specified in the manner already mentioned. The old paper mark's exchange rate with

---

[29] Ibid., pp. 16–28; Hjalmar H. G. Schacht, *Die Stabilisierung der Mark* (Stuttgart, Berlin, and Leipzig: Deutsche Verlags-Anstalt, 1927), pp. 56–62; Bresciani-Turroni, *Economics*, p. 335; and William Guttman and Patricia Meehan, *The Great Inflation* (London: Gordon & Cremonesi, 1976), pp. 207–209.

[30] Frank D. Graham later called Havenstein's death "a demise which cannot be thought of as other than opportune." Guttman and Meehan called it "timely"; Guttman and Meehan, *Great Inflation*, p. 215.

[31] Schacht, *Stabilisierung*, pp. 70–71.

the Rentenmark and other currencies, however, still was not fixed. When Schacht took office on November 12, the dollar rate in Berlin was 630 billion paper marks; on November 15, it had risen to 2.52 trillion. The official Berlin quotation remained far behind rates abroad or on the free market. For example, on November 12 in Cologne, which under Allied occupation was not subject to German foreign-exchange legislation, the dollar rate stood more than six times as high as in Berlin. Schacht believed that such discrepancies could not long be maintained and that the official Berlin quotation would have to be adjusted upward toward the world-market rate. The Berlin dollar rate was set up to 840 billion old marks on November 13, to 1,260 billion on November 14, to 2,520 billion on November 15, and to 4.2 trillion on November 20. The latter rate was equivalent to 1 trillion paper marks for 1 gold mark or 1 Rentenmark.[32]

This trillion-for-one rate had the convenience of a round number, but it was not secure for some time. The dollar rate hit a record of 12 trillion in Cologne on November 23.[33] Many people in official circles thought that the tentative stabilization rate overvalued the paper mark and undervalued the Rentenmark and foreign currencies, and they called for further adjustments in the direction recently taken. At a conference with Schacht at the end of November, the spokesman for the Rentenbank initially called for depreciating the old mark still further against the dollar, while the spokesman for the Reichsbank called for maintaining the rate set on November 20. Schacht also wanted to hold the line but believed that doing so would require a contraction of the paper-money circulation, including a regularization of the emergency moneys that had been put into circulation by so many different issuers.[34]

There was no guarantee that the old mark would not fall further, dragging the Rentenmark with it. Two reasons have been suggested why this did not happen. First, Germans were desperate for some stable means of payment and anxious to believe in the reform. Second, moves toward a tight purse signaled that the government was at last serious about stabilization. The reform scheme provided that the total issue of Rentenmarks would be strictly limited to 2.4 billion, half of that amount going to the government and 300 million of that half going to pay off the government's previously incurred

---

[32] Ibid., pp. 72–73; Lüke, *Stabilisierung*, p. 22; Karl Elster, *Vom Rubel zum Tscherwonjez* (Jena: Fischer, 1930), p. 215.

[33] Charles S. Maier, *Recasting Bourgeois Europe: Stabilization in France, Germany, and Italy in the Decade After World War I* (Princeton: Princeton University Press, 1975), p. 397.

[34] Schacht, *Stabilisierung*, pp. 74–75 and passim.

floating debt. Once the money showed a reasonable prospect of remaining stable, the public's demand for real cash balances recovered rapidly. Previously, the public had been economizing on holdings of melting money to the point of extreme inconvenience. With the demand for money recovering, it was possible for a great increase in its quantity to take place while its value was maintained.[35]

Price indexes in terms of the new currency begin with December 1923 or January 1924 and show near stability—only mild fluctuations—in the immediately ensuing years.[36] Furthermore, the trillion-to-one peg of the old currency to the new did ultimately hold. It does seem, then, that the German stabilization was a sudden one. Still, some questions of interpretation remain. One might argue that the German experience, like the Austrian experience of fifteen months before, was one of inflation suddenly terminated by exchange-rate pegging; the old paper mark was pegged against the Rentenmark and against gold and dollars at 4.2 trillion per dollar. The Rentenmark, along with its replacing the old mark in being issued to finance the government, though in strictly limited amounts, could be regarded as a kind of gimmick to aid the exchange stabilization of the old mark. On the other hand, one might argue that what was done was not so much the stabilization of the old money as its near abolition in real terms. The numerically convenient trillion-to-one ratio of old to new marks represented a marking up of the price of the dollar beyond what it had actually reached in Berlin. The old paper money was not so much being stabilized as being nearly wiped out in real terms.[37]

Furthermore, the stabilization of the vastly devalued old mark was not secure at once. Continuing speculation against the paper mark on unofficial markets in late November carried the dollar rate far above the official rate. Speculators did not have to pay for their dollar purchases at once but only a few days later. Payment, however, could only be made in old marks, whose further issue the Reichsbank was restricting, and not in Rentenmarks or in emergency money. For lack of paper marks, the speculators had to resell the foreign exchange that they had bought. The dollar rate was back down to the official figure by December 3 in New York and by December 10 in Cologne. From then until the end of the month, the winding up of bearish speculation against the paper mark brought no less than 200 million gold marks worth of foreign exchange into

---

[35] Maier, *Recasting*, pp. 379–380; League of Nations, *Course*, pp. 62–63.

[36] League of Nations, *International Statistical Year-Book, 1926*, pp. 170–174.

[37] Lüke, *Stabilisierung*, p. 23, makes some remarks hinting toward this interpretation: Choice of the exchange rate amounted to determining the extent of contraction in the real quantity of money.

the Reichsbank. The success of this action strengthened public confidence in the entire reform program.[38]

Although loans for passive resistance in the Ruhr had been completely suspended on October 15 and although the government strove for other economies and also required taxes to be paid according their gold value, balancing the budget still was not easy. It appeared that all of the Rentenbank's 900-million-Rentenmark credit to the government (the other 300 million of this credit being reserved to cover the government's old debt to the Reichsbank) would be spent by the end of December. It was uncertain whether the government would be able to meet its next payroll. The Finance Ministry asked the Rentenbank for further loans. With the moral support of the Reichsbank and Currency Commissioner Schacht, the board of the Rentenbank, in its session of December 20, refused, thereby intensifying the pressure on the government to consolidate its budget with its own means. The government did manage to get through the last days of December and the first weeks of January until revenues newly calculated in gold marks or Rentenmarks began flowing in regularly.

The monetary stabilization itself eliminated the problem of expenditures rising in step with the price level while taxes, collected with a lag, eroded in real value. Whereas debt service had previously been the heaviest item of German government expenditure, the depreciation of money had by now nearly wiped the debt out in real terms; interest and amortization on the public debt amounted to little more than 3 percent of total expenditures budgeted for 1924. Dismissal of many government employees and the financial recovery of the state railroads eliminated other sources of deficit. Furthermore, the government in a sense granted itself the reparations moratorium that the Allies had until then always refused; it temporarily suspended certain types of reparations payments and deliveries. In January 1924, for the first time since the start of the war, government receipts and expenditures were brought into balance.[39]

While the problem of money issues to finance the government was thus brought under control, the Reichsbank, the Rentenbank, and private note-issuing banks kept expanding credit to industry.[40]

---

[38] Ibid., pp. 80–81; Lüke, *Stabilisierung*, p. 25.

[39] Bresciani-Turroni, *Economics*, pp. 355–357; Lüke, *Stabilisierung*, pp. 26–27; Schacht, *Stabilisierung*, p. 87.

[40] The Rentenbank granted loans through the Reichsbank rather than directly. It imposed a so-called constant-value clause on borrowers, that is, the obligation to repay the gold value of the amount originally borrowed. Bresciani-Turroni, *Economics*, p. 353.

In mid-November, the paper marks in circulation amounted to 93 quintillion. By November 30, the amount passed 400 quintillion. It reached 496 quintillion on December 31, 690 quintillion on March 31, 1924, 927 quintillion on May 31, and 1,211 quintillion on July 31. At the same time, the volume of new Rentenmarks was also increasing—in millions, to 501 on November 30, 1,049 on December 31, 1,760 on March 31, and 1,803 on July 31;[41] these figures are to read as quintillions for their equivalents in old marks. Thus monetary stabilization was achieved without contracting the money supply or even stopping its expansion. The rate of expansion, however, was drastically reduced from what it had been during the hyperinflation: the figures just quoted imply that the combined circulation of old marks and Rentenmarks grew at a 214 percent annual rate in the first seven months of 1924.

Recognition, even though belated recognition, that the stabilization was in danger of coming undone helped keep the monetary expansion that relatively moderate in the end. While the stabilization was still new and confidence in it incomplete, the Reichsbank's liberality in granting credit interacted with people's eagerness to borrow as much as they could. The Reichsbank and Schacht hesitated to tighten industrial and agricultural credit for fear of provoking a crisis and impairing the food supply. Consumption and imports rose while exports sagged. The abundance of credit stimulated speculative purchases of foreign exchange, or at least freed many holders of it of the need to sell it to obtain working capital for their businesses. One trillion paper marks, supposedly worth 23.8 U.S. cents, was quoted at only 20.4 cents in New York by February 9. The official exchange rate in Berlin was not entirely meaningful because the Reichsbank was not satisfying demands for foreign exchange in full at that rate; the dollar rate in paper marks generally stood about one-tenth higher in occupied Cologne, where the official rate did not prevail. Furthermore, the Rentenmark was becoming subject to free-market quotations abroad, especially in Holland, and sank to a discount of 12 to 15 percent during February. The wholesale price index rose from 117.3 in January to 120.7 in March and to 124.1 in April. People began to speak of new inflation.[42]

Currency Commissioner Schacht later admitted that he had not paid prompt enough attention to what turned out to have been an

---

[41] Ibid., p. 337.

[42] Ibid., pp. 337–338, 350–351; Schacht, *Stabilisierung*, pp. 106–107, 113–115. The wholesale price index quoted by Schacht is evidently the old one. The new index, printed side by side with it in League of Nations, *International Statistical Year-Book, 1926*, p. 170, does not show such a rise.

excessive expansion of credit. One excuse offered was that international financial negotiations—he was also president of the Reichsbank—kept him away from Berlin for weeks on end. As soon as he was again able to remain steadily in Berlin, though, around the end of March, he took steps to overcome the emerging crisis.[43] The Reichsbank determined to limit its outstanding credits to its end-of-March total. From April 7 on, it would extend no further credit except as funds became available from the repayment of earlier loans. A storm of indignation blew up throughout the business world, yet the Reichsbank held firm for weeks and even months. (This policy was reflected on the balance sheet of the Reichsbank, which showed issues of means of payment of 2,955 million gold marks on April 7, 2,854 million on May 7, and 2,919 million on June 7.)[44]

The squeeze on money and credit induced a brief but sharp reduction in imports, more rapid delivery to the Reichsbank of foreign exchange earned by exporters, and some repatriation of flight capital. Businessmen were impelled to unload stocks of commodities or of foreign exchange that they had been holding from the time of rapid inflation or that they had speculatively built up in the early months of 1924 in fear of a new inflation. The gold and foreign-exchange holdings of the Reichsbank grew. The wholesale price index declined some 7 percent between April and July. By June 3, the Reichsbank could abandon foreign-exchange rationing and satisfy demands in full at the official rate. Quotations on the mark abroad and in the occupied territories improved from the middle of April. According to Costantino Bresciani-Turroni, even official papers that had earlier shown little sympathy with quantity-theory ideas recognized the obvious connection between credit abundance and exchange depreciation in the first quarter of 1924 and between credit restriction and the firming of the mark thereafter. According to Schacht, the success of the policy was not only substantive but also psychological. Gone, he says, were all fears that the Reichsbank would again subordinate currency stability to any other economic or political interest; gone were speculators' hopes of profiting from renewed inflation.[45]

[43] Schacht, *Stabilisierung*, pp. 114–115.

[44] Ibid., p. 121.

[45] Ibid., pp. 117–123; Bresciani-Turroni, *Economics*, pp. 315–353; League of Nations, *Course*, pp. 104, 106.

During the squeeze, the Reichsbank rationed credit directly while continuing to hold its discount rate artificially low at 10 percent. Rightly or wrongly, Schacht maintained that rationing by a sufficiently high interest rate would have been unbearable for the long-term capital market, yet would not have sufficed to ward off speculative attacks on the currency on the foreign-exchange market. Schacht, *Stabilisierung*, pp. 118–120.

As several commentators have suggested, perhaps the German stabilization should be dated not on November 15, 1923, when the Rentenmark was introduced, nor on November 20, 1923, when the exchange rate of the old paper mark was set at the level that ultimately prevailed, but on April 7, 1924, when a credit squeeze was introduced that rescued that exchange rate and the entire monetary system from the threat of renewed inflation.

Stabilization brought side effects. The period of inflation had brought a search for inflation hedges, an emphasis on clever trading, and a proliferation of financial and trading firms. The "false flowers," as Schacht calls them, that had bloomed during inflation were bound to wither when stabilization came and especially when credit was squeezed in the spring of 1924. The natural (that is, competitive) selection of the fittest firms, which had been weakened when people were desperately trying to unload money onto goods of almost any sort, came back into operation. Stabilization meant that resources had to shift from an inflation-distorted pattern of allocation into a more economic pattern again, but the very process of shifting resources created scope for frictional unemployment and idleness of capacity.[46]

Stabilization ended the process that had provided entrepreneurs with abundant financial means at the expense of owners of liquid assets, owners of rent-controlled housing, small stockholders, and wage- and salary-earners. No longer forced saving but now only voluntary saving could provide capital for businesses.[47]

During the credit squeeze of 1924, while the Reichsbank rationed funds directly, private banks charged commissions of up to 1 percent a month, making an effective interest rate of 20 to 25 percent a year. Stock prices reflected the squeeze, an index falling from 31.5 at the end of March to 20.2 at the end of May. Bankruptcies climbed.[48]

The shortage of working capital obliged industries to cut back their orders for capital goods. As a result, the engineering, iron and steel, and coal industries bore the brunt of the stabilization crisis. The heavy unemployment that resulted in these industries reportedly shifted bargaining power from employees to employers. Employers were able to restore the eight-hour shift in the mines and the ten-hour shift above ground; labor unions were weakened. At the same time, many workers, capitalists, and house owners regained real purchasing

---

[46] Schacht, *Stabilisierung*, p. 123; Bresciani-Turroni, *Economics*, pp. 391–393 and passim.

[47] Bresciani-Turroni, *Economics*, p. 367.

[48] Maier, *Recasting*, p. 416.

power and were able to increase their demands for consumer goods. The repatterning of demand resulted for a while in both overproduction of capital goods, evident in unsold accumulations of coal and iron, and underproduction of goods for direct consumption.[49]

The remainder of the story concerns mopping-up operations. The Dawes Plan of 1924 not only brought some order into the wrangle over reparations but brought Germany an international loan of almost $200 million that helped fortify the monetary reserves and consolidate a gold-exchange standard. Under a law of August 30, 1924, Rentenmarks were gradually withdrawn from circulation and replaced with Reichsmarks of the same gold and foreign-exchange value. The stability of the Reichsmark was presumably supported by its conformity to the requirements of the evolving international gold-exchange standard and by the Dawes committee's role of watchdog over the Reichsbank. Elements of partial exchange control introduced during and after the war were removed at various times. Mortgages and other financial claims denominated in the all-but-wiped-out old paper marks had their real value partially, but only partially, restored by law.

Summary and Comment. Not so paradoxically, the very extremeness of German inflation favored the success of stabilization efforts. The catch-up element was practically absent from so rapid an inflation, and expectations were ripe for being turned around. The real value of mark notes and claims held by foreigners was practically wiped out, as was the real value of the government's debt, which facilitated restoring budget balance. The total real value of the money supply had shrunk to a small fraction of the amount normally demanded. This left room, once a measure of confidence in money had been restored, for further money issue issue to help cover the government's budget deficit during a transition period and to continue providing loans to industry and agriculture. Once the authorities perceived that excessive ease of credit and money was threatening renewed inflation, they resolutely applied a credit squeeze until success was assured.

Political changes in the broad sense facilitated stabilization. The Cuno government was replaced in August 1923 by the Stresemann government, which was reorganized in October with Hans Luther as finance minister. The new government discontinued the policy of passive resistance in the occupied Ruhr district, a policy whose costs were generally recognized as fateful for the extreme degree that the inflation had reached. The Reichstag passed a law authorizing the finance minister to issue the decree establishing the Rentenbank and

---

[49] Bresciani-Turroni, *Economics*, p. 369; Maier, *Recasting*, p. 445.

introducing the new currency. Hjalmar Schacht, who was to display considerable courage and resoluteness, was appointed currency commissioner and soon afterwards, upon the "timely" death of Rudolf Havenstein, president of the Reichsbank also. During this period, reaching into the time of the credit squeeze of the spring of 1924, studies and negotiations were going forward to settle financial issues outstanding between Germany and the Allies.

Poland in the 1920s

Poland, in part a successor state of the Austro-Hungarian monarchy, stabilized its currency three times within five years, 1921–1926, but the first two stabilizations broke down.

The budgetary problems of the new republic were worsened during its first few years by fighting with Russia, Czechoslovakia, and Lithuania and wrangling with Germany over the drawing of boundaries. The tax collection mechanism was ineffective. For generations, Poles had regarded the tax collector as the agent of an alien oppressor; thwarting him had been a patriotic act. Since the country was made up of parts of three former empires, the administrative machinery was disorganized, and political influence was splintered among many parties.

The first attempt at currency stabilization came in September 1921, when an index of wholesale prices stood at 602 times the level of 1913. (Not all the figures that one might wish are available. A retail price index had stood at 112 times the level of 1914 in December 1920 and continued rising throughout 1921, reaching 467 in December, a 318 percent increase over the year.)[50] Parliament granted the finance minister, Professor Michalski, almost dictatorial power in the realm of finance. His program—actually implemented only in part—called for government assistance for new industrial production, strict economy in public administration, and a capital levy whose proceeds were to go for withdrawing half the currency from circulation. Public economies turned out less massive and the capital levy produced less revenue than had been expected.[51]

Even so, the program showed signs of initial success. The announcement of measures aiming at budget balance apparently supported hopes for financial rehabilitation and currency stabilization.

---

[50] League of Nations, *International Statistical Year-Book, 1926*, pp. 172, 176.

[51] Jack Taylor, *The Economic Development of Poland, 1919–1950* (Ithaca: Cornell University Press, 1952), p. 36; Ferdynand Zweig, *Poland between Two Wars* (London: Secker & Warburg, 1944), p. 35.

The dollar rate fell from 4,550 Polish marks in mid-November 1921 to 4,232 at the beginning of March 1922 and further to 3,957 at the beginning of June 1922; thus the mark's dollar value rose 15 percent in six and one-half months. The quarterly wholesale price index showed a 5 percent dip between September and December 1921, then resumed its rise; the Warsaw retail index dipped 5 percent between June and September 1922.[52]

Severe side effects accompanied the apparent financial improvement. Unemployment rose. When employers tried to cut wages as prices fell, a wave of strikes developed. The cabinet collapsed. Efforts at budget balance were relaxed. The currency depreciated again in the second half of 1922, the dollar rate soaring from 3,957 marks in June to 18,075 by the end of 1922. At least one critic blames the failure not only on the weakness of the government but also on its having overreached itself in aiming not merely at stabilization but at actual deflation.[53]

The currency depreciation apparently reacted unfavorably on the real size of government revenues, and price inflation again became extreme.[54] Successive weak cabinets drew up reform programs but accomplished little. The depreciation reached its most extreme degree under a center-right cabinet between late May and mid-December 1923, when the dollar rate rose from 53,375 to 6,050,000 marks,[55] meaning exchange depreciation of the mark at a 99.98 percent average annual rate. The wholesale price index was multiplied by 126 between May and December 1923, by 463 over the longer period between January 1923 and January 1924, when prices appear to have peaked, and by 1,655 over the still longer period from September 1922 to January 1924. The sharpest month-to-month jump appears to have taken place between September and October 1923, when wholesale prices were multiplied by 3.75.[56]

The government, in a desperate attempt to stabilize, had refused to grant raises to railway workers and other government employees. A wave of strikes followed in the autumn of 1923, sharpening incentives for a second stabilization attempt. In December, Wladyslaw Grabski formed a nonparliamentary ministry of experts, taking the portfolio of finance minister. Hilton Young's "Report on Financial Conditions in Poland," submitted to Grabski in February 1924, em-

---

[52] League of Nations, *International Statistical Year-Book, 1926*, pp. 172, 176.
[53] Zweig, *Poland*, pp. 35, 37.
[54] League of Nations, *Course*, pp. 25–26.
[55] Zweig, *Poland*, p. 36.
[56] League of Nations, *International Statistical Year-Book 1926*, p. 172.

phasized the unhealthy influence of banknote issue to cover government deficits.[57]

Around this time, two schools of thought about stabilization were dominant. One wanted to enlist the cooperation of either the League of Nations or the United States. Grabski, however, believed in recovery through the country's own means and efforts alone. He aimed at a drastic increase in revenues to earn public confidence in the government's forswearing of its earlier inflationary policy.[58] His first efforts were directed at the budget situation. Taxes were to be reckoned in gold francs but paid in Polish marks at the exchange rate prevailing on the day of payment.[59] Loans were floated in Italy and the United States.[60] Property and income taxes were strengthened in January 1924. Tax revenues grew, the slowing of inflation itself had a healthy effect on government finances, and the government was able to announce that from February 1 it would have no further recourse to note issue to cover its deficit.[61]

Direct exchange stabilization played a part in the improvement, although, according to a League of Nations study, the chain of causation ran from fiscal reform to the exchange rate and not the other way around.[62] Previously, in June 1923, the Polish State Loan Bank had suffered heavy losses when it intervened to try to check the decline of the mark. When it tried again early in 1924, the results were different. Although the exchange rate stood at about 6.5 million marks per dollar at the beginning of the year, the Bank retreated to a 9.3-million rate to make its stand, partly to moderate the business slump that stabilization was expected to entail. The action succeeded, and speculators lost heavily.

The gold franc had already been introduced as a unit of account for tax purposes. Now, after the State Loan Bank was reorganized as a joint stock company into a State Bank, it became the basis of a new currency. One zloty (meaning "golden"), although not actually redeemable in gold, was defined to have the same gold content as one prewar franc of the Latin Monetary Union. The relation to the old currency, corresponding to the stabilized exchange rate, was 1.8 mil-

---

[57] Zweig, *Poland*, p. 38; Robert Machray, *The Poland of Pilsudski* (New York: Dutton, 1937).

[58] Zweig, *Poland*, p. 39.

[59] Lawrence Smith, "The Zloty, 1924–35," *Journal of Political Economy*, vol. 44 (April 1936), p. 148.

[60] Zweig, *Poland*, p. 40.

[61] League of Nations, *Course*, p. 26; Zweig, *Poland*.

[62] League of Nations, *Course*, p. 26.

lion marks per zloty. The bank began issuing zloty notes on May 1, 1924.[63]

The note circulation rose from 125 trillion marks at the beginning of 1924 to about 600 trillion at the time of the conversion to the zloty. Although printing money to cover the government's deficit ended in February, note issues continued for supplying loans to industry and for acquiring foreign-exchange reserves. Yet the exchange rate held. This phenomenon again illustrates why it is relatively easy to stabilize from a stage of hyperinflation. The flight from the currency has shrunk real balances so severely that their reconstitution allows scope for further nominal issues of money provided people do believe that price inflation is being stopped.

Soon, however, the new-found monetary stability was threatened. Whereas a good harvest in 1923 had aided the stabilization program, a poor harvest in 1924 directly pushed up some prices, put the trade balance into deficit through imports of grains, and impaired tax revenues. Although the government did not resort to issues of banknotes, it did cover its renewed deficit by using its authority to issue small-denomination notes in lieu of coins. Germany and Poland got into a tariff war in the second half of 1925, which made for a fall in coal exports, a rise in unemployment, and a worsening of industrial unrest. Internal prices rose about 28 percent between December 1924 and March 1925; and according to one interpretation at least, the indexing of wage rates to the cost of living worsened the precarious condition of the currency. The fixed exchange rate, which had initially undervalued the zloty on the exchanges, was now coming to overvalue it. Critics blamed the policy failure, as it turned out to be, on light-hearted optimism, on failure to consolidate government finances, and on a search for a stabilization by measures that were too drastic for the infant economy.[64]

A new exchange depreciation of the zloty began at the end of July 1925. When the president of the central bank refused to continue supporting the zloty at 5.98 per dollar—already a 13 percent depreciation from parity—Finance Minister Grabski resigned (November 13, 1925). He claimed no party allegiance and was criticized by all parties. His fall was considered a failure of even "semi-democracy." The zloty immediately began sinking further.[65]

The period running from then until May 1926 was marked by bankruptcies, unemployment, strikes, and exchange depreciation. The

---

[63] Zweig, *Poland*, p. 39.

[64] League of Nations, *Course*, pp. 26–28, 111; Taylor, *Economic Development*, p. 39; Zweig, *Poland*, pp. 40–41.

[65] Zweig, *Poland*, p. 41.

dollar rose to 10.55 zlotys, representing a 43 percent depreciation from the zloty's previous official support level. Although the resumption of depreciation in July 1925 had kindled fears of renewed hyperinflation, the rise of prices was in fact moderate, less than in proportion to the exchange rate. Toward the end of 1925, the government took steps to cut expenditures, and in April 1926 it took action on the revenue side also, imposing a 10 percent tax surcharge, enacting some new taxes, raising railway rates, and so forth. The deficit shrank after the end of 1925.[66]

In mid-May 1926, General Jozef Pilsudski seized power in a military coup, supported by a general strike, and ruled thereafter essentially as a dictator. Pilsudski had been a charismatic leader in the Polish liberation struggle and had served as chief of state for the first four years of the republic; he had resigned in December 1922 because the new constitution gave the president only limited powers. He had been a leader of the Polish Socialist Party but quickly disillusioned his left-wing supporters and relied for support on the army and on the conservative nobility of eastern Poland. He sought to create a stable framework conducive to long-term investment and has been credited by some with providing the political stability, previously lacking, for financial stabilization.[67]

A report prepared for the Polish government by E. W. Kemmerer proved influential in shaping the final reform. It blamed earlier breakdowns squarely on the government's issue of large quantities of treasury notes and recommended that the government, as distinguished from the central bank, be allowed to issue coin only.[68]

Pilsudski abolished the indexation of wages, separated the railway budget from the regular budget, revalorized taxes, and raised ad valorem taxes.[69] A British coal strike helped Polish exports in 1926, and the index of industrial production rose almost 48 percent from January to December.[70]

In July 1926, just at about the time that the budget deficit disappeared, a de facto exchange stabilization of the zloty was achieved at 58 percent of its former value. The de jure stabilization, with the gold content of the zloty redefined to correspond with the exchange rate, did not come until October 1927. Not until the following month,

---

[66] Ibid., pp. 41–42; League of Nations, *Course*, p. 27, citing V. J. Zbijewski, *La Stabilisation monétaire en Pologne* (Paris, 1928), pp. 54–62.

[67] Zweig, *Poland*, p. 44; *Encyclopaedia Britannica*, s.v. "Pilsudski."

[68] Mildred S. Wertheimer, "The Reconstruction of Poland," *Foreign Policy Association Information Service*, vol. 6 (June 11, 1930), pp. 141–142.

[69] Zweig, *Poland*, p. 49.

[70] Smith, "Zloty," pp. 156–157.

with stabilization an accomplished fact, did Poland receive the support of a foreign loan for that purpose.[71]

This time the exchange rate held. Poland clung to it, in fact, for years beyond the time when its prosperity of 1926–1929 gave way to depression shared with the rest of the world.

Summary and Comment. The Polish experience illustrates the possibility of rapid stabilization, particularly when started from a stage of extreme inflation, as the first two efforts were. It also illustrates the helpfulness but insufficiency of a turnaround of expectations. The first two efforts failed because they did not remedy the underlying causes of deficits and resort to the printing press. The third effort was more thoroughly planned. Although his reforms were called a failure, Grabski did accomplish much; at least, he brought hyperinflation to an end. As for the importance of political change, it is noteworthy that Parliament surrendered some of its powers during all three stabilization attempts. Pilsudski's role in the final, successful, effort appears noteworthy.

Russia in the 1920s

Russia stabilized from a stage of hyperinflation by introducing new currency units in a process that stretched over several years. Ultimately, 50 billion rubles of the type circulating in 1921 were replaced by one new gold ruble, so called.[72] For a while, Russia exhibited a phenomenon almost unique in monetary history, two different paper currencies circulating side by side with a fluctuating rate of exchange between them.

The Russian experience might seem irrelevant to us because it occurred in a noncapitalist country. It is of interest, however, to see whether similar monetary principles hold true under widely different conditions. Furthermore, the Russian economy did largely, though temporarily, slide back into capitalism in the 1920s under the New Economic Policy.

The issue of paper money, which the tsarist government had resorted to during the war, grew more intense under the democratic provisional government ruling from March to November 1917. During the eight months of its rule, the quantity of paper money almost doubled and the ruble depreciated fourfold. In real terms (in nominal

---

[71] League of Nations, *Course*, pp. 27, 72; Smith, "Zloty," pp. 157–158.

[72] Throughout this section and the whole study, the words "billion," "trillion," and so on are used in the American (and French) sense, translation being made from the British-German-Russian system where used in the works cited.

terms deflated by the price index), the monthly rate of money issue was greater under the provisional government than under both the tsarist government that preceded it and the Communist government that succeeded it. Even before the overthrow of the provisional government, the sharp depreciation of money was causing the disappearance of coins from circulation, a chronic deficiency of money of small and medium denominations, the appearance of a variety of money substitutes, and a tendency to resort to barter. The smaller real money issues under the Communists were presumably not due to any reluctance to raise revenues in this way but to hyperinflation's erosion of the real value of note issues. During the first few years after the Bolshevik Revolution, political, military, and economic conditions made stopping or limiting inflation a practical impossibility. The paralysis of the tax mechanism during the civil war led to greater activity of the printing press and also to the requisitioning of goods as a form of taxation.[73]

Soviet writers are inclined to distinguish inflation in their country, where it served to expropriate the capitalists, from inflation in capitalist countries, where it supposedly enriches the capitalists at the expense of the broad working masses. The interests of the workers were protected while money was depreciating during the first few years of the Soviet system by payment of wages in kind. The share so paid amounted to 64 percent in 1919, 84 percent in 1920, and 93 percent in the first quarter of 1921. From 1920 on, workers received their food rations without paying in money, and payment for communal, transport, and other services was also abolished.[74]

During 1918, Lenin launched a currency reform intended to eliminate the huge stocks of money accumulated by the bourgeoisie, kulaks, and speculators, so called, and to stop the rise in prices. The money supply was to be shrunk by exchanging only small holdings of old currency for new on a ruble-for-ruble basis, while exchanging large holdings only in part. The financial requirements of the civil war forced abandonment of the reform until later.[75]

Meanwhile, the paper money of the tsarist government and of the provisional government became objects of bullish speculation and hoarding. Tsarist rubles came to be worth fifty to sixty Soviet rubles.

---

[73] Karl Elster, *Vom Rubel zum Tscherwonjez* (Jena: Fischer, 1930), pp. 208, 228 (quoting in part from a Russian authority, Sokolnikov); V. S. Gerashchenko, ed., *Denezhnoe Obrashchenie i Kredit SSSR* (Moscow: "Finansy," 1966), pp. 26, 35.

[74] V. V. Ikonnikov and others, *Denezhnoe Obrashchenie i Kredit SSSR* (Moscow: Gosfinizdat, 1952), pp. 148–149.

[75] Ikonnikov, *Denezhnoe Obrashchenie*, pp. 143–144; Gerashchenko, *Denezhnoe Obrashchenie*, p. 28.

TABLE 1

SOVIET COMMODITY PRICE INDEX, 1921–1922

Date	Index (1913 = 1)
December 1, 1921	138,000
January 1, 1922	288,000
February 1, 1922	545,000
March 1, 1922	1,150,000
April 1, 1922	2,520,000
December 1, 1922	17,226,000
End of 1922	21,000,000

SOURCE: Elster, *Rubel*, pp. 169, 180, and footnote.

Two reasons have been suggested for this premium. First, many people expected the Communist government to be overthrown and its notes to be no longer recognized. Second, the old Russian money continued to circulate as a means of payment in the Baltic states and Poland. Later, after the civil war had ended and after the neighboring states had replaced Russian money with new money of their own, the old notes lost their premium, became intermingled with the newer issues, and eventually disappeared after continuing inflation had made their denominations too small to be useful.[76]

The scrappy figures assembled in table 1 convey an impression of how extreme the rise in prices had been by December 1921. They also suggest that prices were roughly doubling each month in the first quarter of 1922 and rising at an average monthly rate of about 27 percent during the remainder of the year. The reported total circulation of Soviet currency—sovznaks, as distinguished from the chervonets currency to be mentioned later—grew by 8,932 percent in 1922, that is, at a monthly average rate of 45.5 percent.[77]

The extreme degree that inflation had reached led to two attempts to cut down the awkwardly large numbers. By a decree of November 3, 1921, 10,000 old rubles were replaced by 1 new ruble; and by a decree of October 24, 1922, 100 of the new rubles were replaced by 1 still newer ruble. The two reforms combined thus replaced 1 million of the rubles circulating before November 1921 with 1 of the "model 1923" type authorized in October 1922.[78]

---

[76] Elster, *Rubel*, pp. 106–107.

[77] Calculated from figures in Ikonnikov, *Denezhnoe Obrashchenie*, p. 157.

[78] Elster, *Rubel*, pp. 181–182; Ikonnikov, *Denezhnoe Obrashchenie*, p. 157.

A less merely arithmetical reform also came late in 1922. A decree of October 11, 1922 authorized the State Bank to start issuing notes denominated in a new and supposedly stable unit of value. The bank paid the first such notes into circulation on November 27, 1922. The new unit was the chervonets, having the same gold content, according to the inscription on the notes, as a prewar ten-ruble gold piece. This specification was hardly operational, since redemption in gold not only did not take place but also could not be expected. Since the chervonets was intended to be a stable currency unit, it hardly could have—and for fifteen months did not have—a fixed rate of exchange with the still inflation-prone Soviet (sovznak) ruble. On December 1, 1922, a few days after its introduction, one chervonets was worth 117 rubles of the "model 1923." Since the pound sterling was the currency in which Russian payments abroad were generally made at the time, the managers of the State Bank decided to choose that currency as the one from whose quotations in terms of the two domestic paper units the official rate between the latter two units would be calculated. In addition to this calculated rate, a free-market rate between the sovznak and the chervonets was determined by supply and demand. During 1923, the State Bank employed market intervention to keep the rates between pound and chervonets in the general vicinity of 1 to 1 (the extreme rates reached that year were 1.26 and 0.86 pounds per chervonets). The stability of the chervonets was relative only—relative to the much greater instability of the ordinary paper ruble. Between January 1 and September 1, 1923, the chervonets lost 36 percent of its purchasing power as measured by the wholesale price index and 28 percent as measured by the retail index.[79]

Even so, the advantages of using and holding chervonets currency were widely recognized, which reportedly intensified people's efforts to get rid of old rubles. In the six months after the chervontsi were first issued, the commodity price index in terms of ordinary rubles was multiplied approximately by six (implying a rate of inflation definitely greater than experienced during most of 1922). Because merchants were obliged to accept payments for goods in ordinary rubles at the officially calculated rate between the two currencies, yet expected to have to buy chervontsi at the free-market rate and take a loss in doing so, they were inclined to include an allowance for this risk in the prices that they charged for goods. In the countryside, where the ruble remained the dominant means of payment even after people in cities had largely shifted over to the chervonets, the peasants

---

[79] Elster, *Rubel*, pp. 172–173, 176, 188–190, 198, 200, and passim.

began reckoning in nails or cotton and showing reluctance to deliver their products to the cities. In the last two months of 1923, price indexes rose 544 percent for agricultural commodities and 387 percent for industrial commodities.[80]

As a relatively stable unit, the chervonets gradually displaced gold as a unit of account and various makeshifts as media of exchange. Previously, tsarist gold coins and foreign moneys had come into circulation and even threatened to displace paper rubles, especially in border regions where foreign trade was active.[81]

The Soviet Union's parallel circulation of two distinct paper currencies from late 1922 until early 1924 invites comparison with the situation in Germany in 1923–1924. The first steps toward a stable-value parallel currency were taken in Germany in the second half of 1923 with the issue of government bonds linked to the dollar and available even in small denominations.[82] The chervonets and the Rentenmark were similar in some respects. Both had a link with gold—a more indirect link for the chervonets, which was rather meaninglessly defined in terms of a gold coin, than for the Rentenmark, which was exchangeable for bonds denominated in gold marks possessing a specific dollar exchange rate. The chervonets and the Rentenmark were similar in not being legal tender but in being more eagerly sought than the old legal-tender currency. In each country, the new currency was issued by a different agency from the issuer of the old (in the Soviet Union, the State Bank issued the chervonets, the People's Commissariat of Finance the old ruble),[83] a circumstance intended to promote confidence in the new currency. A major difference is that although in Germany the two currencies were linked together at a fixed exchange rate within a few days after the introduction of the new one, in Russia the old kept depreciating against the new for more than a year.[84]

This anomalous situation was terminated by reforms of February and March 1924. The old paper ruble was given the coup de grâce by an enormous final increase in its circulation, from 333 to 813 quintillion in February; then its issue was terminated. In its place, the government treasury began issuing legal-tender notes in denominations of 1, 3, and 5 "gold rubles" of unspecified gold content. (This move represented resurrection or activation of a unit of account that

---

[80] Elster, *Rubel*, p. 201.

[81] Gerashchenko, *Denezhnoe Obrashchenie*, pp. 41–42.

[82] See the section on Germany, above.

[83] Gerashchenko, *Denezhnoe Obrashchenie*, p. 43.

[84] Elster, *Rubel*, pp. 197–198, 213–215.

had been used for some government budgeting and planning and private calculations.) Although the new unit did not initially have any legally fixed relation with the chervonets, 10 gold rubles were in fact equal to one chervonets, and the State Bank officially recognized this relation. The two units thus came to be linked together in much the same way as dollars and cents or rubles and kopecks are linked. The old paper rubles were to be taken out of circulation at the rate of 50,000 rubles of "model 1923" for 1 gold ruble.[85]

In the early months of the monetary reform of 1924, the issue of the new treasury currency was severely limited despite the great demand for it associated with withdrawal of the old paper rubles from circulation and the rebuilding of real cash balances. This restraint created a famine of small currency, a so-called small-change crisis, a proliferation of local money substitutes, and appearance of a premium on the new notes. In the second half of 1924, the issue of sufficient quantities of coins and treasury notes overcame the small-change crisis.[86]

Thanks to successful efforts at financial discipline—or so says a Soviet authority—the issue of treasury notes to help cover government expenditures was discontinued from July 1, 1924. From the end of 1925, all operations for putting money into circulation were entrusted to the State Bank. Meanwhile, during 1924, the State Bank successfully intervened on the market to strengthen the currency's foreign-exchange value. Market maneuvers with stockpiles of commodities belonging to the government also supposedly contributed to the stabilization and reduction of prices. An index of Russian wholesale prices peaked in February 1924, dropped 14 percent in three months, and, after intermediate fluctuations in both directions, ended the year 1926 well below the 1924 peak.[87]

Summary. Against a background of hyperinflation, a relatively stable currency, the chervonets, was instituted late in 1922. It circulated for more than a year in parallel with and at a floating exchange rate against the old paper ruble (which had already undergone two reforms of the merely arithmetical or lopping-off-zeros type). A further reform of 1924 introduced a new ruble soon recognized as one-tenth of a chervonets, and the old ruble was dropped. As things worked out, the chervonets proved to be a transitional device leading to re-

---

[85] Elster, *Rubel*, pp. 232, 237; Gerashchenko, *Denezhnoe Obrashchenie*, pp. 40–41, 46.

[86] Gerashchenko, *Denezhnoe Obrashchenie*, pp. 46–47.

[87] Gerashchenko, *Denezhnoe Obrashchenie*, pp. 47–51; League of Nations, *International Statistical Year-Book, 1936* (Geneva, 1937), p. 172.

placement of the old ruble with a new ruble worth a great many of the old one. Government discipline in budgeting and money issue made the stabilization stick.

Colombia around 1900

Colombia's experience around 1900 is worth a few brief paragraphs by way of a footnote to better-known stories. Colombia suffered what was, at the time, one of the most extreme inflations in history.[88] The episode is an example of inflation being stopped at the end of the war that had caused it.

Largely because of money issues occasioned by the expenses of the civil wars of 1876 and 1885, Colombia was definitively on a regime of inconvertible paper money by 1886. Another civil war, said to be the most destructive armed revolt in the country's history, broke out in mid-October 1899. Between then and June 1903, when the central government declared public order reestablished and lifted the state of siege, the money circulation was multiplied by approximately twenty-three. Including further issues made in 1904, the money stock was multiplied by about twenty-five. (These figures presumably do not take account of irregular money issues and issues by regional authorities.)

In October 1899, when the war broke out, the Colombian peso was quoted on the foreign-exchange market at about one-fifth of its metallic parity. In the month of deepest depreciation, October 1902, foreign exchange was quoted at 190 times the peso's parity. (Some individual transactions were reported at a multiple of about 200.) In three years, thus, the peso lost over 97 percent of its gold value.

Exchange-rate movements during the war reflected not only the quantities of paper money issued, which neither the public nor even the government itself knew at the time, but also changing expectations associated with the changing fortunes of war. The central government's peso tended to rise with a defeat and fall with a victory of the revolutionary forces.

---

[88] According to Guillermo Torres García, Colombia came "to occupy the first place in world history of depreciation of paper money"; the premiums on foreign exchange reached levels never before exceeded in the world history of paper money. Torres, *Historia de la moneda en Colombia* (Bogotá: Imprenta del Banco de la República, 1945), pp. 275, 283–284. Torres's remarks are something of an exaggeration, since the eighteenth-century depreciations of both the American Continental currency and the French assignats were of the same order of magnitude.

The facts in these paragraphs are taken from Torres's book, and some of the numbers are calculated from his tables. Internal evidence, such as slight contradictions regarding exchange rates and exchange premiums, calls for regarding Torres's figures as rough indications rather than as precise measurements.

After the revolution was put down and the war ended, the price of foreign exchange fluctuated generally downward until the rates leveled off with the peso worth about one one-hundredth of its theoretical gold content, that is, about one twentieth of its immediate prewar value.

In 1903, Congress adopted a plan aiming at reestablishing the gold standard with a gold peso equivalent to a U.S. dollar and at gradually raising the value of the paper money further by reducing the amount in circulation. This law proved to have little constructive effect because the government did not have and could not readily obtain the gold necessary for carrying out the plan. Furthermore, the plan condemned the paper peso to continued instability during the period when its value was supposedly to be raised. Actually, one early step was taken in the other direction: 100 million more pesos were issued under a law of 1904, raising the money supply a further 11 percent or so.

In August 1904, Congress had second thoughts about aiming at revalorization and decided to stabilize the paper peso at approximately the prevailing exchange rates. One hundred old pesos were set equal to one new peso. This measure constituted not so much a devaluation as a legal recognition of an already accomplished depreciation. The government managed to stabilize the paper money on this basis without any foreign loan or any substantial gold reserve. Colombia continued with a regime of irredeemable paper money whose quantity was now practically rigid.

In 1905, with the organization of a central bank, the government intended to transform the money into banknotes convertible into coin. This plan was not in fact carried out.

A law of 1907 provided for a new monetary unit, the peso fuerte, with a gold content equivalent to that of one-fifth of the British pound sterling. Thus, Colombia had three different monetary systems or units in the course of four years: the old paper peso, the peso supposedly worth one U.S. gold dollar, and a peso worth slightly less, namely, one-fifth of a pound sterling. Subsequent years brought a series of measures aiming at eventual gold convertibility.

Colombia's experience is interesting for our purposes as an example of stabilization after what in its day must have counted as hyperinflation—stabilization by introduction of a new unit worth a large number of the old paper units.

3

Pulling Back from the Brink
of Hyperinflation

Czechoslovakia, 1919–1923

Unlike other main remnants of the Austro-Hungarian empire, Czecho-
slovokia stopped short of hyperinflation. It even partially reversed
the depreciation of money. Its inherited unit, the crown, had been
worth about 20.3 U.S. cents before the war, sank below 1 cent at the
worst, and was stabilized at about 3 cents.[1]

After the war, offices of the Austro-Hungarian Bank were continuing to issue new banknotes on the security of the practically
worthless Austro-Hungarian war loan. Dr. Alois Rašín, finance
minister of newly independent Czechoslovakia, sought to check inflation by preparing a separation of currencies. Late in 1918, the government declared the Bank's new series of 25, 100, and 10,000 crown
notes unacceptable in Czechoslovakia, and it temporarily restricted
cash payments out of bank accounts.

Two alternatives had been suggested to the plan finally adopted.
First, the Czech government might repudiate the old currency and
introduce a new currency of its own, leaving each holder of old notes
a mere creditor of the Bank. Second, the government might take over
the Bank's liability for the notes, then restore the gold standard at a
devalued parity. The view that prevailed favored monetary contrac-

---

[1] The chief sources used for this section are Antonin Basch, "Economic and Finan-
cial Policy of Czechoslovakia, 1918–1938," in Miloslav Rechcigl, ed., *Czechoslo-
vakia Past and Present* (The Hague: Mouton, 1968), vol. 1, pp. 158–169; Karel
Karásek, "Banking," and Vilibald Mildschuh, "Currency Conditions," both in
Josef Gruber, ed., *Czechoslovakia* (1929; reprint ed., New York: Arno Press and
New York Times Press, 1971); Leo Pasvolsky, *The Economic Nationalism of the
Danubian States* (New York: Macmillan, 1928); and Alois Rašín, *Financial Policy
of Czecho-Slovakia During the First Year of Its History* (Oxford: Clarendon
Press, 1923).

tion, and Dr. Rašín wanted deflation to go far enough to restore the prewar parity.

As in some other successor states, the government proposed to convert the old banknotes in circulation into national money by officially overprinting or stamping it; unstamped notes would not be valid as local money. Under the Czech reform of March 1919, each note would be stamped only upon retirement of an equivalent note from circulation. In other words, a note holder would have to surrender half of his money (receiving a nonnegotiable bond in return) to get the other half validated. Because of exemptions for small currency holdings, only about 30 percent of the notes were actually withdrawn. The monetary reform continued with a law passed in April 1919 to limit the circulation of "uncovered" banknotes.

Adequate money-supply and price-level statistics apparently do not exist (the wholesale index published by the League of Nations does not begin until 1921 and the retail index not until 1923), but it does seem (for example, from continuing exchange depreciation) that the contractionary measures did not have the desired shock effect in reversing or even stopping the inflation. A supposed scarcity of money impelled the government to return some of the withdrawn notes to circulation. Furthermore, fraudulently stamped banknotes flooded into the country in unknown volume. The greater value of the Czech than the Austrian crown made forgery profitable. Unstamped notes were also reportedly worth more than Austrian stamped notes, presumably because they could be forged into Czech notes more easily.[2]

Finance Minister Rašín operated with some questionable economic ideas. He was concerned that too many payments were being made in cash and that the credit system was being insufficently used. He felt that a contraction of the currency stock would force a greater use of the credit system, which would be antiinflationary. This idea was tied up with his acceptance of the real-bills or needs-of-trade doctrine:

> A paper currency without a gold basis is certainly possible, but it can be sound only if such a quantity of bank notes uncovered by private legal liability is in circulation as is just requisite for the daily necessities of life, all other business requirements being met by credit dealings with a bank of issue. For then the circulation is elastic and adapts itself readily to the needs of business, while the bank of issue is

---

[2] Karl Schlesinger, "The Disintegration of the Austro-Hungarian Currency," *Economic Journal*, vol. 30 (March 1920), pp. 26ff.

in a position to regulate such a circulation by raising or lowering the discount rate.[3]

Rašín took apparent satisfaction when, in 1919 and 1920, the total of bills discounted by the bank appeared to fluctuate in accordance with the "monetary requirements of trade," as, for example, with the changing seasonal requirements of the sugar industry; he took satisfaction that "this variation of the bill holdings . . . corresponded to the monetary requirements of trade and that the circulation was becoming elastic."[4] He saw depreciation of the currency as largely the result of big wage increases due to labor unrest and to what he called "dry Bolshevism." Czechoslovakia supposedly could not obtain credit abroad because it was viewed as a Bolshevized country. Only Germany would provide credit, so the Czech economy became dependent upon the German; and the crown's exchange rate moved for a time with that of the mark.[5] Also to blame were a deterioration of productive capacity, the straining for unearned profit, the excessive rise in incomes of certain sectors of the population, which led to excessive buying, "the pursuit of pleasure," "the life of ease led by the productive classes in the enjoyment of high incomes," and a trade balance deficit "accentuated by greed for what is not available at home but has to be imported from abroad."[6] To stabilize the currency, everyone had to work and save.

Rašín thus was guided by moralistic, even puritanical, ideas, perhaps more than by sound economic theory. He believed in not merely stopping but even reversing inflation. A policy stance based on such thinking may well have influenced the state of confidence and international movements of capital. A money supply behaving more or less in accordance with the real-bills doctrine tends to reinforce trends otherwise established, such as a stabilization or decline of prices initiated by stabilization or appreciation of the currency on the exchanges.

If the figures can be trusted, the currency circulation was not expanding after around 1921, though the volume of bank deposits continued increasing. Notes in circulation on September 15 in millions of Czech crowns amounted to 9,891 in 1920, 11,254 in 1921, 9,837 in 1922, and 8,925 in 1923. The total of time and sight deposits in banks,

---

[3] Rašín, *Financial Policy*, pp. 41–43.
[4] Ibid., p. 79.
[5] Ibid., pp. 72–73, 75.
[6] Ibid., p. 74.

TABLE 2

Exchange Rates of the Czech Crown in U.S. Cents

Year	Month	U.S. Cents
1919	July	5.63
1920	January	1.43
	February	0.98
	July	2.20
1921	January	1.30
	July	1.31
1922	January	1.73
	July	2.19
	October	3.29
	December	3.10

Source: Pasvolsky, *Economic Nationalism*, p. 211.

again in millions, was 844 in 1914, 4,016 in 1918, 12,508 in 1920, 17,567 in 1921, and 19,492 in 1922.[7]

Table 2 shows behavior of the exchange rate.[8] Over the seven months from July 1919 to February 1920, the crown depreciated against the U.S. dollar at a 95.0 percent annual rate. It recovered sharply by July 1920, then sank again, but by July 1922 was back practically to the same level as two years before. It recovered still further and in October 1922 was quoted 3.4 times as high as in February 1920.

Not only the exchange rates but also available price indexes suggest that inflation came to an end late in 1921, after already experiencing interruptions. One official wholesale index stood at 14.6 times the prewar level in January and February 1921, then dropped by 14 percent (at an annual rate of 30 percent) by July, and then rose by 33.5 percent (at a 128 percent annual rate) by November. After the substantial rekindling of inflation thus indicated late in 1921, the index

---

[7] Mildschuh, "Currency Conditions," p. 182; Karásek, "Banking," p. 170.

[8] A chart in League of Nations, *The Course and Control of Inflation* (Princeton, 1946), p. 127, shows the price of the dollar peaking in early 1920 at slightly over 5 times the rate of early 1919, then declining, then peaking again just slightly higher at the end of 1920 and late in 1921. After 1921, the rate on the dollar definitely declines, leveling off late in 1922 and in 1923 at about twice the level of early 1919. Thus the crown—to switch points of view—recovered to 2.5 or more times its weakest quotation.

generally sagged, standing 41 percent below its peak thirteen months later.[9]

One influence reportedly tending to reduce prices in the first half of 1921 was the liberalization of trade; then the abolition of price controls allowed them to rise in the second half of the year. After that, external influences seemed to dominate. The Czech crown appreciated rapidly, in striking contrast with the collapse of the Austrian and German currencies and with the previous tendency of the three currencies to move together. The flight of capital from Austria and Germany was said to be largely directed toward Czechoslovakia because of its tight budgetary policy and favorable trade balance.[10]

Influenced by considerations of prestige, the Czech government had been pursuing a policy of deflating back to the prewar standard, but it had to recognize that the goal was unattainable. Late in 1922, the Ministry of Finance seized the opportunity provided by the crown's recent appreciation and decided to stabilize the currency at about 3 U.S. cents. This appreciation had occurred under the influence of capital inflows, had not yet been fully reflected in the crown's domestic purchasing power, and had carried the crown's exchange quotation to a level widely believed to be too high to be maintained. As a result of this circumstance and also of tensions surrounding the impending clash between France and Germany over reparations, a currency crisis developed late in 1922. Exports suffered from the high exchange rate. To support the currency, the government sold large amounts of foreign bills and securities accumulated during the period of appreciation. By February 1923, the crisis eased. Continuing internal deflation worked toward bringing the crown's purchasing power into line with its exchange rate. A severe business depression, with unemployment reaching about 20 percent at the worst, also occurred. According to Antonin Basch, the policy was generally recognized as wrong; stabilization of the crown at a lower level could have limited the severity of the adjustments necessary in any stabilization after inflation. The industrial crisis was eased by the fact that French occupation of the Ruhr increased Germany's demand for Czech coal and metallurgical products.[11] Prices did eventually adjust to the exchange

---

[9] Mildschuh, "Currency Conditions," p. 180. The table in League of Nations, *International Statistical Year-Book, 1926* (Geneva, 1927), p. 172, does not show wholesale prices before the end of 1921, when they stood at 16.5 times the level of 1914, then declining by 43.0 percent by July 1923. The retail index (p. 176) begins in June 1923 at 7.2 times the 1914 level, then declines 7.2 percent further in the following eleven months.

[10] Pasvolsky, *Economic Nationalism*, p. 212.

[11] Ibid., pp. 212–216; Basch, "Economic and Financial Policy," p. 160.

rate, which was maintained until the devaluation of the crown in 1934 under greatly changed circumstances.

Summary and Comment. Czechoslovakia's experience is interesting for the contrast that it provides with the experiences of other successor states of the old Habsburg monarchy. The crown was saved from hyperinflation by a policy guided, if not by sound economic theory, at least by an instinct for financial conservatism. Under the influence of capital movements responding partly to that policy and partly to monetary disorders in neighboring countries, the Czech crown appreciated substantially from its low on the foreign exchanges. A stabilization that overvalued the crown in relation to its purchasing power brought downward pressure on the price level, but also business depression. In that respect, the episode resembles Great Britain's return to the prewar gold parity of the pound in 1925.

France in 1926

France in 1926 presents an example of an inflation being stopped suddenly, after approaching the panic stage. As shown in table 3, wholesale and retail price inflation had reached substantial double-digit rates by late in 1925; between May and July 1926, wholesale price inflation was running at a triple-digit annual rate.

The French government had financed its expenses in World War I mostly by issuing bonds, particularly short-term bonds, and by resort to the printing press. Between mid-1914 and the end of 1918, the note circulation of the Bank of France was multiplied by 5.2; the average annual rate of increase was thus 44 percent. The rate of growth of the note circulation slackened after the war but between the ends of May and July 1926 again reached an annual rate of 44 percent.[12]

The prewar exchange rate of the franc had been 19.3 U.S. cents. Late in March 1919, just after abandonment of wartime pegging, the franc was down to 16.9 cents. It fluctuated further downward to the end of 1920, reaching 5.9 cents, recovered to 9.2 cents late in April 1922 (the highest quotation ever reached after December 1919), and thereafter generally fell, reaching an average of 2.4 cents in the last weeks of July 1926 and falling practically to 2 cents at the worst. Between late May and late July 1926, the rate of the dollar in Paris was rising at a 491 percent annual rate.[13]

---

[12] Calculated from James H. Rogers, *The Process of Inflation in France, 1914–1927* (New York: Columbia University Press, 1929), p. 62.

[13] Calculated from ibid., p. 59.

TABLE 3

Price Increases in France, 1925–1926

Annual Percentage Rates

Year	Dates of Wholesale Index	Wholesale Index	Dates of Retail Index	Retail Index
1925				
			June-Sept.	11.8
	Sept.-Oct.	42.5		
	Oct.-Nov.	97.2	Sept.-Dec.	21.5
	Nov.-Dec.	70.2		
1926				
	Dec.-Jan.	1.9		
	Jan.-Feb.	3.8	Dec.-Mar.	31.7
	Feb.-Mar.	−7.2		
	Mar.-Apr.	41.7		
	Apr.-May	95.0	Mar.-June	33.7
	May-June	135.7		
	June-July	345.7		
	July-Aug.	−63.6	June-Sept.	52.5
	Aug.-Sept.	33.2		
	Sept.-Oct.	−42.3		
	Oct.-Nov.	−68.2	Sept.-Dec.	4.5
	Nov.-Dec.	−64.7		

Source: Calculations from League of Nations, *International Statistical Year-Book, 1926*, pp. 171, 175.

Price inflation, like exchange depreciation, was not uninterrupted. At the end of the war, the wholesale price index stood about 3.6 times as high as at the beginning. Between November 1918 and May 1919, the index declined by 9.2 percent, then rose by 80.7 percent by April 1920, then fell by 47.8 percent by February 1922. Only then did inflation get going again. From its low in February 1922 to its high in July 1926, the wholesale index rose by 173 percent; between May and July 1926, it was rising at a 223 percent annual rate.[14]

Inflationary government finance was continuing, punctuated at times by gestures of reform. New taxes were levied and noninflation-

[14] Calculated from ibid., p. 57.

ary loans floated in 1920, and the government obligated itself to repay earlier advances from the Bank of France at a rate of 2 billion francs a year. Although these repayments were later made either only partially or by means of subterfuges (such as borrowing from private banks to which the Bank of France had to lend the necessary funds), the announced policy did at first help promote confidence in the currency.

Expenditures on postwar reconstruction from 1919 to 1926 resulted in government budgets that were as large as or larger than wartime budgets (larger in nominal francs, though smaller in purchasing-power terms). These expenditures, together with war-related pension and interest costs, produced a "consecrated deficit" in a confusing morass of special budgets. France had had to pay an indemnity to Germany after the Franco-Prussian war; now the victorious French expected that it was their turn to collect. As Finance Minister Klotz said, "Taxpayers need not worry, Germany will pay."[15]

> In a sense the special budget of recoverable expenses was the cause of the collapse of the franc. The result was not only to involve the country in continuous borrowing which the investment market was at times unable to absorb, but also tie up the prospects of the Franch franc with the prospects of the German mark in the minds of the public.[16]

The franc was thus vulnerable when reparations discussions broke down in June 1922. It suffered from the inclination of the Americans and British to postpone further reparations collections until the collapsing German mark had been strengthened. In January 1923 the French sent troops into the German Ruhr to collect payments by force. The Germans responded with passive resistance, and the revenue obtained hardly covered the costs of the French troops. Slowly it began to dawn on the French people that *they* would have to pay the debts and expenses of war and reconstruction. "This bitter awakening lent a new and frightening significance to the rise in prices in France and the drop in the exchange value of the franc."[17]

The franc suffered notable spells of weakness in February, August, and November 1923. On the latter occasion, it became known that the government would again be unable to comply with the law and convention of 1920 regarding debt repayments to the Bank of

---

[15] Quoted in Eleanor Lansing Dulles, *The French Franc, 1914–1928* (New York: Macmillan, 1929), p. 114.

[16] R. G. Hawtrey, *The Art of Central Banking* (London: Cass, 1962), p. 3.

[17] Martin Wolfe, *The French Franc between the Wars, 1919–1939* (New York: Columbia University Press, 1951), p. 33.

France. January 1923 saw the failure of a loan floated by an association of French banks that had been set up to sell its government-guaranteed bonds to the public and use the proceeds for loans to industry and to war-damage victims.

The failure of this loan was ominous because the government was dependent on the willingness of the public to buy its obligations if it were to avoid outright inflationary finance. The manager of the public debt had already pointed out more than a year before that the short-term debt represented a "potential inflation." If it could not be continually renewed—that is, if the government could not succeed in continually borrowing from Peter to pay Paul—an actual inflation and a panic would result, whose first symptom would be crisis on the foreign-exchange market.[18]

In March 1924, as the continuing slide of the franc dramatized an atmosphere of crisis, Parliament accepted several fiscal reforms called for by Raymond Poincaré's new coalition government, including government economies and a 20 percent increase in most taxes. This law symbolized Parliament's first official recognition that the "Germany-will-pay" program had been wishful thinking.[19] Largely thanks to this show of fiscal realism, the government was able to borrow private funds in New York and London. These funds were promptly used to strengthen the franc and engineer a "bear squeeze" that inflicted heavy losses on speculators who had sold francs short. This success proved only temporary, and the franc's quotation slid again. Furthermore, the public's dismay at the impending tax increases probably influenced the outcome of the May 1924 elections, in which a leftist coalition defeated Poincaré's government.

The election result helped make investors increasingly apprehensive and increasingly inclined to let their maturing treasury securities run off, rather than invest in new ones, and transfer the proceeds abroad. By late in 1924, current government deficits, having shrunk year by year, had become a less crucial inflationary factor than past deficits in the form of government debt. Borrowing from Peter to pay Paul was becoming increasingly difficult. The volume of bonds coming to maturity would be especially heavy in 1925. Furthermore, the floating debt, represented by *bons de la défense nationale*, "was so sensitive to the condition of public confidence that any adverse opinion as to the future led to the failure to reinvest the cash received for redemptions, which meant a decline in holdings amounting often

---

[18] Charles S. Maier, *Recasting Bourgeois Europe* (Princeton: Princeton University Press, 1975), p. 464.

[19] Robert Murray Haig, *The Public Finances of Post-War France* (New York: Columbia University Press, 1929), pp. 97–98.

to hundreds of millions of francs a month."[20] As Finance Minister Doumer said in 1925,

> the debt is not only terrible by its weight. It is also terrifying by its nature. The resources that the *bons de la défense nationale* bring to the Treasury are essentially precarious. Their flow depends on factors both economic and moral, and these variations, which are difficult to anticipate, condemn our Treasury to live in a state of intolerable insecurity. . . .[21]

As a recent scholar said, "Any lack of confidence in money deterred holders [of *bons*] from renewing their lendings, thus depriving the government of vital funds and forcing it to look elsewhere, mainly to the Bank of France."[22]

During 1925, when six different finance ministers held office, two different theories regarding the *bons* formed the basis of rival policy recommendations. The theory of the *plafond unique* held that the *bons*, which came in denominations as small as 100 francs, were used as money. The Treasury could save itself problems if it worked within only a single ceiling, the total of the outstanding *bons* and the existing note-issue ceiling, and allowed newly issued notes to replace unrenewed *bons* within this total. Supporters of this view did not expect any further price increases to result, since the moneylike *bons* had already had their effect on prices. Actually, indications are that the *bons* were *not* circulating as money,[23] and replacing them with actual money would have tended to be inflationary.

The theory of the *circuit fermé* supposed that loans to the Treasury should be renewed in an almost automatic manner: ". . . the sums of money drawn from the Treasury are rediffused among the public who reinvests them and so on. Thus subscriptions should normally compensate for maturities; and a large scale demand for repayment is not to be feared." Since renewals were "automatic," interest payments on the *bons* could safely be reduced. Unfortunately, the theory presupposed certain conditions that did not in fact hold: "It is essential that the general level of prices shall not be so high as to call out a larger volume of monetary instruments; that confidence in the treasury be absolute; and that the fear of a rapid depreciation of the monetary unit be avoided."[24]

---

[20] Dulles, *Franc*, p. 183.

[21] Quoted in Haig, *Finances*, pp. 131–132.

[22] Tom Kemp, *The French Economy, 1913–39* (London: Longman's, 1972), p. 75.

[23] Dulles, *Franc*, p. 246.

[24] Ibid., p. 249, quoting George-Edgar Bonnet.

Three major options were considered in 1925 to deal with the government's financial plight. One was a capital levy. Another was a forced consolidation of debt, which would have spelled partial repudiation: holders of high-interest, short-maturity bonds would have been compelled to accept low-interest, long-term bonds in exchange. The third and actual course was to resort to the printing press to pay off unrenewed *bons*.[25]

A vicious circle resulted. Whenever the expected rate of appreciation of foreign exchange exceeded the interest rate on *bons*, speculators would redeem *bons* to buy foreign exchange. The government would have to turn to the Bank of France for advances, which swelled the note circulation, tending to raise prices and further stimulate shifts of funds abroad.[26] During 1925, the volume of *bons* outstanding fell from 55 to 46 billion francs, and a marked shift also occurred from one-year and six-month *bons* to three- and one-month issues.[27] Wholesale prices and the cost of living continued rising in 1925 at a not yet panicky rate. The decline of the franc on the exchanges, interrupted occasionally by official support, speeded up late in the year.

Political and psychological factors were also at work. In April 1925, when England by contrast was returning to the gold standard, the Herriot government had to confess a subterfuge whereby state borrowing at the Bank of France had exceeded the legal limit, with the excess concealed in the Bank's balance sheet under the heading "portfolio." Herriot's defense was that earlier cabinets had been guilty of similar irregularities. It also came to light that the Bank's end-of-1924 balance sheet, and possibly others, had concealed note issues beyond the legal limit under the heading "miscellaneous liabilities." The general public had grown accustomed to regarding repeated increases in the legal limits to the Bank's "advances to the State" and "note issue" as ominous signs, so the disclosure of actual subterfuges was a particular blow to confidence. These disclosures, together with unpopular proposals for a capital levy or a forced loan, toppled the Herriot ministry in April 1925. Fifteen months of parliamentary agony ensued as successive governments wavered between trying to hold the votes of socialists on fiscal policy and the votes of moderates on monetary issues. The next cabinet tried to issue an internal loan to consolidate the floating debt and to borrow money in America. The

[25] Haig, *Finances*, pp. 115–116.
[26] S. C. Tsiang, "Fluctuating Exchange Rates in Countries with Relatively Stable Economies," International Monetary Fund *Staff Papers*, vol. 7, no. 2 (Washington, D.C., October 1959), p. 267.
[27] Wolfe, *Franc*, p. 60.

internal loan was poorly received, and the American loan negotiations fell through in October. A reconstructed cabinet suggested left-wing financial remedies, including postponement of the December treasury bond redemptions and a new property tax. Desertion by the conservative wing of the leftist coalition brought the government down in November 1925.[28] "By the end of 1925 the seemingly uncontrollable wave of exchange depreciation had brought a hysterical note" into financial discussions. A general flight from the franc and monetary assets into commodities and foreign assets was getting under way.[29]

All this background information is relevant to understanding the nature of the inflationary situation in which expectational or psychological factors could play such an important part in the remedy. Here is a good place to summarize what happened before the climax of 1926. Though actual government budget deficits and increases in the national debt remained moderate (with the deficit actually shrinking somewhat), they were large enough and had persisted long enough to sap confidence. The government kept having trouble selling new securities to pay off old ones as they came due, especially since so much of the debt was of short maturity. With the government having to borrow at the Bank of France, increases became necessary in the limits set to the Bank's advances to the state and to its note issue—either forthright increases or devious subterfuges.

These inflationary omens further discouraged public subscriptions to government securities. By July 1926, the Bank's advances to the state had increased 77 percent, notes in circulation had increased 38 percent, and notes in circulation plus demand deposits with four leading commercial banks had increased 43 percent over the levels of only eighteen months before (as annual rates, these increases amount to 46, 24, and 27 percent respectively).[30] Business as well as government borrowing fed the inflation. The French banking system was dangerously responsive to the "needs of trade": as rising prices swelled the nominal volume of transactions, bank credit expanded correspondingly. Banks could meet their customers' demands for loans by drawing on their deposits previously made with the Treasury, by cashing government securities as they matured, or by discounting at the Bank of France. Their doing so caused the government all the more financial embarrassment. The political situation was also awkward. Finance minister replaced finance minister in a "waltz of the port-

---

[28] Leland B. Yeager, *International Monetary Relations*, 2nd. ed. (New York: Harper & Row, 1976), p. 326; Maier, *Recasting*, pp. 499–500.

[29] Wolfe, *Franc*, pp. 38–39.

[30] Calculated from a table in Tsiang, "Fluctuating Exchange Rates," p. 269.

folios." From October 1925 to July 1926, a new minister took office every thirty-seven days on the average.[31]

In the spring of 1926, the franc declined even more alarmingly than before (as reflected in the price figures of table 3). In just two weeks, between May 5 and May 19, it depreciated 15.7 percent against the pound sterling. Observers linked the new depreciation with recent adverse trade-balance figures and new taxation of dividend income. At a meeting early in May, Edouard de Rothschild, regent of the Bank of France, opined that no market intervention could promise success until a conservative government had returned to power; and American authorities, including the president of the Federal Reserve Bank of New York, effectively endorsed this rather self-fulfilling estimate. The latter, as well as the governor of the Bank of England, pointed out that bearish speculation had taken on a character different from what it had had in the spring of 1924. Then the speculators had been foreigners. Now, French holders of capital were demonstrating lack of confidence.

> . . . in 1925 and 1926 every grocery man was considering the effect of the exchange rate on coffee, every stenographer was trying to build up a savings account in a gold standard country. . . . The cost of the dollar was the subject of conversation in every corner cafe, and one could hardly make a purchase without some discussion of the exchange rate. There was, in fact, a general increase in money consciousness. . . .

People well remembered what had happened to the German mark only two and three years before.[32]

The French war debt to the United States placed an additional constraint on the French government in the spring of 1926. The U.S. Treasury had informally embargoed private as well as public loans until repayment terms were settled. A number of French financiers and political experts were recommending prompt settlement in order to gain American credits and relieve pressure on the franc, but a weak government might not survive parliamentary debate on the issue.[33]

The climax came in July during the debate over ratification of a financial agreement with the United States and over Finance Minister Caillaux's demand, spurred by the urgent tone of a report just released

---

[31] League of Nations, *Course*, pp. 34–37, gives particular emphasis to the floating debt situation, the shaky confidence of the public, and the panicky nature of capital flight at times, particularly in the latter part of 1925 and the first seven months of 1926.

[32] Maier, *Recasting*, p. 501; quotation from Dulles, *Franc*, pp. 45–46.

[33] Maier, *Recasting*, p. 502.

by a nonpolitical committee of financial experts, for power to institute financial and monetary measures by decree. Parliament refused. The Briand-Caillaux government was overthrown and replaced, for two days only, by another Left coalition under Herriot.

The old finance ministry had previously asked the Bank of France to buy from the Treasury $31 million still left from the American loan of 1924. On July 19, the Bank agreed on condition of a corresponding increase in its legal note issue. The new ministry balked at the condition, but the Bank insisted. On July 21, to forestall subterfuges, Governor Moreau of the Bank of France sent a letter to the finance minister warning in effect that the Treasury's small remaining balance at the Bank would probably run out by the end of that day. The balance sheet to be made up that night and published the next day would probably show advances by the Bank to the state in excess of the legal limit, obliging the Bank to cease making payments for the Treasury's account. The only way out, the letter concluded, was immediate parliamentary approval of the proposed transaction on the Bank's terms.

The Treasury's balance did not quite, in fact, run out on July 21. That evening the government was overthrown after submitting a bill to sell the dollars to the Bank *without* raising the note-issue ceiling. Immediately afterward, Parliament enacted a bill embodying the Bank's terms.[34]

That evening's votes signaled the collapse of the Left majority of 1924. Raymond Poincaré now won the support that the Radical Socialists had withheld until the financial and parliamentary situations seemed desperate. He quickly put together a ministry including all the discordant elements of the past years, leaving only the Communists in outright opposition.[35] On July 23, Parliament installed the conservative old lawyer, former premier and president of the Republic, as premier and as finance minister with the special powers recently denied to Caillaux. He promised to save the franc by cutting expenditures, cutting pensions, cutting government payrolls, and raising taxes. His reputation for fiscal conservatism was so great that the mere news of his nomination for office appeared decisive. Scholars have reported the change of scene in words such as the following. "Miraculously the picture seemed to change over night. The presence of Raymond Poincaré at the head of the government apparently was enough to stop the panic." "The assumption of power by Poincaré at the head of a government of National Union had a reassuring psycho-

---

[34] Yeager, *Relations*, p. 327.
[35] Maier, *Recasting*, p. 505.

logical effect on the bourgeoisie and middle-class opinion as a whole." "The sudden recovery of the franc and the political calm after wild excitement were astounding. The franc rose from below 2 cents to 2½ cents in five days."[36]

Poincaré's measures were drastic but not strikingly original or ingenious. Besides dropping proposals for such "radical" measures as a capital levy or forced debt consolidation, he adopted measures based largely on the recommendations of the expert committee. The business turnover tax was applied to more transactions; the luxury tax was increased; an inheritance duty and a tax on the first transfer of real estate were instituted; and a new institution, the Caisse d'Amortissement, with funds coming from the government tobacco monopoly, was created to administer the floating debt. Poincaré attached the question of confidence in himself to his proposals, making it clear to the deputies that he would accept no compromises and that his defeat would mean collapse of the franc. Parliament quickly complied. To clinch his success, Poincaré convoked the two chambers at Versailles as a National Assembly to enact some of his basic fiscal reforms into constitutional law, safe from any future left-wing government.[37]

Poincaré's measures would take time to be fully effective, but the confidence that he inspired provided the time. His task was not unduly difficult. Speculation had brought the franc lower than current fundamentals justified, so it had room to rise. Unlike Germany during its inflation, France relied primarily on indirect taxation and on the revenue of fiscal monopolies instead of on taxes on incomes of the year before, so government revenues rose with the price level. Government expenditures rose more slowly: approximately 53 percent of them in 1926 went for service on the internal debt and for pensions and so were fixed in nominal terms. The budget moved into balance and even into surplus.

In December 1926, after recovering on the exchange market from its panic level of two cents to about four cents, that is, to about one-fifth of its prewar parity, the franc was stabilized de facto by official intervention. To restrain the franc's further recovery, the Bank of France bought foreign exchange heavily under its new legal authority to buy gold and foreign exchange at premium prices and to issue banknotes against them that would not count against the legal ceiling.

---

[36] Respectively, Wolfe, *Franc*, p. 44; Kemp, *French Economy*, p. 79; Dulles, *Franc*, p. 195.

[37] League of Nations, *Course*, p. 38; Hawtrey, *Art*, p. 9; Wolfe, *Franc*, p. 45; Dulles, *Franc*, p. 345; Maier, *Recasting*, p. 505.

During the ensuing year and a half, small creditor interests kept pressing for an upward revaluation of the franc; and Poincaré too had some qualms, concerned with national honor, about officially writing off four-fifths of the franc's prewar gold value. Spurts of bull speculation on a possible revaluation forced the Bank of France to absorb foreign exchange from time to time in amounts that threatened to inflate the French money supply. Prodded by the resignation threat of the governor of the Bank of France, Poincaré moved legally to consolidate the stabilization already achieved. He recited the arguments against pursuit of prewar parity that he had formerly resisted. A law of June 25, 1928 put the franc on a gold-bullion standard at an appropriately redefined parity.[38]

The end to price inflation was not quite as dramatic as the turn-around on the foreign-exchange market, but it was quick. The wholesale price index, like the dollar rate, peaked in July 1926; by December it stood 25.1 percent below and by October 1927 29.7 percent below the peak level. The retail price index registered rises over the preceding three months of 7.5 percent in June 1926 and of 11.1 percent in September but of only 1.1 percent in December.[39]

Some side effects accompanied stabilization. The number of unemployed on public relief rolls rose from 17,000 in December 1926 to 80,000 in February 1927. Thereafter the number fell rapidly. The effects were presumably lessened by the "safety valve" of immigrant workers. Even though France admitted 64,325 in 1927, mainly to harvest crops, 89,982 foreign workers were refused an extension of their visas.[40] Industrial production averaged 12.6 percent lower in 1927 than in 1926. The monthly index peaked in October and November 1926, then reached a trough 17.8 percent lower in April through July of 1927 before beginning a mild recovery.[41] In assessing the side effects, one must of course consider what would have happened if a stabilization program had *not* been adopted.

Summary and Comment. The situation from which France stabilized in 1926 exhibits some similarities with but probably greater differences from the current U.S. situation. Both countries had been suffering inflation for many years—France from 1914, but with major

---

[38] Yeager, *Relations*, pp. 328–329; Maier, *Recasting*, pp. 507–508; Wolfe, *Franc*, p. 59.

[39] Calculated from tables in Rogers, *Process*, p. 57, and League of Nations, *International Statistical Year-Book, 1926*, pp. 171, 175.

[40] Wolfe, *Franc*, p. 56.

[41] Calculated from a table in Rogers, *Process*, p. 172.

interruptions right after the war and again in 1920–1922. The stage of triple-digit wholesale-price inflation lasted only a few months. France was not suffering the supply shocks—oil, for example—to which the United States has recently been exposed, though the problems of reconstruction and of trying to collect reparations perhaps are a counterpart. Labor unions seem to have been weaker in France in the 1920s than in the United States nowadays. France suffered political instability of a kind that the United States has not yet experienced.

France provides another example of a stabilization in which political change, together with its expectational or psychological effects, appeared important. France also illustrates the argument—if the argument is persuasive on other grounds—that stabilization from inflation of a moderate or intermediate degree is very difficult and that, as a practical matter, things have to get worse before they can get better. The French Parliament did not take the necessary decisive action until inflation and exchange depreciation had become extreme enough to make the public clamor for a dramatic and credible change of course and until political crisis had compounded the economic crisis.

Belgium and Portugal in the 1920s

The experience of Belgium and Portugal in the 1920s provides a footnote to the French story. In all three countries, control of the money supply was made difficult by a public debt structure sensitive to expectational or psychological factors.

In Belgium, more suddenly than in France, a crisis of confidence developed in the first half of 1926, when the note circulation rose by 16 percent, wholesale prices by 56 percent, and the exchange rate on the dollar by 87 percent. As recently as the last few months of 1925 and the first two months of 1926, the wholesale price index had been declining. Then, over the five months between February and July, the index rose at a 198 percent annual rate. After the resolution of the crisis, the index declined in August and ended the year below the peak reached in July.

During the years 1921–1923, the government had tried, unsuccessfully, to convert its floating debt into long-term obligations. In 1923, the government ran into difficulty selling long-term bonds to cover even current budget needs. Sometimes business recovery and at other times lack of confidence and flight of capital drew funds away from government securities. In the early summer of 1926, redemptions of maturing short-term treasury obligations so far exceeded new subscriptions that the government had to call on the National Bank for an advance of 1.5 billion francs.[42]

The crisis was associated with failure of an attempt at exchange stabilization in the early months of 1926. Foreign financiers had made a stabilization loan conditional on simultaneous flotation of a domestic long-term loan, but Belgian bankers refused their support. As the difficulties of the stabilization scheme became apparent, banks and private investors were increasingly inclined to let their short-term government securities run off and use the proceeds to buy foreign exchange. Although the National Bank sold large amounts of gold and foreign assets in efforts to support the Belgian franc, these sales failed to shrink the domestic money supply, as the government had to borrow from the Bank to pay off its maturing securities.

In May a new government came into power, and in July the king was given temporary dictatorial power to solve the financial problem. The government was able to obtain a foreign long-term loan to stabilize the currency. (A new unit was introduced, the belga, equaling five francs.) The floating debt held by the public was drastically reduced through a compulsory funding operation.[43]

In Portugal, also, a large floating debt made monetary conditions sensitive to the state of public confidence. In the fiscal year 1923–1924, despite a reduced budget deficit, the government considerably increased its borrowing from the Bank of Portugal. The public was losing confidence in the currency, failing to renew treasury bills as they matured, and converting the proceeds into foreign currencies. The exchange value of the escudo fell 20 percent, and commodity prices rose. In July 1924, the authorities were able to check the depreciation by selling silver stocks abroad and raising foreign credits. In the second half of the year, funds returned from abroad, the escudo recovered sharply, sales of treasury bills to the public increased, and government borrowing at the banks stopped. A small-scale replay of the 1923–1924 disturbance occurred in 1927–1928, with exchange depreciation, run-offs of treasury bills, and government borrowing at the central bank. Negotiations for a long-term foreign loan to pay off the domestic floating debt broke down. In April 1928, however, a new finance minister (Salazar) came to power. He achieved a long series of budget surpluses, which, along with issue of long-term funding loans, permitted mastery of the floating debt.[44]

---

[42] League of Nations, *Course*, pp. 39–41, citing Henry L. Shepherd, *The Monetary Experience of Belgium, 1914–1936* (Princeton: Princeton University Press, 1936), p. 29; cf. the wholesale price index in League of Nations, *International Statistical Year-Book, 1926*, p. 171.

[43] League of Nations, *Course*, pp. 40–41.

[44] Ibid., pp. 41–42.

In Belgium and Portugal, then, as in France around the same time, political change apparently played a part in a turnaround of expectations that contributed to overcoming a rather sudden flare-up of inflation and exchange depreciation.

Italy in 1947

Italy stopped a severe inflation within a few months. A credit squeeze, rather than immediate budgetary action, was the key measure.

Statistics for Italy around 1945 are unreliable, some contradicting others. Still, it appears that the country came out of World War II with real national income cut to little more than half the prewar level, the money supply multiplied ten- or fifteenfold, prices multiplied some fifteen- to thirtyfold, and the structure of relative prices twisted by controls. "A violent inflationary process developed during the last two years of the War when the fighting split the country and completely disrupted its economy and administration while the two opposing armies financed themselves by issuing vast amounts of currency." Issues of lira notes by the invading Allied forces were reflected in a rise in the share of currency in the total money supply (from 52 percent of currency plus bank deposits in 1938 to 71 percent in 1945).[45]

For the first twelve to fifteen months after the end of fighting, the currency circulation expanded little further. After the liberation of Italy, the lower prices in the north began adjusting to the higher level of the south. Price inflation practically came to a halt around the turn of the year 1945–1946. Between January and August 1946, the cost-of-living index fluctuated mildly at a level about twenty-seven times as high as before the war; the food index actually declined. In June 1946, before starting upward again, the wholesale index stood at about twenty-six times the level of 1938. Relief shipments of food and the restoration of contact between north and south helped mitigate shortages, and people were said to be willing to hold onto their money balances while awaiting the expected reappearance of scarce goods on the market. The government was able to cover its deficit with the proceeds of a successful postliberation loan and by borrowing from the banks. The banks had considerable excess reserves and

---

[45] Albert O. Hirschman, "Inflation and Deflation in Italy," *American Economic Review*, vol. 38 (September 1948), pp. 598–606 (quotation from p. 598); Bruno Foa, *Monetary Reconstruction in Italy* (New York: King's Crown Press, 1949); and Sima Lieberman, *The Growth of European Mixed Economies, 1945–1970* (New York: Halsted/Wiley, 1977), chap. 4 and table on p. 102 (based in turn on Paolo Baffi, "Monetary Developments in Italy," Banca Nazionale del Lavoro *Quarterly Review*, December 1958, p. 417).

faced only light demands for credit from business firms, whose activities were limited by fuel and materials shortages.[46]

This pause in inflation in the first half of 1946 means that the stabilization after the rekindling of inflation was a stabilization from a relatively brief burst rather than from an inflation that had been persisting uninterrupted for years. Anyway, the period of pause proved to be the calm before the storm. Previous monetary expansion had greatly increased the liquidity of the public. The public was depositing currency holdings and government checks in the banks, increasing the reserves of the banking system. No system of required reserves was effective at the time, so the banks had a great capacity to expand their loans and deposits whenever a strengthening of the demand for credit (or, presumably, a mere recognition by the banks of the profits that they had been missing by holding excess reserves) should touch off the expansionary process.[47]

Depreciation of the lira on the exchanges foreshadowed a renewal of price inflation and perhaps played some role in the process. The exchange rate had been implicitly pegged by American and UNRRA aid but was unpegged in the spring of 1946. The lira started falling in May, forcing the government to change the official rate on the dollar from 100 in 1945 first to 225 and then to 350 in August 1947.[48] (See table 4.) From June 1946, when it reached a low, to September 1947, the wholesale price index was multiplied by 2.39, thus rising at a 101 percent annual rate.[49] Between February and October 1947, the official wholesale price index was rising at a 95 percent annual rate, the effective wholesale price index at 113 percent annual rate, and the cost-of-living index for Milan at a 72 percent annual rate. Between March and April 1947, the respective annual rates were 344, 927, and 220 percent.[50] Thus inflation was on, and sometimes beyond, the brink of triple digits.

A new wave of money-supply expansion also got under way around mid-1946. In the second half of that year alone, the note circulation rose by 27 percent. This increase amounted to 46 percent in the full year between mid-1946 and mid-1947 and to 34 percent in the

---

[46] Hirschman, "Inflation," pp. 598–599; George H. Hildebrand, *Growth and Structure in the Economy of Modern Italy* (Cambridge: Harvard University Press, 1965), p. 18; Foa, *Reconstruction*, pp. 55–56; Lieberman, *Growth*, p. 101.

[47] Hildebrand, *Growth*, pp. 15–16; Lieberman, *Growth*, p. 102.

[48] Foa, *Reconstruction*, pp. 64–65, 101; Lieberman, *Growth*, p. 102.

[49] Calculated from Hildebrand, *Growth and Structure*, p. 18. Hildebrand says that wholesale prices were rising at a rate of 9.4 percent a month from July 1946 to September 1947, a figure that is too high in relation to the levels of the index he cites.

[50] Calculated from a table in Foa, *Reconstruction*, p. 68.

TABLE 4

ITALIAN EXCHANGE RATE, MONTHLY AVERAGES, LIRA PER DOLLAR, 1946–1948

Year	Month	Legal Free Rate	Black Market Rate
1946	May	364	333
	June	377	366
	July	478	401
	August	505	484
	September	596	530
	October	600	523
	November	568	611
	December	568	683
1947	January	528	607
	February	532	590
	March	605	644
	April	697	722
	May	906	801
	June	841	737
	July	775	662
	August	721	637
	September	667	665
	October	618	645
	November	603	584
	December	575	582
1948	January	573	592
	February	573	612
	March	574	663
	April	574	618
	May	575	587
	June	575	582

NOTE: The legal free rate was the free-market rate at which exporters sold 50 percent of their foreign-exchange proceeds (selling the other half at the official rate). The free and official rates coincided from February 1948 and remained at 575 through August 1949, while the black-market rate fluctuated in the range of 582 to 681.

SOURCE: Lutz and Lutz, *Policy*, p. 46.

second half of 1947 alone.[51] From mid-1946 through September 1947, currency in circulation expanded at an average rate of 4.7 percent a month; the total volume of currency plus checking accounts increased

---

[51] Calculated from Foa, *Reconstruction*, p. 72.

during the fifteen months from mid-1947 through September 1947 at an average monthly rate of 5.6 percent (equivalent to a 92.3 percent annual rate).[52] The period, according to Friedrich A. and Vera C. Lutz, showed all the typical signs of an inflation: a sharp increase in the velocity of circulation (sharper even than the contrast between the rates of increase of prices and money would suggest, since production and transactions were also increasing over the period), a flight into inventories and other "real values," a rise in share prices and fall in bond prices, and a decline in the propensity to save, as reflected in a lag of savings deposits beyond the expansion of currency and checking accounts.[53]

Among the factors feeding the rekindled inflation were said to be expectations (which proved wrong) of a currency reform, inducing holders to get rid of money for real assets. Banks responded as demands for credit soared to finance the recovery of imports, investment, and production (industrial production doubled between March 1946 and September 1947), as well as speculation in inventories and on the stock market, which become feverish with the rise in commodity prices. (The banks' loan/deposit ratio rose from 0.42 to 0.75 between June 1946 and September 1947.) Credit expansion for the private sector overshadowed government deficit financing as the main element in monetary inflation.[54]

Government deficits and the currency printing press were to blame, however, in the sense that they had earlier loaded the banks with the ample reserve funds that they were now putting to fuller use. The government still was running a deficit, furthermore, and price inflation itself was pushing up expenditures ahead of revenues. In addition, the Bank of Italy was creating money in buying wheat bills, as it was obliged to do under a price-support and subidy program.[55]

Late in the spring of 1947, a major financial and foreign-exchange crisis developed. As already mentioned, price increases were particularly sharp between March and April. By May, the average legal free rate on the dollar was up to 906 lira from the rate of 528 only four months before,[56] implying depreciation of the lira at an 80 percent annual rate.

The lira's subsequent recovery seems not unconnected with

---

[52] Friedrich A. and Vera C. Lutz, *Monetary and Foreign Exchange Policy in Italy* (Princeton: Princeton University Press, 1960), pp. 3, 5, 11. The price index used by the Lutzes was increasing at a 9.3 percent monthly rate over the same period.

[53] Ibid., p. 11.

[54] Lieberman, *Growth*, pp. 102–103; Hildebrand, *Growth and Structure*, pp. 18–20.

[55] Lutz and Lutz, *Policy*, pp. 8–9; Hildebrand, *Growth and Structure*, pp. 18–20.

[56] Table 4 and Foa, *Reconstruction*, p. 103.

political changes. On May 30, Premier de Gasperi succeeded in reconstructing his government without the participation of the Communists, whose activity in and out of government had been disruptive and whose purpose would be served by rampant inflation. Developing shortly afterward, the hope of Marshall Plan aid and the attendant easing of external pressures against the lira also improved prospects of stabilization.[57] A turn toward monetary and fiscal responsibility was signaled by appointment of Professor Gustavo del Vecchio as minister of the Treasury and of Professor Luigi Einaudi as deputy premier and budget minister, the latter post being newly created. Einaudi had been governor of the Bank of Italy. Although aware of the problem of credit inflation, he had had little authority to cope with it.

In essence, although the banks were awash with liquidity, there was no effective system of required reserves. In January 1947, Governor Einaudi had made the gesture of notifying the banks that they would thereafter be required to observe the reserve requirements imposed by a 1926 law that had been allowed to become a dead letter. That effort to check credit expansion had failed; obtaining the necessary powers depended on the political resoluteness only now beginning to take hold. Einaudi was given authority over financial and monetary matters and, in August 1947, was put in charge of the Inter-Ministerial Committee on Credit and Saving, whose task was to design a workable system of credit control and formulate overall monetary policy. In the technical execution of the plan that he worked out, Einaudi was powerfully aided by Treasury Minister del Vecchio and by his successor at the Bank of Italy, Donato Menichella.[58]

On August 22, Einaudi's committee put the banks on notice that credit restraint was finally under way. Effective at the end of September—thus giving the less liquid institutions more than five weeks to prepare themselves—the banks would be required to hold reserves in the form of specified government securities or deposits at the Bank of Italy. Since the committee was aiming at credit restraint but not actual contraction, it took care to set the requirements in such a way that they could be covered—but only slightly more than covered—by the banking system's existing aggregate holdings of the specified reserve

---

[57] Hildebrand, *Growth and Structure*, pp. 24–25; Charles S. Maier, "The Politics of Inflation in the Twentieth Century," in Fred Hirsch and John H. Goldthorpe, eds., *The Political Economy of Inflation* (Cambridge: Harvard University Press, 1978), p. 58.

[58] Foa, *Reconstruction*, pp. 98, 103–104; Hildebrand, *Growth and Structure*, pp. 24–25. Hildebrand describes Einaudi, de Gasperi, and Menichella as men of almost puritanical devotion to principle, especially in matters of money and public finance.

assets. The immediate effect of the new requirments was to freeze some 110 billion lire of the banks' reserve funds, leaving only 3.2 billion still free. At first, required reserves amounted to 14.7 percent of the commercial banks' total deposits. Over the next eighteen months, this ratio was steadily raised nearly to the 25 percent target set. The stiffened reserve requirements would not have slowed down bank credit expansion if the banks had been able to borrow at the Bank of Italy, but they were clearly warned in August 1947 not to count on being able to do so except in special circumstances. (Moreover, the discount rate was raised early in September.)[59]

Credit expansion did slow down. During the last quarter of 1947, bank loans to borrowers other than the government expanded at a monthly rate of only 0.7 percent, as against a 14.2 percent monthly rate in the preceding fifteen months. The expansion of checking deposits slowed to only about 1 percent.[60] Growth of the total money supply also slowed, although less conspicuously—from a monthly average rate of 3.9 percent from September 1946 to September 1947 to monthly rates of 3.0 percent over the following twelve months and 2.0 percent from September 1948 to the end of 1949.[61] The growth of the total money supply slowed less than the growth of bank credit and demand deposits because the Bank of Italy continued issuing banknotes in connection with loans to the government.[62]

It is noteworthy what the new policy did not include. It did not include trying to balance the budget by slashing expenditure and raising taxes. Such an approach was judged politically intolerable, and it would have brought results too slowly anyway. In fact, the deficit for the financial year running from mid-1947 to mid-1948 was larger than the deficit of the preceding financial year. Not until 1948–1949 and

---

[59] Lieberman, *Growth*, p. 103; Foa, *Reconstruction*, pp. 107–108; Lutz and Lutz, *Policy*, pp. 12–13; Hildebrand, *Growth and Structure*, pp. 26, 30, 32.

[60] Lutz and Lutz, *Policy*, p. 13. Somewhat different concepts show qualitatively the same change: bank credit had expanded by 14.7 percent and bank deposits by 8.3 percent in the third quarter of 1947; in the fourth quarter, these increases were 7.2 and 4.8 percent respectively. Foa, *Reconstruction*, p. 108. Some slowdown had in fact already occurred in the third quarter, when banks experienced some drainage of cash and decline in their free reserves. Hildebrand, *Growth and Structure*, pp. 22–23.

[61] Hildebrand, *Growth and Structure*, pp. 37, 39.

[62] Lutz and Lutz, *Policy*, p. 14. Furthermore, growth of the total money supply (here defined as demand deposits plus currency, including circular checks, in contrast with deposit money only) did not slow down immediately. Growth of total money in the December quarter of 1947 amounted to 10.9 percent, as against 14.4 and 10.7 percent in the two preceding quarters. Growth in the four quarters of 1948 amounted to 4.7, 7.0, 7.7, and 9.4 percent. Calculated from Hildebrand, *Growth and Structure*, p. 21.

1949–1950 did budgetary measures actually show up in shrinkage of the deficit. Italy therefore provides an example of an inflationary process broken by working on private bank credit while the central bank was still printing money to help cover a growing government deficit.[63]

The new policy reportedly had sensational effects on expectations and, through them, on exchange rates and prices. The dollar rate and the free price of gold had already dropped around the time when the government was reconstructed in May and June 1947, when some measures were taken to restrain the budget deficit, and when the Marshall Plan came into prospect. The export rate of the dollar peaked at 939 lira around the end of May and dropped rather steadily thereafter, the free price of gold reached its peak shortly before, and the stock-market boom also climaxed and went into reverse in the late spring. Observers attributed the reversal of the lira's depreciation first to a change of expectations and later, after midsummer, to the pressure that tightening credit put on holders of foreign exchange to liquidate some of their holdings. The rapid fall in the price of foreign exchange shrank the lira equivalent of the sales proceeds of the export industries. To alleviate that situation, the official exchange rate of the lira was devalued to 350 to the dollar on August 2. (The effective rate for exporters was the middle rate between the legal free rate and the official rate, so marking up the latter was to the advantage of exporters.) As it became apparent that the improved foreign-exchange situation was no longer temporary but rested on improved fundamentals, the time seemed ripe for reforming and simplifying the whole foreign-exchange mechanism. Late in November, the official rate of 350 per dollar was abolished, the lira officially (if temporarily) became a floating currency, and the official and free-market rates moved very nearly together.[64]

Prices peaked in the autumn of 1947, sagged, and then fell quite rapidly. The index of official wholesale prices peaked at 52 times the 1938 level in October, then dropped 7.9 percent by December. The index of effective wholesale prices peaked at 106 times the prewar level in June, then sagged and oscillated, peaked again at 108 times in October, and then fell 26.1 percent by December. From its peak in October, the index of the cost of living in Milan fell 13.2 percent in the following two months. Alternative wholesale and cost-of-living

[63] Hildebrand, *Growth and Structure*, pp. 26–27; Lutz and Lutz, *Policy*, pp. 11–12 and table on p. 7.

[64] Foa, *Reconstruction*, pp. 108–113; Lutz and Lutz, *Policy*, table on p. 46.

indexes both peaked in September, then declined by 17.1 and 13.7 percent respectively by the following July.[65]

This price behavior was attributed to the interplay of expectations, the fall in the prices of foreign exchange and hence of imports, and inventory liquidation. The credit squeeze both signaled the government's firm intentions and also directly penalized the further accumulation of inventories by traders. This end to the temporary diversion of part of current output away from consumer markets would itself have brought downward pressure on prices. In addition, signs of initial and then continuing price declines led traders to unload parts of their inventories. Falling prices motivated the public to rebuild its shrunken real cash balances; that is, a decline in velocity could absorb continuing growth of the nominal money supply.[66]

This phenomenon is familiar at the ends of severe inflations. The rebuilding of real cash balances permitted a restrained and noninflationary credit expansion by the banks and gave the government a breathing space during which it could gradually shrink its budget deficit to a size that could be financed mostly out of the savings of the public. The decline in velocity continued over the longer run. Over the period of 1948 through 1961, the stock of money grew by 363.3 percent in all, or at a fitted trend rate of 11.6 percent a year. Yet price increases were moderate. The wholesale index actually fell 4.5 percent in total between 1948 and 1961, and export prices also showed a slight decline. The success of the stabilization policy was less clear as judged by the gross national product (GNP) deflator and the cost-of-living index. Their exponential trend rates of increase between 1948 and 1961 were 2.3 and 3.13 percent a year respectively.[67] This "scissors" between opposing movements of wholesale and export prices on the one hand and the GNP deflator and the cost of living on the other hand apparently reflects the growth pattern of the Italian economy.

George H. Hildebrand suggests three reasons why Italy was able to absorb continuing monetary expansion with only trivial price inflation. One was the sheer productive potential of the economy; another was the translation of this potential into growth of real output at a remarkable trend rate of 5.9 percent a year. Third was the already mentioned rebuilding of real cash balances, indicating restoration of

---

[65] From and calculated from Foa, *Reconstruction,* pp. 68, 110, and Hildebrand, *Growth and Structure,* p. 32.

[66] Foa, *Reconstruction,* p. 111; Lutz and Lutz, *Policy,* pp. 13–14; Hildebrand, *Growth and Structure,* pp. 32–34.

[67] Lutz and Lutz, *Policy,* p. 16; Hildebrand, *Growth and Structure,* pp. 57–60, 86.

confidence in the lira. The ratio of money stock to current GNP rose from 26.4 percent in 1948 to 41.7 percent in 1961.[68]

The Italian record of approximate price-level stability began coming to an end in 1962, but that is another story.

There is no denying that the successful stabilization had initial side effects. Bruno Foa speaks of a "very serious industrial and business recession." Industrial production declined by some 20 to 25 percent on one estimate. Other figures show a decline of about 12 percent between June and December 1947, with recovery following in 1948, or of 11 percent over the two quarters following the credit squeeze, with recovery to nearly 6 percent above the 1947 peak by the fourth quarter of 1948, or of 15.2 percent between October 1947 and January 1948, with a strong recovery beginning in February. These estimates are seasonally unadjusted and no doubt include an element of mere seasonal decline. For the whole years 1948 and 1949, industrial production recorded substantial increases; real gross domestic product rose 5.8 and 7.5 percent in those two years. Agricultural output apparently held steady during the period of industrial slump.[69]

Although the recession, lasting less than half a year, did add to the number of people out of work, unemployment became no worse than at the worst of the inflation. By March 1949, the number of unemployed stood below the level of two years before. Italy had a longstanding unemployment problem anyway, with or without inflation and with or without a stabilization program; one strand of explanation ran in terms of a scarcity of the real capital stock relative to labor.[70]

Failures and discouragement swept through the business world and made Einaudi, del Vecchio, and Menichella distinctly unpopular. Yet Foa, who so reports, judges that the recession was the inevitable result of antiinflationary actions and of the lira's recovery on the exchanges and was a price well worth paying for stopping inflation.[71]

Nevertheless, the program drew severe criticism at home and abroad. Usually the critics acknowledged that it had succeeded in ending inflation. They contended variously, however, that it made interest rates too high, that it was deflationary, that it denied industry fully warranted credits, that it caused high unemployment and excess capacity, and that it obstructed both recovery and correction of regional imbalances.[72]

[68] Hildebrand, *Growth and Structure*, pp. 86–87.

[69] Foa, *Reconstruction*, p. 116; Hildebrand, *Growth and Structure*, pp. 4–5, 39–40.

[70] Hildebrand, *Growth and Structure*, pp. 4–5, 41–42, 185–186.

[71] Foa, *Reconstruction*, p. 116.

[72] Hildebrand, *Growth and Structure*, p. 35. Hildebrand goes on (pp. 36–37) to

Yet Italy went on during 1948–1961 to achieve one of the highest and best sustained growth rates in the world. She rebuilt her obsolete and damaged industries, raised per capita incomes, and became a strong competitor on world markets. People came to speak of the "Italian miracle." As Einaudi had expected, saving and investment played an important part in this record, and the termination of inflation had played an important part in the recovery of private saving. Hildebrand characterized Italy's impressive expansion as a capital-formation and export boom.[73]

Summary and Comments. Italy's wartime inflation was followed by a pause. The definitive cure followed a severe rekindling of monetary and price inflation running approximately from June 1946 to September 1947. In large part, the diagnosis focuses on the activation, for purposes of private credit expansion, of the great liquidity that had been thrust onto the banks by previous government and military financing. Before this renewed inflation could become deeply entrenched, it took on ominous aspects reminiscent of France in 1926 (although the mechanisms were different). Again, as in France, the threat to the currency became frightening enough to prompt dramatic action well calculated to turn expectations around, including political and administrative change. The new policy—essentially a credit squeeze—and the way that expectations responded brought a rapid turnaround of the price rise, partly by halting and reversing speculative inventory building. (This experience suggests a further reason why it may be easier to stop an inflation approaching the crisis stage than a long-ingrained moderate inflation. Traders may have built up commodity hoards as a substitute for holding monetary assets. If confidence in the currency can be restored, the unloading of commodities can have an almost immediate impact on prices.) Once expectations had been turned around, the resulting rise in holdings of money relative to income and the associated rise in the propensity to save could facilitate consolidating monetary stability and real growth over the longer run.

cite a document prepared in 1948 and published in February 1949 by the American authorities responsible for the European Recovery Program. The document expressed impatience with the Italian government's supposed excessive worry about renewed inflation and its consequent neglect of public investment for development and housing. In 1950, the United Nations Secretariat for the Economic Commission for Europe expressed similar views and called for more expansionary policies.
[73] Ibid., pp. vii, 56–57.

4

Some Latin American Experiences since World War II

Bolivia

In Bolivia, as table 5 shows, inflation was rapidly brought down from triple-digit rates to a price increase of hardly more than 3 percent between 1957 and 1958.[1] Although price inflation heated up again somewhat after that, it remained moderate for several years by Latin American standards and in a few years even by U.S. standards.

When the Bolivian stabilization program was launched late in 1956, the country was suffering the most acute inflation in Latin America and probably in the world. The inflation traced back to the Chaco War of 1932 and had accelerated after the seizure of power in 1952 by leftist revolutionaries, who nationalized the tin mines and the petroleum industry and who kept printing money to cover the deficits of the government and its numerous development agencies and nationalized enterprises. The boliviano had fallen by the beginning of 1952 to an official rate of 60 to the dollar and a free-market rate of 210. By July 1956, when the official rate was 190 (having been adjusted in 1953), the "street rate" had soared to 14,000 per dollar.[2]

---

[1] See, however, pages 113–114 and note 4.

[2] Centro de Estudios Monetarios Latinoamericanos, *Aspectos monetarios de las economías latinoamericanas, 1956* (Mexico City: 1957), p. 68; idem, *Aspectos monetarios de las economías latinoamericanas, 1959*, p. 152; G. A. Costanzo, *Programas de estabilización económica en América Latina* (Mexico City: Centro de Estudios Monetarios Latinoamericanos, 1961), p. 78; and George Jackson Eder, *Inflation and Development in Latin America, A Case History of Inflation and Stabilization in Bolivia* (Ann Arbor: Bureau of Business Research, University of Michigan, 1968), passim. Most of the information in this section comes from the book by Eder, the architect of the Bolivian stabilization program. Detailed citations to that book will be given only where specific reasons recommend. Some of the price and exchange-rate figures come from International Monetary Fund, *International Financial Statistics Yearbook, 1979*, and from earlier issues of *International Financial Statistics*.

TABLE 5

INCREASES IN CONSUMER PRICES
AND MONEY SUPPLY IN BOLIVIA, 1950–1978

Year	Price Index, Percentage Change from Previous Year	Money Supply, Percentage Growth during Year
1950	24.0	(Not available)
1951	32.4	20.0
1952	24.5	51.7
1953	100.9	80.2
1954	124.4	67.1
1955	80.0	104.4
1956	178.8	251.8
1957	115.1	47.8
1958	3.1	3.2
1959	20.3	28.3
1960	11.5	8.6
1961	7.6	18.4
1962	5.9	12.2
1963	−0.7	19.6
1964	10.2	20.8
1965	2.9	17.4
1966	6.9	22.3
1967	11.2	3.4
1968	5.5	8.0
1969	2.2	5.7
1970	3.9	12.6
1971	3.6	15.3
1972	6.5	25.1
1973	31.6	34.3
1974	62.7	43.4
1975	8.0	11.8
1976	4.5	36.5
1977	8.1	20.9
1978	10.4	12.4

NOTE: The price figures are percentage changes from the preceding year's average index to each current year's average index; the money figures are percentage changes from the end of the preceding year to the end of each current year.

SOURCE: From or calculated from International Monetary Fund, *International Financial Statistics Yearbook, 1979*, pp. 58–59, 112–113, and *International Financial Statistics, 1963/64 Supplement*, p. 18.

Exchange and price controls were pervasively disrupting the economy. Black-marketing was rampant. Literally hundreds of rates composed a multiple-exchange-rate system; but the principal rate and the one applicable to imports by the government and its agencies was 190 bolivianos per dollar, far below what a free-market rate would have been. The resulting apparent extreme cheapness of imports in terms of bolivianos encouraged lavish spending by government agencies on locomotives, tractors, road-building and other equipment, materials, and all sorts of goods. Corrupt politicians and their associates could make huge profits by smuggling imported goods, including American aid goods, out of the country. Peasants found it profitable to desert their fields and engage in smuggling rather than soberly continue to grow their crops. Not only were staple commodities such as sugar and flour smuggled out of the country; even bread, some 200,000 loaves a day, was smuggled to Peru. This, says George Eder, was possibly the only example in history of so bulky and perishable a commodity being smuggled on so large a scale. With a controlled price of 30 bolivianos a loaf in Bolivia and free-market prices equivalent to 500 bolivianos obtainable across the border, though, such smuggling was inevitable.

American aid contributed to economic disorder, partly by fostering an atmosphere of unreality that diverted Bolivians from taking responsibility for their own problems. (This, anyway, is one of the leading themes of Eder's book, just cited.) American aid contributed to inflation in a more mechanical way also. A recipient government is supposed to sell the goods donated to it by the United States for local currency. A small part of these funds goes to the American aid mission to cover its expenses, while the bulk is to be used for purposes, such as development projects, agreed to with the Americans. The Bolivian government, however, was receiving much smaller amounts of these so-called counterpart funds than it should have been receiving because of the ridiculously low prices for which the aid goods were being sold, notably to politicians and their associates. Where, then, was the rest of the counterpart funds required by the Americans to come from? From the printing press.

These disorders traceable to controls and corruption are relevant to the question of how inflation might be stopped, since they suggest scope for, in effect, restoring the economy's real efficiency. A reform program might, in effect, increase the supplies of goods available for a restrained flow of money to chase.

Under the threat of otherwise suspending its aid, the U.S. government induced the Bolivian government to invite a commission from the United States, headed by George Eder, to assist it in launching a program of reform and stabilization. Eder arrived in the country on June 1, 1956, "as an invited, but scarcely welcome, guest of the Bolivian government."

Already in May 1953, the Bolivian government had enacted a series of so-called stabilization measures on the advice of a United Nations mission headed by Arthur Karasz. When Eder met Karasz in 1956, he requested figures for Bolivia's note circulation, bank deposits, free-market exchange rates, and commodity prices. Karasz replied that he had never assembled such data; apparently they were irrelevant in the light of his monetary theories. As for the impact of printing-press currency, Karasz maintained in a lecture of July 1956 that "the increase in note circulation, and the increase in the free-market rate of exchange, are the consequences and not the causes of inflation. They are merely statistical data and nothing more."[3] Eder judged the 1953 "stabilization" measures "as useless as a bladeless knife without a handle." It may not be irrelevant that Karasz, the architect of those measures, had been president of the Hungarian National Bank during that country's record-smashing hyperinflation of 1945–1946.

The first task of Eder's mission was to convince the leading Bolivian government figures and their advisors that the country's runaway inflation was due to government spending financed through the central bank and the printing press. Although this diagnosis ran counter to everything that the revolutionary government had said or done for three years, Eder was able to convince its leaders of his diagnosis because, as he says, they instinctively knew that it was correct.

The Bolivian Congress was persuaded to pass a law establishing the National Monetary Stabilization Council and empowering the president, on the council's advice, to issue decrees with the force of law and take the measures necessary to carry out the objectives of the stabilization program. By December 1956, the entire program, with all its necessary laws and decrees, had been drawn up and made ready to go into operation. It was essential for the program's success, Eder argued, that it be a complete and instantaneous break with the past and that its key measures be enacted simultaneously. If the stabilization measures had had to be enacted piecemeal by Congress, then political pressures and ordinary legislative delays would have resulted in continuation of the existing disorder.

The recently inaugurated president, Hernán Siles Zuazo, announced the stabilization program in a radio broadcast on Sunday,

---

[3] Quoted in Eder, *Inflation*, pp. 480–481.

December 16, 1956. An all-inclusive budget was being prepared for the national government and all its agencies and enterprises. All government borrowing from the central bank was to cease. The finance ministry was authorized to fix legal reserve requirements of banks. All exchange controls were removed and a single rate of exchange established, with a $25-million stabilization fund being made available from the United States and the International Monetary Fund to help maintain an orderly market. (The foreign-exchange market was to reopen on Wednesday, December 19, after the banks had remained closed on Monday and Tuesday.) Import and export controls were all but removed. Price controls were removed. Subsidized commissaries in the nationalized and private mines and in the government and private railways were abolished and workers' wages raised in compensation. (The transition might have been made easier by effective public explanations of what had been causing the inflation and how the new program would cure it. Eder judged it a shortcoming of the stabilization program that it did not include a consistent program of information.)

A decree approved by the Stabilization Council on December 31, together with regulations issued under it, established double reserve ratios for private commercial banks and the banking department of the central bank. Besides the 40 percent reserves already required, banks were required to keep a marginal reserve of 50 percent against any increase in their deposit liabilities. A qualitative credit restriction was introduced prohibiting banks from makng consumer and construction loans or other loans that would not contribute immediately to speeding up production. In view of the small role that the private sector had played in causing the inflation, it might have seemed unfair to impose these drastic credit restrictions on private banks and business. Nevertheless, Eder says, if private credit had been unrestricted, speculators would have been quick to obtain bank loans to buy the dollars freely available under the new regime. A flight of capital would have wiped out the exchange stabilization fund and nullified efforts to stabilize the boliviano.

One key issue facing the Stabilization Council was how to set the new unified exchange rate. Eder would have preferred to take the advice of Edwin Kemmerer, the peripatetic "money doctor" of the 1920s and 1930s, that "the way to stabilize is to stabilize," that is, to fix a firm dollar rate of the domestic currency and enlist the discipline of that fixed rate in support of the entire stabilization program. Against the background of price controls, multiple exchange rates, black marketing, and smuggling, all of which was being altered, however, there was no way of knowing in advance what would be an equilibrium rate. Either too high or too low a rate would undercut the new program. It was therefore necessary to let the boliviano "find its own level" or, more exactly, to experiment with rate fixing while responding flexibly to market pressures. On the eve of the reopening of the banks and the foreign-exchange market, the Stabilization Council decided on 7,700 and 7,750 bolivianos as the rates at which the central bank would buy and sell dollars (with a narrower buy-sell range applicable to wholesale transactions between the central bank and private banks and exchange houses). The dollar had been unofficially quoted at 13,000 bolivianos three weeks before the stabilization program went into effect and had slumped to around 10,000 the week before. By the end of the first week of stabilization, the rate was down to between 7,590 and 7,650.

Eder had predicted that, within three or four months of the new regime, goods would be abundant at substantially reduced prices. He expected that the one-third or more of commodities being smuggled out of the country would no longer be exported, which would mean a 50 percent increase in supplies available at home. With import restrictions dropped, prices could not long remain above world levels plus transport cost. With the Indians no longer able to earn a living as smugglers, they would return to their farms and grow crops again.

Signs tending to justify these hopes appeared when the Indian markets in La Paz and similar markets throughout the country opened on the Monday after the president's speech. Tuesday's newspapers carried stories of commodities beginning to come out of the dealers' stores and from under the shelves under the influence of ·free prices, which at first approached the previous black-market levels. There had reportedly been an attack on shopkeepers in one of the capital's two largest Indian markets, not by irate housewives but by smugglers retaliating for loss of their livelihoods. On December 24, a newspaper printed a table showing bread prices at 300 bolivianos a loaf on the first day of stabilization, 250 on the second day, 200 the third day, and between 180 and 200 at the end of the week. In the same period, meat prices had fallen from 7,500 bolivianos per kilo to between 4,500 and 5,000.

After a temporary rise in living costs in January 1957, the newly unleashed competitive forces carried prices down steadily through the third quarter of the year, which ended with consumer prices some 14 or 15 percent below the level of the preceding December or January. In Eder's words,

> there occurred almost overnight the "miracle" of stabilization, the elimination of shortages of food and other supplies,

the disappearance of the black markets and of smuggled exports of commodities. Prices, free to find their own levels in a free market, gradually dropped to 22 percent below the pre-stabilization levels in just eight months. . . .[4]

Whatever was to happen subsequently, extreme inflation was stopped and reversed suddenly—almost literally overnight—and the reversal persisted for several months.

After that reversal, prices rose again in the fourth quarter of 1957, supposedly in consequence of disguised wage increases and of higher prices of foreign exchange beginning in June. Wage demands in mid-1958 paved the way for an 18 percent cost-of-living increase in the fourth quarter of that year. Even so, the index at the end of 1958 stood at about its level of two years before, and its rise over a two-year period amounted to about 12 percent at the end of 1959— not so bad a record in comparison with an annual average inflation rate of almost 100 percent over the period of 1931–1956.[5]

The governmental situation was not favorable to a determined policy, as events illustrated even during the first month of the new program. The government was more or less shared between the legally elected officials and the Bolivian Workers' Confederation, which held conventions every half-year or so at which delegates from all over the country made demands and complaints. Fiery speeches at the December 1956 convention roundly denounced the stabilization program. Juan Lechín Oquendo, who was both president of the Senate and executive secretary of the Workers' Confederation, said in a speech (falsely, according to Eder) that the Confederation had not

---

[4] Quotation from ibid., p. xi. Costanzo, *Programas*, p. 87, also comments on the decline in prices through most of 1957. This, he says, came after a 473 percent rise in prices in 1956. Eder, pp. 499–501, says that official index numbers published later for the full years 1956 and 1957 show a 13.8 percent drop in the cost of living and a 97.5 percent rise in wages, implying a rise in real wages of nearly 130 percent.

Obviously, there are some contradictions or apparent contradictions among these numbers and with the ones in table 5. The figures in table 5 refer to changes in annual average price indexes, however; and prices could have been rising extremely rapidly *during* all but the last month of 1956, as they were, with their average over the year as a whole nevertheless being no further above the 1955 average than the table shows and also being below the average of 1957, even though prices were lower in that year than at the *end* of 1956. Furthermore, the pre-stabilization index numbers are no doubt distorted by price controls, so decontrol could have brought a rise in some reported prices even while effective prices were declining. Nevertheless, there may well be some outright contradiction. The chaotic nature of statistics relating to any aspect of Bolivia is a recurring theme in Eder's book. He says, for example (p. 4), "In all, Bolivia occupies an area of between 411,000 and 514,000 square miles (accurate figures are hard to come by in any matter relating to Bolivia). . . ."

[5] Eder, *Inflation*, p. 87.

been consulted about the program and that he had had no prior knowledge of it. Faced with this sort of sabotage, President Siles went on a hunger strike. On the evening of the first day, huge crowds milled around screaming for guns with which to kill those responsible for making the hunger strike necessary and stoning the congressional building where they thought Lechín was hiding. Siles was able to end his hunger strike the next day in triumph over his opponents and with expressions of support coming from all parts of the country and all sectors of society.[6]

Then, for the first and last time, says Eder, Siles was strong enough to crush his enemies; yet he let the opportunity slip away. He agreed to a series of "concessions to reality," each one encouraging further demands. The president yielded to political pressure for a cut in gasoline prices and insisted on a cut in kerosene prices, even though the management of the Government Petroleum Corporation complained that these would mean selling below costs. The company's budget was unbalanced, and it was forced to borrow from the central bank. Another early "concession to reality" concerned wage increases.[7] Still another, and one particularly disturbing to Eder, was the president's attempt to conceal from him a number of substantial bits of windfall revenue not anticipated in the government budget. Without consulting the Stabilization Council, the government spent these funds on unbudgeted and improvised projects that would hardly have passed muster if mentioned in Bolivia's application to the International Monetary Fund and the U.S. government for financial assistance.

For the first five months of the stabilization program, the rate on the dollar had been held remarkably stable at or below its initial level of around 7,700 bolivianos, and without heavy drawings on the stabilization fund. In June 1957, however, the Workers' Confederation

---

[6] As Eder later observed, though not about this episode in particular, the United States and the International Monetary Fund had granted Bolivia credits for its exchange-stabilization fund "solely on the hope that a single man, President Hernán Siles-Zuazo, not immune to bullets, would have the courage and ability to impose standards of good faith and responsibility on what was perhaps the most corrupt, incompetent and opportunistic group of politicians that had ever ruled the destinies of the nation." Ibid., p. 241.

[7] Eder mentions throughout his book that wages were subject to control and that wage changes came within the purview of the Stabilization Council. He implies that wage control, while seemingly an interventionist measure incompatible with the new program of economic liberalization, was in fact an appropriate second-best measure in the context of continuing heavy political intervention in the labor market. A free economy and free labor market would have meant employers' freedom to dismiss excess workers, curtailment of the overwhelming power of the labor unions and labor militia, and lower wages for miners. See ibid., p. 459 in particular.

held another convention, Lechín again tried to destroy the stabilization program, and doubts mounted about whether President Siles would have the strength and will to hold the line in the face of wage demands. With confidence in monetary stability flagging, the stabilization fund lost over $1 million in a week. To conserve the fund, the foreign-exchange committee had to let the boliviano drop, first to 8,100 per dollar, then to 8,340, and to 8,375 at the end of June. At the end of November, the depreciation had reached 8,625. Credit restrictions on the private sector were then tightened, and the rate closed the year at 8,565.

President Siles was insisting that the dollar rate not be allowed to rise above 8,600, and the exchange stabilization fund lost a further $6 million in December 1957 alone. By the end of the year, cumulative drawings on the $25-million fund amounted to $12.4 million. This drain is presumably not unconnected with the fact that the government, late in 1957, had returned to its old habits of deficit spending, borrowing from the central bank, and printing banknotes.

By September 1958, the Bolivian government had deviated so far from the stabilization program agreed on with the United States and the International Monetary Fund that the exchange stabilization fund was practically exhausted. Eder's successor as executive director of the Stabilization Council, Victor R. Rose, insisted, as the price of continued aid, on a number of moves toward financial and economic prudence, among them allowing the boliviano to drop to its market-clearing level. On October 1, the central bank let the boliviano depreciate to 11,000 per dollar. The year 1958 ended with a rate of 11,975. That rate was about 55 percent higher than the one initially set in December 1956 (the boliviano had depreciated about 35 percent), while over the same two-year period Bolivia's money supply had grown about 52 percent. However, the stabilization plan had provided from the beginning that market forces would be allowed to determine the exchange rate; so the departure from that plan was not the boliviano's depreciation but the resistance to it that had drained the stabilization fund. In July 1962, after de facto stabilization since 1959, the exchange rate was legally fixed at 11,880 bolivianos per dollar. At the same time, a new currency, the peso boliviano, was introduced, equivalent to 1,000 bolivianos; both denominations were printed on the face of the new banknotes. There the fixed rate held firm until the fourth quarter of 1972, when the peso was devalued to 20 per dollar.

In the nine years of 1957 through 1965, the money supply (notes in the hands of the public plus demand deposits) more than quadrupled, yet the dollar rate rose only 53 percent (all during the first two years, holding steady thereafter), and the cost of living rose only 52 percent.[8] This contrast is explained, Eder suggests, partly by a strong world market for Bolivian tin but perhaps more significantly by continued U.S. aid. After about 1960, the United States provided Bolivia with whatever amounts the government needed to balance its budget. Stabilization was maintained not by a return to reality—as the first year of the program had proved possible—but by return to a new world of unreality in the shape of continuous deficits covered by U.S. subsidies.[9] Money-supply and price-level inflation worsened again in 1973–1974, as table 5 shows, but this development was in large part a consequence of world conditions.

These later developments do not alter the fact of prime significance for us, namely, that Bolivia stopped price inflation in December 1956 and the ensuing months by fairly orthodox monetary and fiscal measures and by getting rid of many of the inefficiencies that controls had been causing. Furthermore, the end to inflation, together with had been causing. Furthermore, the end to inflation, together with the turnaround of expectations that presumably aided it, came suddenly.

Stabilization apparently did not seriously impair economic activity. Between 1956 and 1957, total gross domestic product dropped from 354.8 to 342.9 million U.S. dollars of 1958 purchasing power. This drop of 3.35 percent is too small, says Eder, to be statistically significant. (More recently compiled figures of gross domestic product in Bolivian money at 1975 prices show a drop of 3.3 percent between 1956 and 1957, following a drop of 5.9 percent the preceding year, when inflation had still been raging. Evidently stabilization came not so much as a net disruption to the economy as the replacement of one sort of disruption by another and more temporary sort. The 1955 output peak was surpassed in 1960, and an uptrend continued in the succeeding years.)

The only sectors of the economy unmistakably operating at a lower level in 1957 as a consequence of the stabilization measures were government and manufacturing. Insistence upon a balanced budget as one of the postulates of stabilization forced the government to restrain itself as never before. In manufacturing, gross domestic product fell between 1956 and 1957 from 51.4 to 36 million dollars of 1958 purchasing power, that is, by 30 percent. Textile firms were particularly hard hit, since they had to pay for imported raw materials at the new realistic exchange rate, whereas the old rate had

---

[8] Ibid., p. 587; the figures in *International Financial Statistics* are not greatly different.

[9] Eder, *Inflation*, p. 585. A chart on p. 596 shows that for the years 1954 through 1964, except only for 1957 and 1960, U.S. aid exceeded Bolivian tax revenues.

made materials extremely cheap in bolivianos. Now that textiles had to be sold at prices reflecting their true costs, workers could no longer afford to buy them in such quantities as when they were practically being given away. Domestic retail trade fell for the same reasons that affected domestic manufacturing: consumer products, like materials, could no longer be brought into the country at fictitious rates of exchange.[10]

Gross domestic product in constant dollars recovered and then rose steadily. From 1956, the last year before stabilization, to 1964, the increase amounted to 26 percent, chiefly reflecting a spectacular advance in agriculture. The latter was largely a consequence of the return of the peasants to the land, largely attributable in turn to the elimination of price controls and of imports subsidized by exchange rates. Even hard-hit manufacturing production recovered to well over its prestabilization levels and in 1964 stood 51 percent above its 1957 low. Government expenditures, after being curtailed at first, rose even more rapidly than manufacturing. On the other hand, the growth of population apparently outstripped the advance in production, so that, despite heavy U.S. aid, the people became poorer in real terms.[11]

Eder, the architect of the stabilization program, wavers between satisfaction and despair in his own appraisal. The experiment in economic liberalization and financial prudence was not maintained over the long run, and genuine economic development—a sustained rise in the well-being of the people—did not take place. Corruption, graft, and governmental meddling with the economy continued, though perhaps to a lesser extent than before. The consequences of backsliding from the reforms, and in particular the exchange depreciation and rapid inflation that would probably have otherwise resumed, were masked by U.S. aid that continued to cover budget deficits.

Summary and Comment. Backsliding does not set aside the noteworthy example, however, of extreme inflation being stopped practically overnight. De facto exchange-rate pegging at approximately an equilibrium rate was one of the steps taken. The Bolivian experience contrasts with some of the others that we have reviewed in that the stabilization measures came against a background so bad in real terms that it offered plenty of scope for improvement: economic activity had been so badly distorted and disrupted by wrong exchange rates and by price and other controls that removal of these controls would

---

[10] Ibid., pp. 503–508; International Monetary Fund, *International Financial Statistics Yearbook, 1979*, pp. 114–115. Eder warns about the unreliability of the figures he cites.
[11] Eder, *Inflation*, p. 527.

bring about the equivalent of a quick rise in productivity. Another distinctive feature of the Bolivian experience was the importance of U.S. aid.

Although political turmoil continued when the stabilization program was launched and for years afterward, a political change, or something akin to one, did, after all, facilitate ending inflation, presumably in part through a change of expectations. Hernán Siles Zuazo succeeded Víctor Paz Estenssoro as president when the stabilization program was being put together in 1956. Furthermore, foreign and international authorities, wielding the weapon of being able to grant or withhold economic aid, prodded the Bolivian government into accepting a foreign advisory mission and into appointing the National Monetary Stabilization Council with an American executive director. Congress empowered the president, on the advice of this council, to enact stabilization measures by decree without further legislation. A presidential hunger strike adds a touch of the exotic to the story.

Paraguay

In 1956–1957, Paraguay embarked upon what the *New York Times* soon afterward called "the most effective monetary stabilization of any country in South America."[12] Inflation and economic and political disorder had a long history in Paraguay, marked, for example, by the disastrous wars of 1865–1870 and 1932–1935, thirty-one overthrows of government between 1870 and 1940, six months of revolution in 1947–1948, and six presidents between 1948 and 1954. General Alfredo Stroessner gained power in 1954, inaugurating a quite untypical period of governmental continuity. The country had enjoyed an exceptional period of economic growth during World War II, when demand for its primary products was strong, but since 1950 it had experienced both inflation and economic stagnation. The rate of price inflation was fluctuating widely in the double-digit range and occasionally rose above 100 percent a year. Between 1949 and 1957, average annual rates of increase were 41 percent for the money supply and 47 percent for prices. The monetary expansion traced mainly to extensions of central-bank credit to the government, economic development institutions, and the private sector.[13]

---

[12] "Paraguay Resists Argentine Slump," *New York Times*, January 13, 1960, p. 62.

[13] Joseph Pincus, *The Economy of Paraguay* (New York: Praeger, 1968), pp. 7–8; Leovigildo González García, *Las actividades bancarias y de seguros en el Paraguay (Década de 1957 a 1966)* (Asunción and Buenos Aires: Nizza, 1969), pp. 24–30; Werner Baer, "The Paraguayan Economic Condition: Past and Current Obstacles to Economic Modernization," *Inter-American Economic Affairs*, vol. 29,

Particular difficulties in the second half of 1955 helped motivate a change of policy the following year. A low level of the Paraguay River impeded exports, while prices of several important export products declined on the world market. Currency devaluation in October by Argentina, Paraguay's chief trading partner, interacted with the provisions of bilateral trade agreements in such a way as to worsen Paraguay's terms of trade. Paraguay's dollar claims on the Argentine central bank were blocked under trade agreements, and freely usable foreign exchange was scarce. The country was unable to pay for imports of essential raw materials, and a foreign-exchange crisis occurred around the end of the year. A decision was made early in 1956 to embark on a transition from inflation to stability in stages, with trade and exchange controls being retained for the time being.[14]

The multiple-exchange-rate system was simplified, however, when the first phase of the reform went into effect on February 29, 1956. The rate applicable to exports was devalued from 21 to 60 guaraníes per dollar (the parity originally declared with the International Monetary Fund having been 3.08 per dollar). Paraguay obtained a loan and technical assistance from the fund. The government decided to reorient its trade policy from reliance on bilateral agreements and toward multilateralism and currency convertibility.

The centerpiece of the 1956 reform was establishment of a monetary budget for the purpose of estimating the effects of credit measures on the money supply and in due course limiting money-supply growth to meeting the real requirements of the economy at stable prices. After years of acute inflation, the government did not aim at immediate stability; it hoped to limit money-supply growth to 10 percent during the first year of the program and price increases to some 5 to 15 percent. A ceiling was set on growth of central-bank credit in 1956, with shares allocated to various sectors of the economy. To limit the growth of bank loans, portfolio ceilings were also established for the commercial banks, and the system of reserve requirements against bank deposits was modified.

The program achieved only partial success in 1956. Money-supply growth was about three times as large as budgeted. The rise in the cost of living was cut to about 18 percent (20 percent in Asunción). Prices rose some 10 percent in the first quarter of 1956

---

no. 1 (1975), p. 62; Costanzo, *Programas*, pp. 91–93; César Romeo Acosta, *Diez años de estabilización monetaria en el Paraguay* (Asunción: Banco Central del Paraguay), p. 8; Joachim Ahrensdorf, "Central Bank Policies and Inflation: A Case Study of Four Less Developed Economies, 1949–57," International Monetary Fund *Staff Papers*, vol. 7, no. 2 (Washington, D.C., October 1959), pp. 278–279.

[14] González, *Actividades*, p. 42; Costanzo, *Programas*, pp. 95–96.

alone, reflecting the direct consequences of the currency devaluation, which included a 25 percent increase in wages. The annual rate of price increase then declined to about 8 percent over the remainder of the year. The cost of living rose a further 8 percent in the first quarter of 1957 as a result of increases in minmum wages and minimum agricultural prices; then its rise slackened off.[15]

By mid-1957, the monetary situation seemed to be under control, with the net issue having increased only 2 percent in the first half of the year. The second stage of the program went into effect on August 12. Import and export controls were relaxed. Exchange control, in effect since 1946, was simplified almost to the point of being abolished. A unified and relatively free exchange rate was established, but with an exchange stabilization fund financed by credits from the International Monetary Fund and the United States on hand to moderate seasonal and erratic rate fluctuations. Because stocks of imported articles had been run down, the demand for foreign exchange was strong at first, requiring drawings on the International Monetary Fund. The free-market rate, opening at 95 guaraníes to the dollar, depreciated to 110 by November 1957 and to 122 by January 1959, where the guaraní was then pegged. Realism in exchange rates extended to the rate applicable to government purchases and so tended to increase government spending; accordingly, luxury taxes and a temporary export tax were enacted. The charges of public enterprises were adjusted upward to reflect higher costs at the new exchange rate, subsidies on agricultural products were reduced or partially eliminated, and price controls were eliminated except for items traded in only limited competition. Wage policy aimed at avoiding increases unless the cost of living should rise more than 5 percent because of the exchange-rate reform.[16]

As the Central Bank and its president later summarized the broad sweep of the program of stabilization and liberalization, its main features were these: limitation of money-supply growth through a closer approach to government budget balance and restriction of government borrowing at the Central Bank, credit-expansion ceilings imposed on the Central Bank and the commercial banks, use of deposit reserve requirements, and (during the first few years) use of advance import deposits requirements as a weapon of monetary policy; a

---

[15] González, *Actividades*, pp. 42–45; Centro de Estudios Monetarios Latinoamericanos, *Aspectos monetarios, 1956*, pp. 132–138; Costanzo, *Programas*, pp. 99–100.

[16] Costanzo, *Programas*, pp. 101–104; International Monetary Fund, *Annual Report, 1957–1958* (Washington, D.C.), p. 133; *New York Times*, January 13, 1960, p. 62.

shift from bilateralism to multilateralism in foreign-trade policy; movement toward a unified exchange rate at an equilibrium level; transfer to the commercial banks of foreign-exchange operations previously monopolized by the Central Bank; simplification and re-laxation of trade controls; near-abolition of trade and exchange con-trols (though export taxes and surcharges on foreign exchange for imports were kept or introduced); an end to most subsidies and price controls; and a principle of not granting wage increases unless the cost of living had increased by 10 percent or more during the preced-ing year. Freer trade, the Central Bank reported, permitted prudent inventory formation. Wholesale prices no longer underwent upward jumps, as they had during the period of exchange control, when short-ages created uncertainty about the continuity and the cost of produc-tion. Producers could count on uninterrupted supplies, including supplies of machinery, and business planning could become smoother. The climate for saving and investment, domestic and foreign, became healthier.[17]

Early signs of success appeared. Money-supply growth during 1957 amounted to only 2.9 percent, and in 1958 wholesale and con-sumer prices averaged only 8.0 and 6.3 percent above the average levels of the year before. Gross domestic product in constant prices registered gains of 6.1 percent in 1957 and 6.5 percent in 1958, sug-gesting that no stabilization slump occurred. Difficulties, however, were developing. Money-supply growth rose to 19.4 percent in 1958 and 9.4 percent in 1959; in 1959 wholesale and consumer prices aver-aged 17.7 and 9.9 percent above levels of 1958; and 1959 and 1960 brought dips (but only of 1 percent or less) in real gross domestic product.[18]

In part, the trouble seems due to a contraction of export demand because of a stabilization program being applied in Argentina. Ex-ports of wood were particularly affected. Paraguay's total sales to Argentina fell in half between 1958 and 1959, and recovery in 1960 left them still 42 percent below the 1958 level. Unfavorable weather affected agricultural production in 1959 and 1960; and in 1960, the world-market prices of several of Paraguay's exports declined. The tightness of money and credit was also blamed, rightly or wrongly, for the difficulties for many business firms. Foreign-exchange reserves dropped sharply in 1959 and 1960. As already mentioned, the guaraní was allowed to sink to 122 per dollar in 1959; in 1960, it sank further,

---

[17] Banco Central del Paraguay, Memoria 1957–1960, pp. 57–58, 63–64, 81–83, Memoria 1967, pp. 41, 43, 79, 95; Acosta, Diez años, pp. 10–15.

[18] Calculated from International Monetary Fund, International Financial Statistics Yearbook, 1979, pp. 338, 340, using the line-34 concept of money supply.

to 126, before being repegged. The country appeared to be losing some of its political stability, also, to judge from Stroessner's reestablishing a state of siege, dissolving Congress, and even jailing scores of leaders of his own political party.[19]

During 1961, growth of the money supply (line 34 in *International Financial Statistics*) jumped to 26.8 percent. The accumulation of international reserves and net extension of credit to the government, whose budget deficit increased, were the factors that, as a matter of arithmetic, contributed most to the growth of central-bank money; but extension of central-bank credit to official entities, though somewhat smaller than in 1960, was also a major factor. The total means of circulation grew somewhat less than in proportion to central-bank money, indicating that the behavior of the commercial banks and the public worked to restrain secondary monetary expansion. Price inflation also spurted in 1961, especially consumer price inflation—18.5 percent on an annual-average basis, as against 8.3 percent the year before. (For wholesale prices on an annual average basis, the index rose slightly less for 1961 than for 1960, 12.6 as against 13.0 percent.)[20]

It is rather puzzling that the price spurt of 1961 was so nearly simultaneous with the money-supply spurt, rather than following with the expected lag. Perhaps a 20 percent wage increase decreed in May 1961 contributed to the rise of prices.[21] Anyway, the annual reports of the Central Bank say little that is helpful on the question. Not until its issue covering 1965 does the *Memoria Anual* include a section on the cost of living and wages, complete with a price index. Yet the Central Bank had been calculating such figures and publishing them in its *Boletín Estadístico*. Their absence from the *Memoria Anual* and their disappearance from the *Boletín* for a while, after showing a steep rise through September 1961, arouses suspicions. One suspects that the authorities were anxious to avoid drawing attention to prices until they were confident that the inflation had been beaten.

Late in 1961, by the way, the government-owned Bank of Paraguay ceased operating as a commercial as well as central bank. Its claims on the private sector were taken over by the Central Bank,

---

[19] Centro de Estudios Monetarios Latinoamericanos, *Aspectos monetarios, 1959*, pp. 154–155, 157–158; idem, *Aspectos monetarios, 1960*, pp. 112–115 and price table on p. 73; idem, *Aspectos monetarios, 1961*, pp. 122–123; Costanzo, *Programas*, pp. 105–106, 123–124; *New York Times*, January 13, 1960, p. 62, January 11, 1961, p. 69.

[20] Centro de Estudios Monetarios Latinoamericanos, *Aspectos monetarios, 1961*, p. 123; p. 125 gives a breakdown of the sources of primary monetary expansion in 1960 and 1961.

[21] Ibid., p. 123.

which in return reduced its claims on commercial banks. The remaining assets and liabilities of the Bank of Paraguay were turned over to the newly organized National Development Bank. The Inter-American Development Bank and the World Bank had urged some such reorganization to reduce political interference with sound banking principles.

Probably by way of mere coincidence, efforts toward stabilization were truly rewarded for the first time in 1962. The money supply actually shrank by 2.4 percent during the year; and on an annual-average basis, consumer and wholesale prices rose only 1.4 and 4.9 percent from the year before. Gross domestic product in constant prices was 5.9 percent higher in 1962 than in 1961 and was to continue growing every year in the next decade and beyond; evidently there was no further stabilization crisis.[22] By 1963, when the inflation rate continued quite low, confidence in the stability of the purchasing power of the guaraní had reportedly been established. This was reflected, for example, in the rapid growth of savings accounts and other long-term deposits, which came to represent 38 percent of the liabilities of the country's banking system, as opposed to only 7 percent in 1957.[23]

From 1962 through 1970, each year's annual average consumer price level was never more than 3.8 percent above the preceding year's level, and a minuscule decline actually occurred in 1970. The minimum wage rate was left unchanged from April 1964 to May 1971 (when a 10 percent increase finally became effective);[24] this constancy over seven years reflects both a policy of wage restraint and the slightness of price inflation. For at least twenty years from 1960, the guaraní remained firm against the dollar at 126.

Around 1970, Paraguay began feeling the contagion of world inflation, first in its quantities of central-bank and ordinary money and later in prices. In 1970, the volume of central-bank money (emisión monetaria) grew by 22 percent. The Central Bank estimated that 64 percent of this increase was attributable to growth of its international assets and 36 percent to growth of its net internal assets. During the course of the year, the Bank's international reserves grew by some 94 or 95 percent (depending on the exact definition used), with this growth due in turn to a strengthening of the country's balances of trade and payments.[25] In 1971, the growth of central-bank

---

[22] Calculated from International Monetary Fund, *International Financial Statistics Yearbook, 1979*, pp. 338–341; "money supply" is as in line 34.

[23] United Nations, Economic Commission for Latin America, *Economic Survey of Latin America, 1964*, p. 132.

[24] Banco Central del Paraguay, *Memoria 1967*, p. 32; idem, *Memoria 1971*, p. 34.

[25] Banco Central del Paraguay, *Memoria, 1970*, pp. 48, 49, 53, 57, and the presi-

TABLE 6

PARAGUAY'S INTERNATIONAL RESERVES EXPRESSED AS PERCENTAGES
OF MONEY SUPPLY, ENDS OF YEARS, 1969–1978

Year	Percentage
1969	16.5
1970	27.5
1971	29.1
1972	37.1
1973	49.3
1974	62.1
1975	71.0
1976	80.3
1977	96.4
1978	106.4

NOTE: Gold and foreign exchange plus IMF gold-tranche position plus Special Drawing Rights divided by "medio circulante."
SOURCE: Calculated from Banco Central del Paraguay, Departamento de Estudios Económicos, *Boletín Estadístico*, May 1979, p. 4.

money was again primarily attributable to domestic sources. Afterward, however, the role of external assets became prominent again. This development is reflected in the growth of international reserves expressed as a percentage of the money supply, a figure that had been as small as 2.2 percent at the end of 1961. (Table 6 makes a comparison but carries no implication that international reserves are in any sense a component of the money supply.) The return of Paraguay's inflation was worst in 1974, as judged by consumer prices averaging 25.1 percent higher than the year before.[26]

dent's statement on unnumbered pages between pp. 10 and 11; idem, *Memoria, 1971*, pp. 12–13, 43, 49–54. The attribution of growth in central-bank money in 1970 was slightly revised in the 1971 report, whose figures are quoted above.

[26] Further evidence on the international aspects of Paraguay's renewed inflation appears in an article by Antonio Gómez Oliver and Valeriano García, even though the authors' own emphasis lies on a rather familiar phenomenon, namely, on how the impact of external inflationary factors was magnified by domestic credit expansion on the basis of the expanded monetary base. Furthermore, the authors' argument that the inflation in Paraguay and the seven other countries that they classify together with it—countries of intermediate degrees of economic openness and exchange-rate fixity—was primarily of domestic origin hinges partly on the assertion that these countries devalued their currencies from the dollar values that they had had in 1972. This is not true, however, of Paraguay, which kept its exchange rate fixed. See Gómez and García, "Experiencia inflacionaria reciente en América Latina," *Monetaria*, vol. 1, no. 1 (January-March 1978), pp. 3–34.

Summary and Comments. Despite the events of the 1970s, Paraguay's earlier success in practically stopping a severe price inflation and keeping it practically stopped for almost a decade remains a noteworthy historical fact. One favorable condition was that Paraguay's exports, though overwhelmingly agricultural, are diversified over many products rather than concentrated in one or two; on the other hand, Paraguay had the disadvantage of being highly dependent on the Argentine market. Another advantage in a perverse sense was a great range of exchange, trade, and price controls whose liberalization could bring the equivalent of a rise in productivity. Stabilization was preceded by installation of a government that, whatever else one may say about it, proved durable, in great contrast to the governments that had gone before. Another element of political change was the role of the International Monetary Fund in supervising adherence to various principles and measures of financial prudence that Paraguay had agreed to in connection with standby arrangements for the Fund's financial aid.[27]

Paraguay's stabilization contrasts with a number of other episodes that we have examined in that success did not come suddenly (although a substantial reduction in the inflation rate was quickly achieved). The program was begun in 1956, but price stability did not seem assured until 1962, following a relapse the year before. Perhaps stabilization could not have been sudden, given the intention to relax trade and other controls only in stages. Just how Paraguay's stabilization could ultimately succeed despite apparent absence of anything causing a sudden turnaround of expectations is a question worth further research. Such investigation is impeded, unfortunately, by the cryptic nature of official reports for the years when the outcome of the stabilization program was still in doubt.

Argentina

Argentine authorities achieved partial success with stabilization efforts on several occasions since World War II, only to have inflation speed up again. Table 7 conveys an impression of this record.

Argentina struggled with an inconvertible paper currency until 1899. For the first four decades of the twentieth century, however, the country did not have inflation—not in the sense of an unmistakably and persistently rising price level. Between 1914 and 1939, the Buenos Aires cost-of-living index rose at an average annual rate of only 0.8 percent; between the last years of World Wars I and II, 1918 and

---

[27] On this latter point, see Pincus, *Economy of Paraguay*, pp. 370, 373, and Baer, "Economic Condition," p. 60.

TABLE 7

Year-to-Year Increases in Annual Average Cost-of-Living Index, Argentina, 1940–1978

Year	Percentage Increase	Year	Percentage Increase
1940	2.2	1960	27.3
1941	2.6	1961	13.5
1942	5.7	1962	28.1
1943	1.1	1963	24.1
1944	−0.3	1964	22.4
1945	19.8	1965	28.7
1946	17.7	1966	31.6
1947	13.5	1967	29.3
1948	13.1	1968	16.2
1949	31.1	1969	7.6
1950	25.5	1970	13.5
1951	36.7	1971	34.8
1952	37.9	1972	58.4
1953	4.6	1973	61.3
1954	3.8	1974	23.5
1955	12.3	1975	182.3
1956	13.4	1976	443.2
1957	24.7	1977	176.1
1958	31.6	1978	175.5
1959	113.7		

Sources: 1940–1963, calculated from index for Buenos Aires in Carlos García Martínez, *La Inflación Argentina*, p. 36; 1964 on, International Monetary Fund, *International Financial Statistics Yearbook 1979*, pp. 58–59.

1945, the index actually declined at a 0.16 percent annual rate.[28] With intermediate fluctuations partly reflecting the temporary depreciation of sterling after World War I, the sterling value of the paper peso was practically the same in 1928 as it had been in 1901: 11.47 pesos per pound then as against 11.43 earlier. At around 2.39 pesos, the rate on the dollar was the same in 1939 as in 1914. After fluctuations in the 1930s and 1940s, the free-market rate still averaged no worse than 4.08 pesos per dollar in 1947; the peso still had

[28] Carlos García Martínez, *La Inflación Argentina* (Buenos Aires: Guillermo Kraft, 1965), pp. 36, 38, and calculations from indexes on page 36.

59 percent of its dollar value of 1914. Substantial exchange depreciation did set in after 1947. Between 1949 and 1950, the annual average free-market rate on the dollar jumped from 5.87 to 10.72 pesos; between 1955 and 1956, this rate jumped from 17.36 to 35.18.[29]

Inflation became endemic in Argentina in the late 1940s. At least one observer traces its roots to the campaign preceding and the outcome of the presidential election of 1946. From his key position as secretary of labor and social security (in a government imposed by force of arms), candidate Juan Perón sanctioned a series of labor measures aimed at winning mass support. The mentality that took power in 1946 went beyond simple demagogy and had several ideological aspects. One of them was a doctrine of "promotional money"—belief in using money as a tool of economic change, including expansion of production, full employment of the factors of production, and massive wage and salary increases. In only four years, from the end of 1945 to the end of 1949, the net growth in total credits to official and private sectors of the economy was more than three times larger than the total reached at the beginning of this period. A little more than half of the associated creation of money corresponded to loans to the public sector, a little less than half to loans to the private sector. Inflationary financing was notably employed for housing construction and for the operations of state enterprises, including the Instituto Argentino de Promoción del Intercambio (IAPI), a catchall entity for state trading and development.[30] The expansionary money and credit policies of the Perón regime were facilitated by nationalization of the central bank in 1946 and further developments in 1946–1949 that converted the commercial banks, in effect though not in name, into mere branches of the central bank.[31]

In the ensuing five years, through the end of 1954, creation of money corresponded principally to the extension of bank credit to the private sector. The chief reason for this credit expansion, according to Carlos García Martínez, was business financing requirements expanded by continuation of an inflationary wage policy; under the circumstances, monetary tightness would have brought recession.[32]

Price inflation slowed down remarkably, but only temporarily, in 1953–1954. In 1952, Perón had inaugurated an austerity program, with the public sector setting conspicuous examples. Wages were frozen for two years and price controls imposed. In 1954, faced with

[29] Rafael Olarra Jiménez, *Evolución Monetaria Argentina* (Buenos Aires: Editorial Universitaria, 1968), tables on pp. 182–184.

[30] García, *Inflación*, pp. 100–105, 308–310.

[31] Ibid., chaps. 4 and 7; Olarra, *Evolución*, pp. 6–10, 101–109.

[32] García, *Inflación*, p. 169.

elections and with opposition complaints about the austerity policies, Perón authorized increases in the lowest wages, with the result that increases averaging 18 percent occurred throughout the economy.[33]

The Perón regime was overthrown in September 1955 and replaced by a military government. By then, the means of payment held by the public had expanded 860 percent from its amount at the end of 1944; the cost of living was almost seven times as high as in 1944. The balance of payments had been running a chronic deficit, and net gold and foreign exchange holdings per peso of notes in circulation had dwindled to 0.01 centavo (from 2.04 pesos at the end of 1945). A complicated array of trade and exchange controls, multiple exchange rates, state-trading arrangements, and bilateral trade agreements was causing various inefficiencies. The long-term capital market had been essentially destroyed (as indicated, for example, by the decline of transactions in both government and private securities in relation to gross national income), which had ruined prospects of financing public-sector investments by genuine savings. Much of the country's infrastructure was being consumed without replacement.[34]

Raúl Prebisch, economic and financial advisor of the new government, prepared reports on how the country had imprudently been incurring debts abroad, how inflation had been leading to capital consumption, and why money of stable purchasing power was essential for the country's economic recuperation. Thus, in 1956, began the period of the Prebisch Plan and successor programs. The inflationary mentality of the preceding ten years was to be replaced by an antiinflationary one, to judge from various documents and declarations. Yet the actual results were to prove, if anything, worse.[35]

In 1956 and 1957, wage increases persisted, and devaluation of the peso from 7.50 to 18.00 per dollar also raised business costs. A noninflationary source of mortgage loans for housing construction could not be quickly restored. During the two-year period, about two-thirds of the creation of money corresponded to the extension of credit to the private sector. Furthermore, inflationary financing per-

---

[33] Laura Randall, *An Economic History of Argentina in the Twentieth Century* (New York: Columbia University Press, 1978), pp. 79–80, in part quoting interviews with Alfredo Gomez Morales. (Other books that one would expect to discuss this episode say practically nothing about it.)

Money-supply changes around this time, expressed as percentage changes of the current from the preceding year's average, amounted to 26.8 percent in 1951, 12.5 in 1952, 24.7 in 1953, 17.0 in 1954, and 16.3 in 1955. Calculated from Carlos F. Díaz Alejandro, *Essays on the Economic History of the Argentine Republic* (New Haven: Yale University Press, 1970), p. 489.

[34] García, *Inflación*, pp. 212, 226–227. On the destruction of the capital market, see p. 207 in particular and Olarra, *Evolución*, pp. 151–152, 156, 159–160, 163.

[35] García, *Inflación*, pp. 214–215, where some of the documents are quoted in part.

129

sisted for purchases of crops by IAPI, investment by state enterprises and public departments, covering the deficits of state enterprises, and subsidizing articles of mass consumption.[36]

A vicious circle proved difficult to break: continuing inflation thwarted efforts to reestablish a private market for government securities, so the provisional government felt obliged to keep on resorting to inflationary finance of some of its investment expenditures. It hesitated to take measures that, while beneficial in the long run, would be unpopular in the short run. Beyond the important step of liquidating IAPI, it did little to reduce its budget deficit. An irresolute wage policy was important in frustrating efforts to contain government expenditures, according to García, especially since wages and salaries accounted for 80 percent of the expenditures of the government and state enterprises. A decree did freeze wages for one year and contributed to success in practically stabilizing the cost of living between August 1957 and January 1958;[37] but that stability was lost the following month, apparently because of inflationary expectations touched off by the outcome of the presidential election.[38]

What perhaps had the greatest potential for contributing to success of the provisional government's efforts was the banking reform of the autumn of 1957. It went a long way toward reversing the centralization and nationalization of the banking business accomplished from 1946 to 1949. The banks were again made responsible for their own deposits and no longer accepted deposits as mere agents of the central bank. Their lending capacity was again related to their cash reserves. The central bank no longer determined the money supply directly by allocating its credits to the banks. Its legal independence was restored and the task of maintaining the purchasing power of money again emphasized in its charter. Stricter rules were established for the central bank's rediscounting of paper of commercial or industrial enterprises or of public services belonging to the national, provincial, or municipal governments. The reform of 1957 made antiinflationary modifications in the law of 1946 that had provided for ample extensions of central-bank credit to the National Mortgage Bank.[39]

Despite these and other banking reforms carried out between

---

[36] Ibid., pp. 220–225.

[37] International Monetary Fund, *International Financial Statistics, 1967/68 Supplement*, shows the quarterly average cost-of-living index unchanged from the fourth quarter of 1957 to the first of 1958, while wholesale prices declined slightly.

[38] García, *Inflación*, pp. 240–243.

[39] Olarra, *Evolución*, pp. 11–12, 111–112; García, *Inflación*, chapter 14.

late 1957 and the end of 1963, price inflation became worse than ever. The banks granted credit on an enormous volume of acceptances, principally in 1961.[40]

In 1958, when the Frondizi government replaced the provisional government, the annual average cost-of-living index rose to 32 percent above that of the year before, which was the largest percentage of annual increase since 1945, except only for 1951 and 1952. This acceleration was blamed partly on the policies of the new government, including a massive wage increase amounting to 60 percent of the wages in effect in February 1956 and with extensive retroactivity. The net increase in the means of payment in the hands of the public grew between the ends of 1957 and 1958 by almost 50 percent. In both percentage and absolute amount, this increase was larger than in any previous single year of the twentieth century.[41]

By November 1958, price inflation had reached a rate unknown in Argentine history—some 4 to 5 percent a month—and was still rising. Monetary expansion, indulged in mostly to cover the government's budget deficit, had risen to an annual rate of over 100 percent. Wage increases were swelling demands for credit. The inflation was making the peso increasingly overvalued and was swelling the balance-of-payments deficit. By the end of the year, the country had practically run out of international reserves, and its external debt was already heavy. A flight into gold, foreign exchange, and goods was under way; a deterioration into hyperinflation seemed possible.[42]

These difficulties gave impetus to the Stabilization Program for the Argentine Economy, announced on December 29, 1958. The plan called for a return to freedom of foreign-exchange operations unknown since 1930: a single fluctuating exchange rate would be introduced, with direct controls over trade and payments drastically reduced and simplified. Price ceilings would be eliminated. Wage policy would encourage two-year labor contracts scheduling wage increases but eliminating their automatic link to the cost of living. The government would try energetically to shrink its budget deficit, aided by new taxes and by increases in the prices charged by public enterprises. Bank credit expansion would be limited in line with growth of productive capacity and the availability of goods. Neither the National Mortgage Bank nor the Industrial Bank was to receive any new central-bank credit (whereas such credits had been an important in-

---

[40] García, *Inflación*, p. 232. García maintains that the inflation rate would have been greater still if the banking measures of 1946 had been left in effect.

[41] Ibid., p. 245. The price increases mentioned there reconcile with the table in Felipe Pazos, *Chronic Inflation in Latin America* (New York: Praeger, 1972), p. 14.

[42] Costanzo, *Programas*, pp. 59–60; García, *Inflación*, pp. 246–247.

flationary factor in 1957 and 1958). A ceiling on the domestic assets of the central bank was set at only about 2 percent above the end-of-1958 level (suggesting that the plan aimed at a quick stabilization). Bank reserve requirements were raised to contain the abundant liquidity already created by the central bank. With the intention of expanding productivity and supply capacity, the plan was supplemented by a series of investment projects in basic sectors of the economy. To facilitate maintaining an orderly foreign-exchange market and covering the government deficit without issuing money, important financial aid was obtained from the International Monetary Fund, the United States government, and private banks in North America and Europe.[43]

The plan went into effect on February 1, 1959, and continued through 1961, the last full year of the Frondizi government. The first half of 1959 was a difficult period, bringing sharp adjustments of prices up to realistic levels, as well as labor struggles. (The abolition of price controls and subsidies on consumer goods and increased costs of fuel and other imports as a result of exchange depreciation of the peso all contributed to a spurt in the cost of living, which in turn spurred wage demands and strikes, especially as the government was then backing off from its intervention in wage determination.)[44] A lengthy bank strike and the central bank's losses on its previously granted exchange-rate-insurance contracts allowed excessive monetary expansion to persist. The cost of living rose a further 75 percent in the first half of 1959, and the peso depreciated from 65 per dollar to around 109 in the first days of July. Production suffered in 1959 (real gross national product declined 4.5 percent according to one estimate; according to another, gross domestic product at constant prices was no greater than in 1958.) The decline was not due entirely to the stabilization program, however; for example, the spring of 1959 brought one of the worst floods in Argentine history.[45]

The price situation began showing improvement after mid-year. From September to December 1959, price increases amounted to only around 2 percent a month; in February 1960, the increase was

---

[43] García, *Inflación*, pp. 249–250; Costanzo, *Programas*, pp. 61–66, 75.

[44] The rise in quarterly average indexes, expressed as annual rates, amounted to 401 percent for wholesale prices and 255 percent for consumer prices between the fourth quarter of 1958 and the first quarter of 1959. Increases in earlier and later quarters were much less extreme. Calculated from *International Financial Statistics, 1967/68 Supplement*.

[45] Costanzo, *Programas*, pp. 67–70; CEMLA, *Aspectos monetarios de las economías latinoamericanas, 1959* (Mexico City: 1960), pp. 124, 126; on gross domestic product at constant prices, International Monetary Fund, *International Financial Statistics Yearbook, 1979*, p. 88.

down to 0.9 percent. After August 1959, the free-market exchange rate remained stable at around 82 or 83 pesos per dollar. This strength apparently did not depend on official support, since the balance of payments was equilibrated and the official reserves were growing around the end of the year. In December 1959, the credit arrangements with the International Monetary Fund, the U.S. Treasury, and foreign commercial banks were extended.[46]

By the second half of 1960, the program appeared largely successful. Exchange depreciation had been stopped for a year. The trade balance had become favorable, short-term private capital outflows had given way to inflows, and the foreign-exchange reserves were growing. Price inflation had abated drastically, and between May and October 1960, the cost of living actually declined somewhat (a seasonal rise of about 5 percent in the last two months of the year was half eliminated the following January). Industrial production, which had continued declining in the first half of 1960, recuperated in large measure in the second half of the year. The capital markets showed signs of a return of confidence in the Argentine peso. In August 1960, the government was able to float its first long-term peso bond issue in many years; in December, for the first time since 1946, the National Mortgage Bank successfully launched a long-term peso bond issue. New stock issues grew, as well as time and savings deposits. Argentina's ability to borrow abroad improved fundamentally. Again able to raise funds by borrowing from domestic nonbank sectors and from foreign creditors, the government was less dependent on central-bank credit. An increased rate of investment financed by domestic savings and foreign capital gave promise that the stagnation of the preceding decade was giving way to economic growth. The Argentine experience thus far seemed to provide a counterexample to fears that rapid stabilization brings dire consequences. Strict control of central-bank credit and application of high reserve requirements to the commercial banks did not mean a liquidity crisis or a denial of credit to the private sector. Total bank credits to the private sector rose almost 20 percent in 1959 and more than 20 percent in 1960. Banks could raise funds in relatively noninflationary ways, as by borrowing abroad and serving as intermediaries of increased domestic saving.[47]

From a longer-term perspective, however, the success of the stabilization program was not nailed down after all. A balance-of-payments surplus in 1959 and 1960 was setting the stage for expansion of high-powered money and in turn, through the banking

---

[46] Costanzo, *Programas*, p. 68; CEMLA, *Aspectos monetarios, 1959*, pp. 124, 126.
[47] Costanzo, *Programas*, pp. 111–119.

multiplier, for expansion of domestic credit and money. Wage increases and cost increases related to the foreign-exchange reform were intensifying business demands for credit. At the same time, the government budget deficit and the central bank's implementation of exchange-rate guarantees continued having expansionary effects. Perhaps more importantly, political considerations paralyzed a consistent and resolute antiinflationary policy. Political commotion characterized most of the period 1962–1963. In those two years, regularly elected governments exercised power only briefly (approximately three months in early 1962 and late 1963 under Presidents Frondizi and Illia, respectively); for the remainder of the two years, the military ruled through Dr. Guido.[48]

In 1962 and 1963, the cost of living rose almost 60 percent, one of the largest increases over a two-year period since 1945. Credits from the banking system to the public sector again became the most important element in monetary expansion, with the growth of bank loans to the private sector ranking second. Devaluation of the peso in April 1962 gave impetus to increases in costs, prices, wages, government spending, and the budget deficit.[49]

Carlos García Martínez attributes failure of the stabilization efforts made since 1955 to the absence of the political will to adhere firmly to economic policies that, though advantageous to the people's welfare in the long run, do incur transitional difficulties. More specifically, the key to success—that the new price relations established by an exchange-rate adjustment be allowed to persist—was not assured. Government budget deficits, though occasionally reduced or financed in a relatively noninflationary way, did persist; and appropriate wage restraint was not maintained. Wiping out inflation requires an iron political will, which was lacking.[50]

The inadequacy of wage restraint that García emphasizes so much, along with interactions among currency devaluation, wage and cost and price increases, and growth of the government deficit, are all aspects of the catching-up process, broadly conceived. Devaluation itself, as a delayed price adjustment, is one such aspect. It is unreasonable to expect the new price relations immediately established by a devaluation to persist indefinitely without further adjustment. It is hardly a useful appraisal of a stabilization program to say that it failed because, in effect, it did not somehow immediately overcome the catching-up element of inflationary momentum.

---

[48] García, *Inflación*, pp. 250–270, and chap. 18 in general.
[49] Ibid.
[50] Ibid., pp. 365, 368–369, 371, 373.

In 1963, inflation was running at about the postwar average rate of around 24 percent, unrestrained by significant controls. Between 1964 and 1966, however, the government, dissatisfied with this rate of inflation, introduced selective direct controls on prices in the public sector, agriculture, and some private industries. Inflation was slowed only temporarily, and the controls were abandoned at the end of 1966.[51]

The next stabilization plan—not so much a coherent plan as a collection of policy measures—was launched by a new government in March 1967.[52] As a first step toward stabilizing both variables, the price of foreign exchange was raised 37 percent and wages were realigned upward. Taxes on traditional exports were increased and customs duties were reduced. Fearing the costs of trying to stop entrenched inflation by monetary tightness alone, the government replaced the private negotiation of wages by a legally established mechanism. The initial wage realignments took account of how long ago particular groups of workers had received their last increases. Wages were then to be frozen for the next nineteen months, apart from some further adjustments. Business firms were compensated for the wage increases by cuts in their social security contributions. The government warned the public that the exchange-rate and wage adjustments would speed up inflation at first, but it held out hope that prices could be completely or nearly stabilized afterward.[53]

Although the plan never was made entirely explicit, its strategy, as interpreted by Juan Carlos de Pablo, was to reduce the inflation rate dramatically by freezing the readjusted wages and prices, then to unfreeze them gradually so that relative wages and prices could move toward an equilibrium pattern without getting an overall upward movement going again. Since any frozen pattern of wages and prices was bound to be a disequilibrium pattern, the logic of the strategy implied striving for success quickly—within about one year—before the inefficiencies bred by the throttling of the market mechanism could become really serious.[54]

Because of earlier failures of price control, the government decided to implement its industrial price policy of 1967 by means of voluntary agreement. Firms taking part were expected to hold their prices steady for at least six months. Thereafter, the only justification

---

[51] Ke-young Chu and Andrew Feltenstein, "Extraordinary Inflation: The Argentine Experience," *Finance and Development*, June 1979, p. 32.

[52] Juan Carlos de Pablo, *Política antiinflacionaria en la Argentina, 1967–1970* (Buenos Aires: Amorrortu, 1972), p. 13.

[53] Ibid., pp. 29–30; Pazos, *Chronic Inflation*, pp. 170–171.

[54] Pablo, *Política*, pp. 106–107 and passim.

for a price increase would be an increase in the costs of imported materials; a price increase could not be justified by increased prices of domestic materials charged by nonparticipating suppliers. To persuade firms to take part in the agreement and run the attendant risks of a cost-price squeeze, the government offered rather gimmicky inducements. The government sector would make purchases only from participating firms. From August 1967, the commercial banks were authorized to offer new credits for personal consumption. To grant these credits, the banks could use their otherwise required reserves, as well as ordinary funds. Instead of being paid out in cash or credited to a current account, the loans were to be paid out in the form of vouchers usable only for buying good produced by firms participating in the price agreement. Firms, in turn, could use this special voucher money only for payments to other participating firms. The price agreement was negotiated at the level of producers and was not initially meant to extend to wholesale and retail trade. The response of the business community to the government's proposal was favorable; the most important firms did sign up.[55]

The program of 1967 was hardly a monetarist one, as is reflected in relatively high rates of monetary expansion scheduled for that year and indicated in the letter of intention sent by the government to the International Monetary Fund.[56] One gets the impression that the program centered around the semivoluntary price and wage controls and not on strict monetary restraint, which presumably helps account for the brevity of its apparent success.

In 1968, the program again scheduled substantially larger percentages of increase in central-bank credit and in the money stock than was expected in the price level. An increase in the quantity of money in real terms was targeted in order to depress interest rates in real terms, which the authorities judged to be too high at the time in relation to the thus-far reduced rate of price inflation. Expected reductions in the government budget deficit and the balance-of-payments surplus implied that the planned increase in the money supply had to come from elsewhere, and the policy instrument chosen for this purpose was reduction of the level of required bank reserves.

---

[55] Ibid., pp. 31–33, 37–38.

[56] Ibid., pp. 33–36, 39. Pablo calculates maximum growth rates permitted for 1967 over 1966 for the monetary base, total net internal credit, and central-bank credit to the treasury; these percentages turn out to be in the 20s or 30s, depending on the particular definitions used. Money (as defined in International Monetary Fund, *International Financial Statistics*) grew by 39 percent during 1967.

Not only monetary policy but also public investment policy was intended to be stimulatory in 1968.[57]

At the beginning of 1969, businessmen were asked to extend the price-restraint agreement. They were told that the prices charged by public enterprises, tax rates, and the exchange rate would be held constant during 1969. Firms would have to absorb any increases in labor costs. At its extension, two changes were made in the price agreement. It was extended to retail trade, and a participating firm was allowed to change the prices of individual items provided that it held a weighted average steady. As for monetary policy, no explicit ceiling on the money-supply increase was set, since the standby agreement with the International Monetary Fund was not renewed; but the authorities intended to maintain the system's level of real liquidity in 1969, rather than expand it, as in 1968.[58]

A change of ministers of economics and labor in June 1969 marks the end (in Pablo's judgment) of the first stage of the program of 1967 and provides a vantage point for describing the results to that time. Prices had previously been rising at an annual rate of about 30 percent, and the initial adjustments of the exchange rate and wages briefly speeded up the rise. Then, during the seven months up to February 1968, the annual rate of rise of the cost-of-living index sank to 18 percent. It sank further to an average of 8 percent from the first quarter of 1968 to the first quarter of 1970. On a year-average-over-year-average basis, the cost-of-living increase amounted to 16.2 percent in 1968 and 7.6 percent in 1969, the lowest rate of inflation in the country's recent history. (It rose again to 13.5 percent in 1970.)[59] At times, notably late in 1967 and early in 1968, prices even seemed to be leveling off. The wholesale price index showed actual declines in November and December and again in February, March, and April. The cost-of-living index dropped 3.4 percent between December 1967 and January 1968 and then remained nearly stable for over half a year.[60] After continuing to rise through 1967, the general price index dropped slightly between the first and second quarters of 1968.[61]

The deceleration of the wholesale and cost-of-living indexes has been interpreted as reflecting a decline in primary-product prices that

[57] Pablo, *Política*, pp. 67–69, 73–74, 80.

[58] Ibid., pp. 88–91.

[59] Pazos, *Chronic Inflation*, pp. 170–173; International Monetary Fund, *International Financial Statistics Yearbook 1979*, p. 87.

[60] Pablo, *Política*, tables on pp. 120–123.

[61] Susan M. Wachter, *Latin American Inflation* (Lexington, Mass.: Lexington Books, 1976), table on p. 127.

partially averaged out a continuing rise in other prices. In particular, the world prices of Argentine exports fell in 1968. When the prices of primary products began rising again in the second half of 1968, the balance was broken and the overall indexes began again showing steeper increases.[62]

Throughout the period, both manufacturing production and real gross domestic product continued rising (if the figures can be trusted). Even though a decline in foreign demand for Argentine products depressed activity in the agriculture and livestock sector, total real economic activity rose 7.2 percent from the second quarter of 1967 to the second quarter of 1968.[63]

The deficit of the public sector, measured in real terms, was cut in 1969 to less than half of what it had been in 1967. Government revenues were increased by a surcharge on the export tax, an additional land tax, an increase in the tax on supposedly nonessential consumer goods, and increased efficiency in tax collections. The government froze the number of its employees and reduced its subsidies to government enterprises. The social security system shifted from surplus into deficit during this period, diluting the improvement in government finance. Still, the government became less dependent on money creation.[64]

In 1970, the cost-of-living index again registered an increased rate of rise; and the inflation intensified in the following years, as table 7 shows. By March 1976, the inflation rate briefly reached some 50 percent a month.[65] Money-supply expansion on a year-end-to-year-end basis rose to 19.8 percent in 1970 and 35.9 percent in 1971 and fluctuated at still higher levels thereafter, exceeding 300 percent in 1976 and remaining well above 100 percent at least through 1979. Felipe Pazos blames the collapse of the stabilization program on two deficiencies. First, the government could not keep workers from believing that they had borne the whole burden of the program. This belief created political pressures for wage increases in later years. Second, the decline in relative prices of meat in 1968 and 1969 discouraged cattle breeding in 1970, which not only cut export earnings

[62] Pablo, Política, pp. 63, 74–75.

[63] International Monetary Fund, International Financial Statistics Yearbook 1979, pp. 87, 89; Pablo, Política, pp. 93–94.

[64] Pablo, Política, p. 94; Pazos, Chronic Inflation, p. 171. From rates of 30 percent or more, money-supply growth was finally cut to 17.3 percent in 1969 and 12.0 percent in 1970. (These figures are year-to-year changes from International Monetary Fund, International Financial Statistics Yearbook 1979, p. 55. Changes during years, as calculated from p. 87, line 34, were minus 11.0 percent in 1969 and 19.8 percent in 1970.)

[65] Chu and Feltenstein, "Extraordinary Inflation," pp. 32–33.

but also, by raising meat prices and the cost of living, intensified the pressure for wage increases.[66] In a word, this strand of explanation emphasizes catch-up.

A fuller explanation for the longer run must refer to Perón's return to power in 1973; his policies regarding wages, income redistribution, price controls, a squeeze on profits, and inflationary government financing; and political instability, epitomized by military overthrow of his widow, who as vice president had succeeded him.[67] Although the military government did achieve an impressive cut in the budget deficit in relation to gross domestic product and did manage to reduce the inflation rate to 100 percent or less in the first half of 1980,[68] the problem obviously was far from solved. Economic policy makers reportedly regarded money-supply expansion continuing even at a triple-digit rate as a mere "passive" response to businessmen's habit of raising prices in anticipation of inflation. The policy makers sought to exert pressure on business to cut costs and restrain prices by cutting tariff protection and keeping foreign exchange artificially cheap in terms of pesos.[69]

Surveying the whole period of 1963 to 1976, Ke-young Chu and Andrew Feltenstein attribute the inflation to two main causes. The first was monetary expansion, largely linked with passive expansion of central-bank credit and with the financing of government budget deficits, which were swollen by the lag of tax collections behind price increases. Second, price controls had perverse effects. Either by direct transfers or by bank-credit expansion at low interest rates, the government subsidized public and private enterprises that had incurred losses because of price controls. Furthermore, although Chu and Feltenstein do not explicitly say so, they convey the suggestion that price controls, by distorting relative prices and otherwise causing inefficiencies, made a given flow of spending impinge on a smaller real supply of goods than would otherwise have been available.[70]

Summary and Comment. Argentine experience since World War II illustrates the self-feeding aspects of an entrenched inflation— interactions among prices, wages, exchange depreciation, controls, government deficits, and expansion of money and credit. It provides examples of gimmickry, such as the provision of consumer credit on

[66] Pazos, *Chronic Inflation*, p. 184.

[67] For remarks on Perón's policies, see Chu and Feltenstein, "Extraordinary Inflation," pp. 32–33.

[68] *Business Week*, July 21, 1980, p. 83.

[69] *Wall Street Journal*, July 30, 1980, p. 42.

[70] Chu and Feltenstein, "Extraordinary Inflation," pp. 34–35.

especially favorable terms for the purchase of products of firms complying with the voluntary price-restraint program of 1967. Especially in contrast with episodes of successful antiinflation policy in other countries, Argentine experience illustrates the importance of whether the political situation warrants confidence in a consistent and resolute policy.

5

Stopping Imported Inflation
in the 1970s

Switzerland

Despite its reputation for financial prudence and stability, Switzerland reached inflation rates—measured by the increase of the yearly average consumer price index over the preceding year's average—of 6.5 percent in 1971, 6.7 percent in 1972, 8.8 percent in 1973, and 9.7 percent in 1974. Between the third and fourth quarters of 1974, the annual rate of price increase reached 12.6 percent. As judged by price increases over twelve-month periods, Swiss inflation peaked either in December 1973, when the consumer price index was 11.9 percent higher than a year before, or in April 1974, when the wholesale price index was 18.7 percent higher than a year before. The Swiss money supply in 1970 averaged 10.0 percent above the preceding year's average level and in 1971 averaged 18.5 percent higher; for 1972, the increase was down to 13.3 percent. During the fourth quarter of 1971, the money supply grew at a 36.2 percent annual rate. In relation to the corresponding month of 1970, the money supply was 17.4 percent higher in June 1971, 45.5 percent higher in November, and 39.5 percent higher in December.[1]

Subsequently, the consumer-price inflation rate on a year-average-over-year-average basis declined to 6.7 percent in 1975, 1.7 percent in 1976, 1.3 percent in 1977, and 1.1 percent in 1978. The index actually registered slight declines between the first and second quarters of 1976 and the third and fourth quarters of 1978. The rise of the consumer price index over twelve-month periods apparently reached its low in October 1978, when the index stood only 0.4 percent higher than one year before. As for wholesale prices, the change

---

[1] Figures from or calculated from various issues of *International Financial Statistics* and of Swiss National Bank, *Bulletin Mensuel*.

of the index from the corresponding month one year before averaged —0.7 percent in 1976, +0.3 percent in 1977, and —3.4 percent in 1978. The greatest twelve-month decrease was apparently registered in September 1978, at —4.7 percent. The money supply averaged 0.4 percent lower in 1973 than in 1972. Not until late in 1975 did the money supply exceed the level reached at the end of 1972.

Switzerland thus had the greatest degree of success of any major country and perhaps of any country in all but completely stopping inflation in the 1970s.

Understanding this success presupposes understanding the nature and background of the inflation that was stopped. In brief, the price inflation traces to preceding monetary expansion caused by exchange-rate pegging in the face of balance-of-payments surpluses, notably on capital account. The key to stopping the inflation was allowing the exchange rate to float, which meant that the growth of the Swiss money supply was no longer at the mercy of external conditions.[2]

Expansion of the Swiss monetary base and thus in turn of the Swiss money supply had for many years corresponded to the Swiss National Bank's acquisition of foreign, not domestic, assets. Balance-of-payments surpluses from 1958 through early 1973 added 19 billion francs worth to the foreign-reserve holdings of the National Bank. Of this total increase, 45 percent came shortly before the initial breakdown of the Bretton Woods system of fixed exchange rates in August 1971 and another 16 percent in the system's final three months. The overall payments surpluses corresponded chiefly to inflows of capital, including repatriations of Swiss capital previously placed abroad, especially during international crises when exchange-rate adjustments were expected.[3]

As a balance-of-payments surplus and exchange-rate pegging were creating excess domestic liquidity at times during the 1960s and early 1970s, the Swiss authorities faced a conflict between the internal objective of resisting inflation by policies that might entail high interest rates and the external objective of discouraging capital imports and encouraging capital exports by a low-interest-rate policy.

---

[2] This is the main conclusion of Stuart D. Allen, "The Causation of Inflation in Switzerland, 1952–1975" (Ph.D. diss., University of Virginia, 1977). Allen fitted equations for the price inflation rate quarter by quarter to quarterly data for other variables, notably growth of the money supply, over the 1957–1972 period of fixed exchange rates. Only one variable turned out to be significantly related to the inflation rate: the growth rate of the money supply, or alternatively of the monetary base, currently and over the preceding three or four years. There appeared to be a lag of five to seven quarters from the end of a half-cycle of monetary growth to the end of the corresponding half-cycle of rise in prices.

[3] Ibid., pp. 10, 82, 104, 108, 110, 128, 129, and passim.

The authorities had inadequate weapons with which to try to neutralize the macroeconomic consequences of exchange-rate pegging. Fiscal policy suffered from the splitting of financial sovereignty among the confederation, the cantons, and the communes; and scope for countercyclical manipulation of the federal budget was limited both on the receipts and especially on the expenditure side.

Scope for open-market operations or other monetary-policy actions was also limited. Although the long-term capital market was well developed and active in Switzerland, the reverse was true of the "money" or short-term-credit market. Suitable short-term instruments were lacking. There was no real market in government obligations. Traditionally, the confederation, the cantons, and the communes had only slight resort to borrowing, and hardly any short-term public debt was available in which to invest. Such federal obligations as existed were placed almost exclusively with the banks and the Bank for International Settlements and were rarely traded. Neither was there any substantial market in bills of exchange and bankers' acceptances. The banks preferred to give credit by making loans rather than by accepting drafts. Because of this scarcity of short-term paper, medium- and long-term obligations nearing maturity were much sought. At least 95 percent of the giro balances held at the Swiss National Bank belonged to the commercial banks, and these balances constituted around 60 percent of the banks' liquid assets. Thus, the liquidity of the money market was regarded as practically the same thing as bank liquidity, and the money market was practically the same thing as the market in bank credit.[4]

One fateful consequence of the lack of a developed domestic money market was the frequent recourse of Swiss residents and Swiss banks to short-term investments abroad. In making these investments, the banks were reinvesting funds deposited with them not only by residents but also, and especially, by foreigners. The Swiss traditionally made investments abroad in treasury securities, bankers' acceptances, and money-market paper of the United States and to a lesser extent of England. After around 1965, investments on the Eurocurrency market became important.[5] As long as the Swiss National Bank continued to peg the exchange rate, liquid assets denominated in foreign currencies were almost instantly convertible into Swiss base money. The Swiss National Bank would experience an increase in foreign exchange on the asset side and in giro accounts on

---

[4] Giovanni Antonio Colombo, *Politique conjoncturelle en économie ouverte* (Bern and Frankfurt: Lang, 1973), p. 2 and pt. 2, chap. 2, especially the summary on p. 97, pp. 100–105, 117, and passim.

[5] Ibid., pp. 100–101, 106–108, 139, and, in general, pt. 2, chaps. 3, 4, and 5.

the liability side of its balance sheet. Even if the Swiss authorities had somehow been able to mount effective resistance to inflows of foreign capital, they would hardly have been able to restrict repatriation by Swiss residents and institutions of funds invested in foreign liquid assets. The large mass of Swiss capital held abroad in such forms contributed to the sensitivity of inward capital movements, sensitivity not only to speculation on exchange rates but also to interest-rate differentials.

The National Bank repeatedly mentioned the narrow limits that these circumstances set to its antiinflation policy. Its arguments referred to the permanent inclination of foreigners to place funds in Switzerland, the existence of a great repatriation potential on the part of both bank and nonbank holders of foreign assets, and the necessity of an appropriate differential between Swiss and foreign interest rates to ward off unwanted capital inflows. The Bank further argued, quite questionably, that the narrow scope for its monetary policy was "essentially" independent of the exchange-rate system.[6]

The Swiss experience and similar experiences of Germany and Japan suggest that if a country's authorities are not willing to accept the money-supply expansion caused by speculative inflows of funds and are not willing to accept the consequent rise in prices, the only way out of the dilemma is to set the exchange rate free. Stepwise flexibility, multiplying the occasions when market participants can reasonably expect an adjustment of a pegged exchange rate, is inferior to floating as a way of coping with speculative capital movements; and administrative controls form no genuine alternative either.[7]

The 1960s and early 1970s witnessed repeated efforts to give the monetary authorities effective policy instruments. Faced with an insufficiency of instruments, largely for reasons already described, the Swiss National Bank repeatedly resorted to negotiating "gentlemen's agreements" with the commercial banks. These may be regarded as institutionalized moral suasion. They sought to limit the inflow and promote the outflow of foreign funds by such measures as requiring banks to maintain extra reserves against foreign-owned deposits, banning interest payments and sometimes charging negative interest on those deposits, keeping domestic interest rates below foreign interest rates (though this could clash with the objective of

---

[6] Bruno Gehrig and Beat Gerber, "Hypothesen der schweizerischen Nationalbank: Ein Diskussionsbeitrag," *Schweizerische Zeitschrift für Volkswirtschaft und Statistik*, vol. 110, no. 1 (March 1974), pp. 80–84. In their footnote 39, the authors cite writers who accept the argument mentioned.

[7] Ibid., pp. 87–88.

controlling domestic liquidity), and requiring commercial banks to be prompt in converting funds authorized for capital export from Swiss into foreign currency.

The objective of limiting domestic credit expansion was pursued by asking banks to observe ceilings in their granting of new loans and to deposit in blocked accounts specified percentages of credit extensions beyond the ceiling and by increasing the down payments required and reducing the time allowed in installment purchases. The National Bank raised its discount rate only occasionally. Measures taken by the government included restrictions on the construction industry, tariff cuts to cheapen imports, requirements that certain industries announce in advance and justify any intended price increases, and, finally, upward revaluation (in 1971) and upward floating (in 1973) of the Swiss franc. These measures were adopted and modified at different times and were not all in effect at once.[8] (Some details will be mentioned later.)

Before the floating of the franc, the Swiss authorities, in trying to restrain the inflationary growth of spending, relied more heavily on direct ceilings on the growth of domestic credit than on measures aiming at the quantity of money or at interest rates. Apart from the paucity of other weapons, the chief arguments offered for this approach were that it suffered less interference from external influences than the alternatives would have and that it had a slighter tendency to raise interest rates. Swiss policy was even influenced, according to Bruno Gehrig and Beat Gerber, by a traditional preference for interest-rate stability and by the notion that high interest rates, especially high long-term rates, contribute to high prices. These ideas are dubious. A quantitative credit-limitation policy tends to favor old credit customers of financial institutions over new ones because of the smaller information costs of dealing with old customers. Ceilings on bank credit can be expected to raise the "black" interest rates charged by nonbank lenders, whose relatively less efficient apparatus for acquiring information about borrowers forms a further reason for supposing that borrowers deprived of access to bank credit would suffer from the bank credit ceilings even if they did succeed in getting loans on the nonbank market. Restrictions on access to bank credit and increased interest rates on nonbank loans would be expected to, and apparently did, give holders of liquid foreign assets additional incentives to repatriate their funds into Switzerland. Thus, the policies followed provided no easy answer to the problem of capital in-

---

[8] Facts combined from various periodicals, as well as Colombo, *Politique*, p. 81; pt. 2, chap. 1, goes into detail on Swiss policy weapons and their inadequacy.

flows and involuntary creation of domestic base money under fixed exchange rates.[9]

For years, the Swiss authorities cast about for alternatives to revaluing or floating the franc. After the upward revaluation of the German mark in October 1969, the question was raised in Switzerland whether it should not follow suit as an antiinflation measure.[10] The mark's revaluation tended to have an inflationary impact on Switzerland much as if Switzerland itself had devalued against an important trading partner. Yet a decision was made against impairing the exchange stability of the franc, which had held since 1936. Instead, the credit growth ceiling established in 1969 was tightened in 1970. At the beginning of 1971, the agreement on limiting domestic credit growth was again extended. Its effectiveness was repeatedly undercut by massive inflows of funds from abroad. In the first few days of May alone, the Swiss National Bank had to absorb about $700 million, worth over 3 billion francs. The German Bundesbank's suspension of dollar purchases on May 5 increased the danger of further inflows into Switzerland. The Swiss Federal Council, although still opposed to floating and apparently still regarding a fixed exchange rate as an element of virtue in economic policy, decided on May 9 to revalue the franc upward. The revaluation amounted to 7.07 percent nominally but to 5 percent in relation to the previous lower support level of the dollar.

After the revaluation, the government and Parliament took additional supposed antiinflationary action in the form of direct limitation on construction activity. A supplement to the 1969 gentlemen's agreement with the banks made possible a 100 percent reserve requirement on growth of bank deposits owed to foreigners, as well as a ban on interest payments on foreign-owned deposits. The big banks declared themselves ready in case of need to sterilize the franc counterpart of all dollar amounts sold to the Swiss National Bank for a period of not more than ten days. At the same time, the Bank employed foreign-exchange operations and swaps to try to promote outflow of the funds that had come in in May.

Then came August 1971. In the first two weeks, $2.15 billion were sold to the National Bank. At first, the Bank was able to block 5.6 billion francs of their counterpart by various expedients. Suspension of the dollar's gold convertibility on August 15 compelled Switzerland, like other countries, to give up defense of the fixed dollar

---

[9] Gehrig and Gerber, "Hypothesen," pp. 70ff; Allen, "Causation," pp. 95, 106–107, 117–118; Colombo, Politique, pp. 179–180.

[10] The following paragraphs draw in part on F. Aschinger, "Die schweizerische Währungspolitik, 1969–1973," Aussenwirtschaft, March 1974, pp. 23–39.

rate. To prevent an all too steep decline of the dollar against the franc, though, the Swiss authorities took further defensive measures against capital inflows. They used their recently obtained authority to forbid interest payments on foreign balances denominated in francs and imposed a 100 percent reserve requirement on the net increase in foreign deposits since the end of July. However, repatriations of Swiss funds previously held abroad, which made up a big share of the inflow of funds since the end of July, were not subject to this sterilization requirement. Foreign recipients of officially authorized loans were required to convert the Swiss franc proceeds into foreign exchange at once.

Fixed exchange rates were restored by the Smithsonian Agreement of December 1971.

Further restrictive moves in the first half of 1972 were undercut by the fact that the credit growth ceilings were due to expire at the end of July and that the banks were accordingly making commitments for large new loans. The National Bank responded with new credit guidelines. The sterling crisis and the floating of the pound in June 1972 and the ensuing international currency disorder forced the Swiss National Bank again to suspend foreign-exchange intervention temporarily at the end of July. Meanwhile, direct controls were imposed on capital imports. New foreign investment in Swiss securities and land was forbidden. Interest payments were forbidden on foreign money that had come in since the end of July 1971, and a commission of 2 percent per quarter was imposed on the growth of foreign-owned franc balances since mid-1971. Nonbanks could no longer borrow abroad without permission. Banks were required to balance their obligations and claims in foreign currencies daily. The previous agreement regarding minimum reserves against foreign-owned deposits was replaced by a legal requirement.

Switzerland thus created an arsenal of capital import controls such as scarcely any other country possessed. Despite these barriers, the National Bank had to accept a further inflow of dollars worth roughly 5 billion francs in the first half of July. The inflow did not cease until the members of the European Economic Community reaffirmed their commitment to the fixed-exchange-rate system.

To reduce the liquidity that had been created by capital imports in the second half of 1972, the National Bank raised reserve requirements and liberalized its granting of permission for foreign loans. Next, Parliament enacted a program to resist the inflationary business boom. Minimum reserve requirements were extended from the growth to the level of bank obligations owed to Swiss residents and foreigners. Legal control on security issues was introduced; restrictions on construction tightened; authority established for supervision of prices, wages, and profits; and advertising of installment credit forbidden. (These measures were laid before the voters for retroactive ratification at the end of 1973.)

The ban on advertising for consumer credit seems symptomatic of the general character of Swiss antiinflation policy. One gets the impression (an impression supported by leafing through issues of the Swiss National Bank's *Bulletin Mensuel*) that the country did not have a coherent program but rather an accretion of particular expedients. The short-run focus of policy measures is reflected in the National Bank's frequent references to demands for liquidity at monthly, quarterly, and yearly settlement dates, demands for currency at holidays, and so forth. The authorities seemed to be activists, frequently changing the rules regarding capital imports and exports, reserve requirements, credit growth ceilings, sterilization or desterilization of domestic money created through balance-of-payments surpluses, accommodation of year-end window dressing, and various provisions of gentlemen's agreements with the commercial banks.

On January 23, 1973, amid an international currency crisis, the Swiss National Bank ceased intervening in the foreign-exchange market and allowed the franc to float. The Bank's management and the Federal Council recognized that continued rate-pegging would have required exceptionally large purchases of dollars and the corresponding creation of Swiss francs. This, as the Bank recognized, would have had an unfavorable influence on the political and psychological climate necessary for effective resistance to inflation. The devaluation of the dollar on February 12 is further evidence that the old franc-dollar rate could not have been held even by massive intervention.[11]

The dollar's devaluation, the further upward float of the franc against the dollar and other currencies, and the associated threat to the price competitiveness of the Swiss economy strengthened the desire of the Swiss authorities to return to a stable exchange rate. After a joint session of the Federal Council and the management of the National Bank on February 19, the government instructed the Bank not to let the franc strengthen substantially further against the dollar. The Bank then tried to hold the rate at about 29.9 cents (it had been 26.5 cents at the end of 1972 and 22.9 cents before May 1971). This attempt failed. Up to February 23, the National Bank had to take in no less than $705 million ($530 million spot and $175 million forward). Yet it was unable to prevent a further rise of the

---

[11] Swiss National Bank, *Bulletin Mensuel*, February 1973, p. 5.

franc to a temporary high of 32.8 cents. The Swiss authorities felt obliged to abandon their efforts. Despite their yearning to return to fixed exchange rates, they saw no other possibility than to let floating continue.[12] By early July 1973, the Swiss franc rose to 37.7 cents. By late in October 1978, at a time of particular weakness of the dollar and after wide fluctuations in the meanwhile, the franc stood just short of 68.0 cents. (Subsequent easing still left the rate above 60 cents.)

The floating begun in January and confirmed in February 1973 eliminated the problem of payments surpluses swelling the monetary base. "While Switzerland still has had problems with speculative inflows of foreign capital since the floating of the Swiss franc, the value of the currency, and not the monetary base, has had to adjust."[13]

What might be called speculation, interpreted broadly to include assessments of the likelihood of greater financial prudence and greater price-level stability over the long run in Switzerland than in the United States, apparently did contribute to the Swiss franc's strengthening on the foreign-exchange markets more than in proportion to its gain in current purchasing-power parity. This strengthening of the franc helped hold down local prices of imports. The index of Swiss import prices, even with petroleum included, averaged only 1.5 percent higher in 1978 than in 1973, and between 1974 and 1975 it

---

[12] Aschinger, "Währungspolitik," p. 33; Swiss National Bank, *Bulletin Mensuel,* March 1973, p. 5.

[13] Allen, "Causation," p. 25.

Shortly after the floating began, however, the president of the Swiss National Bank complained that his institution still was not entirely free of compulsion to create base money. Earlier, in granting credit and creating deposits, the commercial banks had become accustomed to paying little attention to their momentary holdings of central-bank money. Under fixed exchange rates, they could obtain it by liquidating funds held abroad, and the National Bank could not escape creating it. Under floating, the National Bank still faced pressure to satisfy the commercial banks' liquidity needs in view of the explosive deposit expansion that had occurred shortly before the float. Under floating, banks were competing for base money by selling foreign exchange or by competing for deposits, tending to drive up the franc's exchange rate or interest rates or both. If the National Bank did not want to accept the attendant risks, including risk of business recession, it could not fully ignore, even under floating, the need for base money created by the preceding expansion of bank deposits. E. Stopper, report to the Bank's general meeting, printed along with Swiss National Bank, *Bulletin Mensuel,* May 1973, separate pagination, especially p. 5.

It should be noted that this argument refers to conditions hanging over from the preceding regime of fixed exchange rates and to how they might impair the National Bank's new-found freedom of action, *not* to any continuing mechanical compulsion to create base money. As a matter of fact, furthermore, the mechanical creation of Swiss money did come to an end.

actually fell by 9.8 percent.[14] Declines in import prices were extremely helpful, in the judgment of Emil Küng, in the fight against inflation. The cheapening of imports

> enormously intensified their competition with goods pro-
> duced at home, forcing domestic producers to reduce their
> selling prices. Since imported raw materials, semi-finished
> goods, food, and investment goods cost less, there was a de-
> cline in the costs of materials and energy to industry, as well
> as to households, serving to dampen wage demands.

These circumstances enabled the National Bank to pursue a more restrictive money-supply policy than the central banks of other countries. The inflationary mentality—pervasive expectations of continuing inflation—was more thoroughly eradicated in Switzerland than elsewhere.[15]

Evidently a "virtuous circle" was at work: the strength of the franc on the foreign exchanges contributed, in the manner described, to slowing price inflation down, while the slowdown of inflation reinforced assessments of future prospects that in turn reinforced the franc's strength. As Küng suggests, these developments facilitated monetary restraint on the part of the central bank.

It is not at all puzzling that Swiss inflation peaked in 1974, some time *after* the franc was floated and the explosive growth of the money supply stopped. (Recall the dates and figures mentioned earlier.) It has become practically a standard general proposition that price trends respond to changes in money-supply trends with a lag of roughly two years. Furthermore, Switzerland, like other countries, was exposed to the oil price shock coming at the end of 1973.[16]

Switzerland's success against inflation was accompanied by apparently severe recessionary side effects. (The entire industrial world suffered its most severe postwar recession at the same time, however, so the Swiss recession was hardly due to Swiss policy alone.) The recession began in the second half of 1974 and worsened in 1975; activity suffered more than in other countries belonging to the Organisation for Economic Cooperation and Development (OECD). The building trades suffered an unprecedented contraction.[17] From peak

---

[14] Calculated from International Monetary Fund, *International Financial Statistics Yearbook, 1979*, p. 393.

[15] Emil Küng, *The Secret of Switzerland's Economic Success* (Washington, D.C.: American Enterprise Institute, 1978), especially pp. 3–5.

[16] On the last-mentioned influence, see Organisation for Economic Cooperation and Development, *Switzerland*, March 1974, p. 51.

[17] Küng, *Secret*, p. 5.

year to trough year, gross national product at constant prices fell 8.1 percent between 1974 and 1976, industrial production fell 14.5 between 1974 and 1975, and manufacturing employment fell 15.9 percent between 1974 and 1976. Although real gross national product recovered by 1979 to 3.7 percent above the 1976 low, it still stood below the 1974 peak.[18] The total number of employed persons (excluding the self-employed) declined by 9.6 percent between 1973 and 1976.[19] The number of persons counted as unemployed, which for many years had run at only a few hundred and at times at even fewer than 100, rose to above 10,000 in 1975 and to above 14,000 in 1976 (August figures).[20]

Even so, the full-time unemployment rate never rose above approximately 1 percent. "Switzerland is the only industrial country that has succeeded in eliminating inflation and maintaining full employment at the same time."[21] The explanation hinges partly on the substantial number of women workers who returned to their households and of workers who retired early on pensions, but it hinges above all on the large numbers of foreign workers who went home. The share of foreign workers in total employment declined from 30 percent in 1973 to 25.6 percent in 1975, 23.7 percent in 1976, and 22.5 percent in 1977. The level of unemployment would have risen to well over 10 percent if the departed foreign workers were counted as unemployed. In general, the foreign workers went home because they themselves had decided to do so, not because they had been dismissed outright by their employers. Existing restraints on the immigration of new foreign workers were tightened, however, to the point of practically cutting off the inflow.[22]

After the Swiss had achieved victory over inflation and had paid most of the costs required, signs appeared that they were about to throw that success away after all. The chief reason appeared to be concern over the high, perhaps uncompetitively high, level of the Swiss

---

[18] Calculated from International Monetary Fund, *International Financial Statistics Yearbook, 1979*, pp. 393, 395; and *International Financial Statistics*, July 1980, p. 370.

[19] Küng, *Secret*, p. 2.

[20] While over 10,000 workers were counted as totally unemployed in August 1975, more than 100,000 were estimated to be on short hours. Report for the session of the National Bank Council of September 19, 1975, printed at end of Swiss National Bank, *Bulletin Mensuel*, September 1975, pp. 1–7, in particular p. 5.

[21] Gottfried Haberler, preface to Fritz Leutwiler, *Swiss Monetary and Exchange Rate Policy in an Inflationary World* (Washington, D.C.: American Enterprise Institute, 1978). Haberler goes on to mention the explanation offered in the text above.

[22] Küng, *Secret*, pp. 1–2.

franc's exchange rate and wide fluctuations in that rate. (Recall the rates mentioned earlier.) The president of the Swiss National Bank recognized the problem in a speech of April 1976. At that time, he rejected suggestions for massive market intervention to restrain the franc's rise. (Some intervention had been resumed at the beginning of 1975, however, after a lapse of almost two years.) Possibilities of keeping interventions from expanding the domestic money supply were too limited. Other suggested solutions were also unattractive: the idea of splitting the foreign-exchange market by introducing two rates, one for commercial and another for capital transactions, was unrealistic, and measures to resist investment of foreign funds in Switzerland could be evaded.[23]

Discussion in the June 1976 issue of the National Bank's *Bulletin*, however, mentioned willingness to undertake massive interventions, along with domestic monetary sterilization measures, to resist a speculative rise of the franc. For reasons connected with the exchange rate, the National Bank cut its official interest rates in July 1977. Subsequently, in coordination with other central banks, it pursued its interventions to moderate exchange-rate fluctuations.[24] In its September 1977 *Bulletin*, it recognized a double task not only of contributing to a stable level of prices and costs in Switzerland but also of resisting excessive fluctuation and appreciation of the franc. In its March 1978 *Bulletin*, the Bank mentioned that, for reasons related to the exchange rate, it had been pursuing a policy of assuring the money market a high supply of liquidity, accepting a temporary departure from its quantity-of-money target. Furthermore, partly to conform to market interest rates and partly to show that it considered high money-market liquidity desirable for reasons of exchange-rate policy, it cut its discount and lombard rates to 1 and 2 percent, respectively, the lowest rates it had ever set. Efforts to resist inflows of foreign funds were broadened by measures announced in February 1978 to encompass the goal of promoting outflows. Rules regarding negative interest rates on foreign balances were reinforced, and rules regarding the commercial banks' foreign money positions and their forward sales of francs to foreigners were modified. Placement of foreign funds in Swiss securities and importation of foreign banknotes were forbidden, and the Bank was authorized to conduct long-term forward exchange operations. The market reacted to these measures by strengthening the

---

[23] Fritz Leutwiler, speech appended to Swiss National Bank, *Bulletin Mensuel*, May 1976, especially pp. 3–4. The resumption of intervention in 1975 is mentioned in *Bulletin Mensuel*, January 1977, p. 6.

[24] Swiss National Bank, *Bulletin Mensuel*, August 1977, p. 5.

dollar against the Swiss franc by 9.5 percent in the first half of March 1978.

In its *Bulletin* of April 1978, the Bank again revealed its short-term preoccupations. It recognized that the monetary base had grown strongly following its dollar purchases, especially in December 1977 and January 1978, and that money-supply growth was already accelerating. Even earlier, the Bank had let the money supply grow to depress interest rates and to resist what it considered an excessive appreciation of the franc. In view of the price-moderating influence that this appreciation, not completely prevented, was exerting, there was no immediate danger to Swiss price stability. When the franc should weaken on the exchanges, as the Bank desired, the just-mentioned downward pressure on prices would disappear. Thus, the Bank found rapid money-supply growth tolerable only as long as the franc's exchange rate should remain too high.

In his speech to the Bank's annual meeting on April 27, 1978, President Leutwiler recognized that, even before the announcement in February of new measures to ward off foreign funds, the Bank had tried to smooth the exchange rate by massive purchases of dollars. The immediate result had not been satisfying, but, in view of hectic market conditions, passiveness on the part of the Bank would have had still worse consequences for the exchange rate. In the six months from October 1977 to March 1978, dollar purchases minus dollar sales for capital export had amounted to the equivalent of over 2 billion francs. Operations to drain off the resulting domestic liquidity could be undertaken only hesitantly, since every withdrawal threatened to raise short-term interest rates and thereby reinforce the rise of the franc. Consequently, the monetary base expanded greatly. In December 1977 and January and February 1978, it registered increases over the levels of one year before of around 25 percent. The resulting abundant liquidity tended to depress interest rates. The expansion of the money supply early in 1978 strongly exceeded the target that had been set. That development, if continued, could impair the credibility of Swiss monetary policy; but a merely temporary deviation from the path of monetary virtue need not reignite inflation. The National Bank should remain alert, the president continued, to throttle money-supply growth in time when a significant weakening of the franc on the exchanges should threaten renewed price increases. By the spring of 1978, after a long period without price increases worth mentioning, some people were inclined to push for economic growth even at the cost of somewhat more inflation. The country needed a long-term-oriented policy of stability commanding confidence. Monetary expansion for the sake of exchange-rate policy should not be allowed to get out of control. In the short run, exchange-rate policy sometimes had to take primacy, but in the long-run the priority was the reverse. Even for an economy as dependent on exports as Switzerland's, a strong currency with a low inflation rate was to be preferred to a weak currency with a high inflation rate. Excessive creation of liquidity should be reversed by small steps, however, not by large ones.[25]

This speech, with its hopes about being able ultimately to reverse policies deemed desirable in the short run but undesirable in the long run, reveals considerable ambivalence.

On occasion, the National Bank did have some success in reversing short-term spurts in monetary growth. Referring specifically to the month from mid-June to mid-July 1978, it reported that a decline in the monetary base had largely compensated for its excessive growth during the past winter, and the money supply had stabilized after its strong recent growth. Even so, the money supply at the end of April stood 16.7 percent above its level of a year before and, at the end of May, 18.3 percent above its year-earlier level (the rise in this percentage reflecting a sharp drop in money in May 1977).[26]

Events of the summer of 1978 again illustrated the tension between exchange-rate-oriented and money-supply-oriented policy. The dollar weakened worldwide; it, the German mark, and other currencies fell to unprecedentedly low quotations against the Swiss franc. The National Bank acted to resist this development. Around the end of July and again in September, it intervened directly in the foreign-exchange market and adopted measures to favor capital exports. It acted to increase money-market liquidity greatly in order to depress interest rates and resist the appreciation of the franc. If the exchange-rate situation required, said the Bank, it would expand liquidity further.[27] In view of the franc's continuing appreciation, the National Bank and the Federal Council decided on October 1, 1978, to adopt a series of measures whose chief component would be intensified foreign-exchange intervention. Although oriented mainly toward the rate with the German mark, the interventions would take the form of purchases of dollars almost exclusively, since the dollar remained the Bank's chief intervention currency.[28]

It is hardly a coincidence that the Swiss money supply grew by the end of 1978 to 19.6 percent above the level of one year before

[25] Fritz Leutwiler, report to the general meeting of April 27, 1978, printed along with Swiss National Bank, *Bulletin Mensuel*, May 1978.

[26] Swiss National Bank, *Bulletin Mensuel*, July 1978, p. 5.

[27] Swiss National Bank, *Bulletin Mensuel*, August 1978, p. 5; October 1978, p. 5.

[28] Report for a meeting of the Bank Council, December 15, 1978, attached to Swiss National Bank, *Bulletin Mensuel*, December 1978, p. 7.

and that it grew during the fourth quarter at a 49.5 percent annual rate.[29]

Around the turn of the year 1978–1979, the National Bank felt obliged to make further purchases of dollars and so create additional liquidity to avoid further increases in the franc rate, even though the franc had already receded from its peak quotations against the dollar. Back in early 1975, supposedly under the monetarist influence of Professor Karl Brunner, the Swiss authorities had begun setting annual money-supply growth targets. Now, for the first time since then, the National Bank and Federal Council decided not to set a monetary target for the new year. This decision was entailed by the three-month-old policy of stabilizing the franc-mark rate.

> The priority accorded to exchange-rate policy implies that the National Bank accepts the development of the money stock resulting from this policy. As before the National Bank intends to provide over the medium run a supply of liquidity that permits our economy to undergo neither inflation nor deflation.[30]

The clear implication was that the exchange rate was the immediate concern of policy; the quantity and purchasing power of money were concerns to attend to later ("over the medium run").

In May 1979, the National Bank reported that a weakening tendency of the Swiss franc in the preceding months had given it an opportunity to sell dollars and to reabsorb the surplus of domestic liquidity that had developed after adoption of its exchange-rate target on October 1, 1978. The growth of the money supply during the preceding twelve months had declined from 20 percent at the end of February to 15 percent at the end of March. The Bank was now even taking measures to keep liquidity from shrinking too much.[31]

Yet the Bank had already recognized a notable rise in the Swiss consumer price index, blaming it on increased world-market prices, particularly of oil. The price increases had already kindled new fears of inflation, reflected in some firming of Swiss interest rates.[32] After an inflation rate of less than 1 percent during 1978, the consumer price index in the first and second quarters of 1979 stood 1.9 and 3.2 percent above the levels of one year before, and by November the increase over twelve months reached 5.2 percent.

---

[29] Calculated from International Monetary Fund, *International Financial Statistics*, July 1980, p. 368.

[30] Swiss National Bank, *Bulletin Mensuel*, January 1979, p. 5.

[31] Swiss National Bank, *Bulletin Mensuel*, May 1979, p. 5.

[32] Swiss National Bank, *Bulletin Mensuel*, March 1979, p. 5.

The Swiss authorities gradually shifted the emphasis of their worries from too high an exchange quotation of the franc to the danger of renewed price inflation. They announced a new monetary growth target late in 1979, this time for the monetary base. With the strengthening of the dollar in early 1980, they became increasingly concerned about a *decline* in quotations of the franc and announced their intention to keep it from depreciating beyond a rate of 0.95 franc per German mark.[33] By June 1980, after the National Bank had again, for a year, been targeting inflation as the number-one enemy and had been welcoming the assistance of a franc still quoted at above 60 cents, the head of its economics department predicted victory. He foresaw reduction of the inflation rate again to under 3 percent in 1981.[34]

Summary and Comment. Whether or not this optimism proves justified, Switzerland's earlier success in getting inflation down practically to zero remains on record. That success is instructive, though it probably offers little encouragement to the United States, since the Swiss enjoyed exceptionally favorable conditions. The chief source of their inflation had been identifiable, namely, the process of importing it at a fixed exchange rate, and this source was removed in a conspicuous way. Money-supply inflation was stopped and even reversed for a while. These sharp changes must have triggered a turnaround in expectations. Changed expectations were borne out by antiinflationary price developments and were reflected in declining interest rates. Exchange appreciation of the franc, restraint on or even declines in import and export prices, and abatement of general inflation interacted in a virtuous circle. The Swiss reputation for financial prudence was a favorable factor, and so, perhaps, were certain sociological conditions that supposedly held down tensions between classes and restrained propensities to grasp for narrow short-run benefits to oneself at the expense of wider interests.[35] Not least important was the opportunity to let most of the recessionary side effects of stopping inflation fall on immigrant workers rather than on the Swiss themselves.

West Germany

The German experience in overcoming the inflation spurt of 1973–1974 was similar to the Swiss and so may be reviewed more briefly. The inflation had been largely imported and was removed by floating

---

[33] Bank for International Settlements, *Fiftieth Annual Report*, 1979–1980, p. 29.

[34] *Wall Street Journal*, June 2, 1980, p. 17.

[35] On these conditions, see Küng, *Secret*, pp. 8–10.

TABLE 8

GERMAN CONSUMER PRICE LEVELS, BY QUARTERS, 1973–1974,
EXPRESSED AS PERCENTAGES OF INCREASE OVER THE LEVELS
OF ONE YEAR EARLIER

Year	Quarter	Percentage of Increase
1973	I	6.4
	II	7.3
	III	6.9
	IV	7.3
1974	I	7.4
	II	7.1
	III	7.1
	IV	6.4

SOURCE: Calculated from International Monetary Fund, *International Financial Statistics*, various issues.

the exchange rate, which permitted bringing the money supply under control. Price inflation, measured as the increase of the annual average consumer price index over the average of the year before, had run around 2 or 3 percent in the 1960s. It rose to 3.4 percent in 1970, 5.3 in 1971, 5.5 in 1972, 6.9 in 1973, and 7.0 in 1974. The largest quarter-to-quarter consumer price increases, expressed at annual rates, were 9.5 percent between the fourth quarter of 1972 and first quarter of 1973 (before the oil price shock) and 9.9 percent between the fourth quarter of 1973 and first quarter of 1974 (at the time of that shock). Table 8 shows quarterly figures for the two years of greatest price increase. (Evidently German price inflation was somewhat milder than the Swiss. A partial explanation may involve the fact that Germany revalued the mark upward in 1961 and again in 1969 and temporarily floated the mark in 1971, before the Smithsonian adjustments of 1971 and the definitive floating of 1973, while Switzerland, before then, sheltered itself against external inflationary pressures only by the slight currency revaluation of May 1971).

German consumer price inflation, measured as already indicated, declined to 5.9 percent in 1975, 4.3 percent in 1976, 3.6 percent in 1977, and 2.8 percent in 1978. (Thus, just as the disease was less extreme in Germany than in Switzerland, so the cure was somewhat less complete.) Price inflation returned in 1979, though milder than before; and by May 1980, consumer prices were running 6.0 percent above the level of one year before.

In conformity with the experiences of other countries, spurts in German money-supply growth came before the price spurts. During the 1960s, monetary growth on an annual-average-over-annual-average basis seldom exceeded 10 percent, and then only slightly, and was well below 5 percent in 1966 and 1967. Growth jumped to 12.4 percent in 1971 and 13.7 percent in 1972, dropping to 5.3 and 5.9 percent in 1973 and 1974 before rising again.

Even before the 1970s, Germany had experienced episodes of imported inflation, transmitted by translation of rising foreign prices at the fixed exchange rate and the creation of base money as the Bundesbank acquired foreign-exchange reserves.[36] The upward revaluations of the mark in March 1961 and September-October 1969 came largely as responses to this problem.

Calculations carried out by Manfred J. M. Neumann indicate that German money-supply growth of 8.6 percent a year over the period 1959–1972 was almost completely accounted for by the 8.4 percent annual growth of the monetary base. The behavior of banks and the public reflected in the money multiplier had essentially no influence on the rate of money-supply growth (although the banks did influence the monetary base and thus the money supply by their operations in foreign assets and their borrowing from the Bundesbank within quotas of rediscounts granted almost automatically). International reserve flows were by far the most important determinant of money-supply growth and of its speedups and slowdowns. This is not to say that monetary growth corresponded closely, even in the short run, with the balance-of-payments position. Policy did have some partial and temporary scope for offsetting the monetary effects of changes in international reserves. This possibility of offsetting lapsed, however, when the discrepancy between German and foreign rates of inflation became large enough to arouse widespread speculation on a correction of the fixed exchange rate.[37]

---

[36] Some of the facts and figures in this section are drawn from Leland B. Yeager, *International Monetary Relations*, 2nd ed. (New York: Harper & Row, 1976), chap. 34, and the sources cited there, including International Monetary Fund, *International Financial Statistics*.

[37] Manfred J. M. Neumann, "A Theoretical and Empirical Analysis of the German Money Supply Process," in S. F. Frowen et al., compilers, *Monetary Policy and Economic Activity in West Germany* (Stuttgart and New York: Fischer, 1977), pp. 73–124; especially pp. 94–97, 99. For further commentary on the predominantly imported character of the German inflation, see the periodic Economic Surveys, *Germany*, published in Paris by the Organisation for Economic Cooperation and Development, for example, the May 1973 issue, pp. 48, 50.

The problem became acute in the early 1970s. In the three years from the second quarter of 1970 through the first quarter of 1973, the 52-billion-mark increase in the stock of domestic reserve money was more than fully accounted for by the growth of the gold and foreign-exchange reserves of the Bundesbank, the latter growth being approximately 50 percent greater than the growth in domestic reserve money. The implication is that the German authorities were trying, but with only limited success, to sterilize the inflationary domestic monetary impact of balance-of-payments surpluses. In 1970, Germany's overall balance of payments settled by official reserve transactions shifted from a deficit of $3.0 billion to a surplus of $6.2 billion, larger than ever before (and not to be exceeded until 1973). Net capital movements shifted from heavily outward to substantially inward.

When the German authorities perceived that this shift was going further than they had desired, they responded by manipulating the banks' rediscount quotas, by complicating the system of bank reserve requirements against foreign and domestic liabilities, and by manipulating the terms offered to the banks in forward swap transactions. So far as these expedients did deter the banks from borrowing abroad to relend at home, they unintentionally led nonbank firms to borrow abroad directly. (Interest rates had been falling in the United States and the Eurodollar market during most of 1970 as the United States pursued an easy-money policy to promote recovery from the business recession.) Although the Bundesbank then felt obliged to try to narrow the excess of German over foreign interest rates by cutting its rediscount rate, it accompanied its cut of November 1970 with further rearrangements of reserve requirements that the banks apparently feared would prove restrictive. Accordingly, they brought funds home from abroad, while German corporations stepped up their borrowing in the Eurodollar market. This set off a groundswell of demand for marks. In just one week of November, the Bundesbank had to absorb more than $1 billion.[38]

The conditions of 1970 grew more intense in early 1971. Scarcely ever before, according to the Bundesbank's annual report for 1971, were monetary developments in Germany as strongly influenced by the balance of payments and by net capital imports in particular as they were then. Short-term foreign borrowing by German nonbank enterprises dominated the capital inflow, although long-term capital imports were significant also. Interest-rate incentives to move funds were increasingly accompanied by loss of confidence in the dollar's foreign-exchange value and so by speculative incentives. The Bundes-

---

[38] Yeager, *International Monetary Relations*, table on p. 504, pp. 510–511.

bank's acquisition of dollars entailed creation of domestic central-bank money and provided the basis for multiple expansion of ordinary domestic money. Speculative sales of dollars for marks grew intense on Monday, May 3, 1971. In three days, before foreign-exchange trading was suspended, the Bundesbank absorbed some $2.1 or $2.2 billion, including about 1 billion in the first forty minutes of trading on Wednesday alone. When the markets reopened on Monday, May 10, the mark was allowed to float upward.

The timing of events in 1971 testifies to the relation between the inflow of funds from abroad and the acceleration or deceleration of German monetary growth. Between January and May, when the inflows were particularly heavy, the increase in the money supply amounted to 16.3 percent at a seasonally adjusted annual rate. When capital flowed out between June and September, after the floating of the mark, the similarly measured monetary growth declined to 8.1 percent. When foreign funds began to flow back in between October and December, the growth rate rose again to 11.5 percent. During 1971 as a whole, the money supply expanded by 12.5 percent, the events of the year's first five months being chiefly responsible.[39]

After the mark was floated in May 1971, the Bundesbank acknowedged that that action had released it

> from the compulsion of having to create Central Bank money by the purchase of foreign exchange even though the internal situation requires action to the contrary. The Bundesbank thus no longer has to fear that its restrictive course in credit policy is more or less automatically undercut by money inflows from foreign countries.[40]

Trade unions reportedly moderated their wage demands in rather prompt response to the disciplining impact of the floating of the mark.[41]

Doubts about the exchange-rate structure, which had been fixed again by the Smithsonian Agreement, were again motivating inflows of funds into Germany early in 1972. Among the countermeasures introduced was a reserve requirement against the foreign borrowings of German firms. June and July brought speculative rushes out of pounds sterling and dollars into marks. To hold the exchange rate within its Smithsonian ceiling, the Bundesbank had to take in $4.5-

---

[39] Alan A. Rabin, "A Monetary View of the Acceleration of World Inflation, 1973–1974" (Ph.D. diss., University of Virginia, 1977), pp. 172–173.

[40] Monthly Report of the Deutsche Bundesbank, June 1971, p. 7, quoted in Rabin, "Monetary View," pp. 173–174.

[41] Organisation for Economic Cooperation and Development, Germany, June 1972, pp. 38–39.

billion worth of foreign currencies. Germany, like Switzerland, again tightened its capital import controls, increasing the reserve requirements against both banks' and nonbank firms' liabilities to foreigners. Incomplete success of these expedients was reflected in the already mentioned exceptional money-supply growth. In 1972, the rise in the German consumer price index was 1.5 percentage points above that of Germany's ten chief trading partners, after having been in line with the international inflation rate in 1971 and below that rate before then. Alan Rabin concludes

> that Germany's rapid growth of the money supply from 1969 on . . . had begun to take effect by 1971–1972; the inflationary trend in Germany may be attributed to the importation of inflation, since most of the rapid growth in the money supply during this period was a direct consequence of the massive capital inflows.[42]

The Swiss float late in January 1973 left the German mark the major European currency neither floating nor trading on a financial market separated from the commercial market. Buying pressure on the mark, the counterpart of bearishness on the dollar, was intense. The Bundesbank took in over $1 billion on February 1 and 2 and a further $4.9 billion the following week. Devaluation of the dollar on February 12 relieved the pressure only briefly. On March 1 alone, trying to hold the mark within its new upper limit against the dollar, the Bundesbank was forced to buy $2.7 billion, "the largest amount of foreign exchange a Central Bank has ever had to acquire within a single day to support the exchange rate."[43]

During and even before the dollar crises of 1973, the German authorities again intensified their capital controls and antiinflation efforts. The crises brought closure of official foreign-exchange markets in Europe between March 2 and March 19. When the markets reopened Germany participated with several other countries in a joint float of their currencies against the dollar. Germany revalued the mark upward by 3 percent then and by another 5.5 percent in late June, when the fixed exchange rates within the joint float came under speculative pressure.

For 1973 as a whole, Germany's overall balance-of-payments surplus measured by official settlements reached $9.2 billion, over which more than 70 percent appeared in the first quarter alone. (The year's last quarter even brought an overall deficit, attributable to transfers

---

[42] Rabin, "Monetary View," p. 182.
[43] Bundesbank, *Report* for 1972, pp. 66, quoted in Rabin, "Monetary View," pp. 182–183.

and capital movements.) With the Bundesbank no longer committed to supporting the dollar at a fixed exchange rate, growth of Germany's international reserves, domestic reserve money, and ordinary money supply was well checked after early 1973.

The Bundesbank commented in its 1973 annual report that it "now controls the creation of Central Bank money directly, whereas previously it had done so only indirectly via the free liquid reserves."[44] Free liquid reserves were the commercial banks' holdings of money-market paper, bills of exchange up to the limit of Bundesbank rediscount quotas, and—under fixed exchange rates—short-term liquid foreign assets. By selling such assets to the Bundesbank, the banks could at any time obtain the central-bank money needed for payments to other banks or for meeting their reserve requirements. Such assets, including, to repeat, liquid foreign assets, had been almost instantly convertible into domestic reserve money. Improved opportunities for borrowing from other banks abroad as well as at home had made the banks feel that they individually could adjust their reserves as needed and thus largely get around the Bundesbank's efforts to control their extensions of credit. Such circumstances enabled heavy inflows of funds from abroad to undermine antiinflationary domestic monetary and credit policy. Now, under floating, the Bundesbank no longer had to create any amount of central-bank money to support the dollar. Practically overnight, the Bundesbank regained its room for maneuver and was able to embark on a severely restrictive policy. Free liquid reserves lost their significance as a policy indicator.[45]

In 1974, the Bundesbank was able to keep the monetary base from rising beyond the extent that it considered consistent with price stability. Most of the emergency restrictions imposed from 1971 on were dismantled.[46] Although Germany's consumer price inflation rate was higher in 1973 and 1974 than it had been for many years, it sank definitely below the average rate of twelve other OECD countries. This divergence demonstrated, said the Bundesbank, "that with the help of a flexible exchange rate a country determinedly pursuing a domestic stabilization policy can—even under difficult external cir-

---

[44] Quoted by Manfred Willms, "Monetary Indicators in the Federal Republic of Germany," in Frowen, *Monetary Policy*, p. 50.

[45] Helmut Schlesinger, "Recent Developments in West German Monetary Policy," in Frowen, *Monetary Policy*, pp. 1–12. Organisation for Economic Cooperation and Development, *Germany*, May 1973, p. 55, and *Germany*, May 1974, p. 43, also comment on how the new money-management techniques precluded the earlier quasi-automatic access to domestic reserve money and greatly reduced earlier external disruptions.

[46] Rabin, "Monetary View," p. 185, citing Bundesbank, *Report* for 1974, pp. 1, 30.

cumstances—manage to detach itself from the convoy of international inflation."[47]

Despite warnings by the Bundesbank to both industry and labor that there would probably be no real economic growth in 1974, wage settlements were providing increases of about 12 percent that spring. A widely accepted prediction that the price inflation rate would rise to 10 percent in 1974 was repeated by the OECD at midyear, yet in fact the rate slackened off. These developments seemed to have a profound impact on the 1975 wage bargaining round. Representatives of the Bundesbank and the Council of Economic Experts attended the bargaining sessions. The Bundesbank warned that it would relax credit only if wage increases were substantially smaller than the previous year. Settlements were in fact held to between 6 and 7 percent, hardly more than half as large as in 1974. The Bundesbank credited this development with breaking the wage-price spiral. The more centralized character of wage bargaining in Germany than in the United States has been suggested as a factor facilitating a break in wage-price momentum.

The decline in the inflation rate in 1975 and 1976 occurred not only in Germany but also in other industrialized countries under the influence of the recession that followed the oil shock. What makes Germany (like Switzerland and also like Japan) an interesting case is that its inflation rate continued to decline in the ensuing business recovery, while it climbed again in the United States and other countries.

Germany's struggle against inflation benefited from a virtuous circle like the one already described for Switzerland. The mark appreciated further against other currencies than could be accounted for by current inflation differentials (as distinguished from expectations of *future* relative purchasing powers); it briefly passed 58 U.S. cents late in October 1978. This appreciation helped keep down import prices—their index actually fell 1.7 percent between 1974 and 1975 and 5.2 percent between 1977 and 1978—and restrain the rise in export prices, which contributed to maintaining the mark's overall purchasing power and to enhancing its image among investors as a stable currency.

The income velocity of money after 1974 behaved contrary to the way one might have expected (and the Bundesbank had expected). Instead of rising during the recovery from recession, as in the United States, velocity fell (to about 13.5 percent lower in 1979 than it had been five years earlier, as calculated from International Monetary Fund, *International Financial Statistics*). This decline kept a given

---

[47] Bundesbank, *Report* for 1974, p. 54, quoted in Rabin, "Monetary View," p. 186.

amount of monetary expansion less inflationary than it otherwise would have been. The Bundesbank offered a number of explanations for what was, in other words, an increase in the relative demand for money, including the influence of lower interest rates and lower expectations of inflation. Another suggestion notes, in addition, the growing use of the German mark as a store of value or reserve currency abroad, especially in East Germany.

The cost to Germany of reducing inflation is hard to evaluate. The gross national product at constant prices rose only 0.4 percent from 1973 to 1974, fell 1.9 percent in 1975, and on the same year-to-year basis rose 5.1, 2.6, 3.5, and 4.4 percent in the four following years. As usual, annual average industrial production showed sharper fluctuations. It fell 2.3 percent between 1973 and 1974, fell a further 6.1 percent in 1975, and then rose by 7.3, 2.5, 2.6, and 5.2 percent in the four following years. Industrial employment actually fell every year after 1970 and through 1978, except only for one insignificant rise. Evidently reflecting structural as well as cyclical changes, it was 12.5 percent lower in 1978 than in 1973.[48] The unemployment rate, which before 1973 never exceeded the 2.6 percent reached in the 1966–1967 recession, hovered around 4 or 5 percent in the new recession. The Bundesbank cited supposed structural reasons for this relatively high unemployment rate, including the fact that foreign workers were not leaving the country on such a scale as in the past.

The construction industry suffered particularly from the recession, following a housing boom in 1973 that the Bundesbank had attributed to an inflation mentality and the attendant desire to hold real assets. As the Bundesbank's antiinflationary measures began to bite, other structural problems that had been veiled over by inflation came to light. Not only construction but also the motor and textile industries were hard hit. Many smaller inadequately capitalized firms also suffered when interest rates climbed as steeply as they did in 1973. The Bundesbank had no real way of using its policy instruments selectively to ease the sectorally uneven pains of making the adjustment away from an inflationary boom.[49]

The recession was not entirely the result of Germany's anti-inflation policy, of course, as the recession's worldwide character and the role of the oil shock testify. During the subsequent recovery,

---

[48] Calculated from International Monetary Fund, *International Financial Statistics*, July 1980, pp. 160, 162; International Monetary Fund, *International Financial Statistics Yearbook, 1979*, pp. 191, 193.

[49] Helmut Schlesinger, "Recent Developments," in Frowen, *Monetary Policy*, pp. 11–12. Schlesinger maintains that there was no alternative that would be satisfactory in the long run to the course actually followed.

Germany incurred some criticism abroad for its alleged failure to do its full share as a "locomotive" of growth in pulling the world economy upward.

After coming so close to complete success in wringing inflation out of the economy—consumer prices averaged only 2.2 percent higher than one year before in the fourth quarter of 1978—Germany, like Switzerland, gave indications of throwing its success away. German consumer prices averaged 3.2 percent above their level of one year before in the first half of 1979 and 5.1 percent higher in the second half; by May 1980, they were 6.0 percent higher. Between the fourth quarter of 1979 and the first quarter of 1980, they were rising at a 7.3 percent annual rate. As usual, this change in the price trend had been preceded by a speedup in money-supply growth. After having been brought below 6 percent in 1973 and 1974, the growth rate, calculated as the change between the preceding and current annual averages, amounted to 14.1, 10.2, 8.3, and 13.8 percent in the four following years. Furthermore, between the end of 1974 and the middle of 1979, the growth of domestic reserve money was matched to the extent of 47.0 percent by growth in the foreign assets of the Bundesbank. In the second half of 1978, a year of renewed rapid monetary growth, growth of the Bundesbank's foreign assets equaled 76.8 percent of the growth of domestic reserve money.

Market intervention to check the rise of the mark has thus at times led to substantial growth of international reserves and domestic high-powered money, causing the Bundesbank to overshoot its money-growth targets. Floating has by no means been complete and free. The mark is tied at fixed exchange rates to the currencies of the other members of the "snake," now reorganized as the European Monetary System; and intervention even on the dollar rate has been heavy at times. Thus, while enjoying a greater degree of independence from external factors than they had before 1973, the German authorities have by no means been using that independence fully.

Possibly connected with the renewed rapid monetary expansion, Germany experienced a strong business expansion in 1979, with investment in plants and equipment in the vanguard. The growth of nominal spending might well have gone more into prices and less into real activity than it did in fact, had it not been for earlier success in wringing out the basis of inflationary expectations. The president of the Bundesbank maintained that Germany was economically much better off than other countries because of its earlier and more energetic fight against inflation.[50]

---

[50] *Business Week*, July 2, 1979, p. 40.

Furthermore, signs appeared in 1979 that the German authorities were again devoting priority attention to inflation and the money supply, allowing interest rates to rise, and, far from struggling as before to hold down the mark's exchange rate, were welcoming a strong mark as an aid in containing price increases.[51] Increases in the money supply from one year earlier were down to 6.2 and 4.1 percent in the third and fourth quarters of 1979.

Summary and Comment. Regardless of the outcome, the earlier success in reducing the inflation rate to scarcely above 2 percent remains instructive. Germany, like Switzerland, had the advantage of being able to discontinue, and in a conspicuous way, the earlier contagion of foreign inflation under fixed exchange rates. The switch to floating against the dollar made possible a sharp tightening of money and credit in 1973. The Bundesbank's warning that it would loosen credit only if inflation were brought under control lent credibility to the new policy and helped reverse inflationary expectations. A virtuous circle of interaction among exchange-rate appreciation, price restraint, and expectations of stability was at work. Other factors, as Wolfgang Kasper explains, have also influenced German attitudes. Voters and statesmen are more alert to the dangers of inflation in Germany than in other countries. They remember how private financial assets were wiped out in the hyperinflation of 1922–1923 and the repressed inflation of 1936–1948. Unemployment, on the other hand, has been a less dominant fear in Germany than in most other western countries. Germany enjoyed a positive experience with externally propelled growth in the 1950s. Accordingly, German policy makers and labor union leaders have been more willing than their counterparts abroad to sacrifice the marginal bit of growth or of wage increase today to gain more price level stability and, in the longer run, more growth and higher real wages.[52]

Japan

Imported inflation and its removal were an element in the Japanese experience of the 1970s, although a less dominant one than in the experiences of Switzerland and Germany. Being not so much a pure case of a particular type, the Japanese case perhaps has a lesser claim on our attention. Nevertheless, Japan's impressive turnaround from an

---

[51] *Business Week*, July 2, 1979, p. 40; idem, November 12, 1979, p. 112; *Wall Street Journal*, May 30, 1980, p. 20.

[52] Wolfgang Kasper in Emil Claassen and Pascal Salin, eds., *Stabilization Policies in Interdependent Economies* (New York: American Elsevier, 1972), p. 271.

inflation more severe than Switzerland's and Germany's does deserve notice.

Japan's consumer price inflation had been running at a rate of 5 or 6 or 7 percent in the 1960s and through 1972; the average rate over the period 1965–1971 was 5.6 percent a year. Increases in wholesale and traded-goods prices had been much smaller over the same period, averaging 1.7 percent for the wholesale index, 1.5 percent for export prices, 1.2 percent for import prices, and 4.7 percent for the GNP deflator. (The spread between the trends of consumer and other prices was attributable to the skewing of Japanese economic growth in favor of sectors where productivity was rising particularly rapidly. The vigor and pattern of Japanese growth, including high rates of saving and investment and improvement in labor productivity, permitted wage increases that would have been "explosive" in other countries.) In 1973, 1974, and 1975, however, increases from the year before in the consumer price index reached 11.8, 24.3, and 11.9 percent. In each quarter of 1974, consumer prices ranged from 22 to 24 percent above the level of one year before. Then inflation was rapidly reduced. In the first and second quarters of 1975, consumer prices were only 14.9 and 13.8 percent above year-earlier levels. By the first quarter of 1979, the one-year increase was down to 2.7 percent; and for the year as a whole, the increase averaged 3.6 percent. (The inflation rate rose again after early 1979.) Wholesale prices were actually below year-earlier levels in 1978, and export and import prices were below year-earlier levels in both 1977 and 1978.[53]

Changes in money-supply growth presaged these changes in the inflation rate. The growth rate on a year-to-year basis had been 16 percent, plus or minus a couple of points, in the late 1960s. It rose to 25.5, 22.1, and 26.1 percent in 1971, 1972, and 1973, then fell sharply to the low double-digit range and to 7.0 percent in 1977 (rising again to around 10 percent in 1978 and 1979). Looking within years, we see that the monetary slowdown began in the first quarter of 1973, when the growth was insignificantly negative; the year ended with the money supply only 16.8 percent above the end-of-1972 level.

The chief cause of monetary expansion in 1971 was Japan's massive balance-of-payments surplus. The external sector was the only contributor to creating domestic reserve money. In nominal money

---

[53] Organisation for Economic Cooperation and Development, *Japan* (Paris, July 1974), table on p. 6; International Monetary Fund, *International Financial Statistics*, various issues. On the divergence between consumer and other price trends, see Yeager, *Monetary Relations*, chap. 25, and the sources cited there, as well as Organisation for Economic Cooperation and Development, *Japan*, July 1973, pp. 64–65.

terms, only the United States in the exceptional circumstances of 1947 had ever recorded larger surpluses on trade and current account. These large surpluses strengthened the general impression that the yen was undervalued and so helped trigger successive waves of speculative inflows of short-term funds—some $5½ billion during the year—despite the tightening of stringent exchange controls. Some $3¾ billion entered in the third quarter of 1971 alone, mainly in the form of advance payments for exports and bank borrowings in foreign currencies. In August, the Bank of Japan continued supporting the dollar at its official parity for two weeks after other major central banks suspended this pegging. Japan's overall (official-settlements) surplus of about $10.3 billion in 1971 was the largest in nominal terms then recorded by any country, and holdings of net foreign assets more than tripled.[54]

The Japanese authorities tried to sterilize most but not all of the monetary impact of the foreign-exchange gains of 1971. Apparently they welcomed monetary ease to help overcome the "Japanese style" or "growth" recession into which the economy had slipped in the second half of 1970. Monetary and credit policy remained easy during the first half of 1972 and beyond. The reserve money generated by the balance-of-payments surplus was allowed to affect the money supply. One reason was official concern about the slowness of the business recovery; another was concern about the continuing payments surplus, coupled with some notion of playing by the "rules of the game."[55]

From the fall of 1972, the rapid absorption of economic slack, sharply rising prices abroad, and the spread of inflationary expectations at home shifted the focus of policy. (The Japanese were thus tardier than the Swiss and the Germans in making inflation their prime concern.) The first official signal of a change in policy came in January 1973, when "window guidance" (moral suasion) regarding bank-credit expansion was resumed and reserve requirements on domestic deposits were raised. The floating of the yen in February 1973, two weeks before the entire system of fixed exchange rates finally broke down, in principle eliminated interference through the balance of payments with the progressively tightening domestic monetary and credit policy. The developments of the two preceding years had so

---

[54] Organisation for Economic Cooperation and Development, *Japan*, June 1972, pp. 21–23, 31, 33; Allan A. Rabin, "A Monetary View of the Acceleration of World Inflation, 1973–1974" (Ph. D. diss., University of Virginia, 1977), pp. 220, 272.

[55] Organisation for Economic Cooperation and Development, *Japan*, July 1973, pp. 15, 18, 63; Rabin, "Monetary View," pp. 218, 220, 223, 272.

gorged the economy with liquidity, however, that the intended restraint on spending did not appear until after around the end of 1973.[56] The oil crisis also obviously delayed any deceleration of prices.

The authorities acted to stimulate the supply side of the economy by encouraging imports, partly under outside pressure to do something about Japan's large balance-of-payments surplus. (Under the changed circumstances of 1973, the balance in fact shrank nearly to zero on goods-and-services account and turned to an overall deficit of about $6 billion as measured by official settlements.) Import duties were cut 20 percent across the board. A campaign against hoarding goods was instituted, and price controls were imposed on fifty-three commodities at the wholesale level. Wage controls, however, were politically excluded.

Exchange appreciation of the yen evidently helped restrain price inflation. Shortly after the float began, the yen appreciated to about 16 percent above its Smithsonian central rate and about 36 percent above its pre-1971 parity. The yen had spells of weakness, too, as during the oil crisis in early 1974. Briefly, late in October 1978, the yen reached twice the value against the dollar of its pre-1971 parity.

The remarkable slowdown in consumer price inflation and the actual decline in wholesale prices during 1977 and the first quarter of 1978 seemed linked to appreciation of the yen. OECD economists offered the following interpretation:

> The downward movement of wholesale prices can largely be ascribed to the sizeable decline in import prices resulting from the marked appreciation of the yen and relatively stable international commodity market conditions. In March 1978, the import price index of the Bank of Japan was down 14.7 percent from twelve months earlier, due largely to the 21.1 percent revaluation of the yen against the dollar over the same period. According to an estimate by the Bank of Japan, in the year to March 1978, the direct negative contribution of the revaluation on wholesale prices amounted to 2.4 percentage points, without allowing for indirect effects on domestic prices.[57]

The side effects of nearly stopping inflation did not seem severe. On a year-to-year basis, gross national product at constant prices declined only in 1974, by 0.6 percent; and industrial production declined only in 1974 and 1975, by 4.0 percent and then by a further 11.0

---

[56] Organisation for Economic Cooperation and Development, *Japan*, July 1973, p. 5; idem, *Japan*, July 1974, pp. 32–34, 56.

[57] Organisation for Economic Cooperation and Development, *Japan*, July 1978, p. 18.

percent. In view of Japan's earlier record of strong growth, however, these declines were more severe than the bare figures suggest. From the preceding to the current quarter, GNP at constant prices declined only in the first quarters of both 1974 and 1975, by 3.0 and 0.3 percent (that is, at 11.5 and 1.0 percent annual rates). Seasonally adjusted industrial production declined throughout 1974 and into 1975; the trough in the first quarter of 1975 was 19.7 percent below the peak in the fourth quarter of 1973 (thus, the decline amounted to 16.1 percent at an annual rate). Manufacturing employment appeared to be in a mild long-run downtrend. The unemployment rate did not go as high as 2.2 percent until around the end of 1975, when business recovery was already under way. Reported unemployment figures, however, are misleading. The tradition of lifetime employment led large Japanese firms to curtail overtime work and make other adjustments to keep workers on the payroll who would have been laid off under the employment systems of other countries. Furthermore, the government granted wage subsidies to promote the stockpiling of workers, so to speak, instead of layoffs. Correspondingly, when business activity recovered, reported employment did not rise in step.

As in Switzerland and Germany, price inflation began increasing again in Japan in 1979. By April 1980, consumer prices were 8.4 percent above the level of one year before.

Summary and Comment. A number of special conditions contributed to Japan's earlier success. Although Japan's chronic consumer price inflation was hardly attributable to an international transmission mechanism,[58] such a mechanism did play a role in a money-supply spurt followed by a spurt of the inflation rate to above 20 percent (and even briefly to 36 percent in wholesale prices). That very spurt (like, for example, the spurts of inflation in France in 1926 and Italy in 1947) must have made people ready to believe that something had to be done and that a meaningful change in policy could be expected. The floating of the yen in February 1973 broke the mechanism of imported inflation, and domestic monetary and credit policy shifted toward tightness at about the same time.

The appreciation of the floating yen, coming in addition to the upward revaluation stipulated in the Smithsonian Agreement, not

---

[58] On the other hand, an argument could be made centering around the linkage of Japanese and world-market *wholesale* prices at a fixed exchange rate, together with the structural divergence between Japanese wholesale and consumer price trends. Gottfried Haberler has explained such an "inflation-transmission multiplier" in several publications, including *A New Look at Inflation* (Washington, D.C.: American Enterprise Institute, 1973), pp. 90–95.

only had its mechanical effect in restraining prices but also presumably signaled a change in conditions that people would take into account in forming their expectations. Political events reportedly helped lend credibility to the government's pronouncements about antiinflation policy. Premier Tanaka appointed the fiscally conservative Fukuda as finance minister late in 1973 (even though the two had had opposing views on economic policy),[59] and Tanaka's resignation in 1974 brought Fukuda to the directorship of the Economic Planning Agency and later to the premiership.

Institutional conditions were favorable to an antiinflation program and to avoiding side effects so concentrated as to arouse strong resistance. (Recognizing this is not enough, of course, to warrant an overall favorable judgment about those conditions.) Government, business, and labor traditionally cooperate more closely in Japan than in the United States. Moderation in pricing policies and wage demands helped make the deceleration of spending bite more on price trends and less on real activity than would otherwise have happened. Japan's practice of lifetime employment gives workers a stake in the future of their firms, and Japanese labor unions are organized at the company level rather than the industry level. Lifetime employment policies and the stockpiling of actually redundant workers helped spread around and dilute the side effects that might otherwise have aroused resistance and might have caused the authorities to lose their nerve in pursuing antiinflation policy. (This circumstance may be regarded as the Japanese counterpart of the Swiss opportunity to send redundant foreign workers home.) In short, Japan stopped inflation under conditions quite different from those that the United States faces nowadays.

Singapore

The experience of Singapore helps show that even inflations running at substantial double-digit rates can be stopped quickly provided they have not been allowed to become entrenched for many years. It bears some resemblance to Swiss, German, and Japanese experience, but the price deceleration was quicker.

As table 9 shows, Singapore's price-level increases were remarkably mild until 1973 and 1974. Then the inflation rate rose to over 20 percent. The percentage rise in the consumer price index over twelve-month periods peaked in March 1974 at about 34 percent. Price deceleration then came rapidly, and in December 1974 consumer prices

---

[59] The significance of this appointment is stressed in *International Currency Review*, November-December 1973, p. 58.

TABLE 9

Consumer Price Index and Money Supply in Singapore, 1966–1978

Year	Percentage Change from Preceding Year's Average		Percentage Change in Money Supply from End of Preceding to End of Current Year
	Price index	Money supply	
1966	1.9	6.5	14.1
1967	3.3	5.0	−2.1
1968	0.7	10.8	21.4
1969	−0.2	17.8	18.5
1970	0.3	16.4	15.1
1971	1.8	13.4	7.9*
1972	2.1	24.2	35.5
1973	26.5	24.8	10.4
1974	22.3	7.4	8.6
1975	2.6	18.6	21.5
1976	−1.9	18.1	15.2
1977	3.3	10.5	10.3
1978	4.7	11.7	11.7

* Figure unreliable because of break in underlying series

Source: From and calculated from International Monetary Fund, *International Financial Statistics Yearbook*, 1979, pp. 57, 61, 365.

stood only 13 percent above the level of one year before.[60] Consumer prices increased only modestly in 1975 and even declined on average in 1976.[61]

The Singapore authorities blamed the sharp price increases largely on the soaring prices of imports, particularly of oil in the first quarter of 1974.[62] Annual-average unit values of imports did rise

---

[60] Singapore, Ministry of Finance, *Economic Survey*, 1974, pp. 22, 25.

[61] However, the Singapore government has been persuasively accused of doctoring its statistics. The impression was widespread that the cost of living was actually rising in 1973—thus before the oil shock—at a rate of 35 to 40 percent. Furthermore, price indexes were not the only figures allegedly doctored. The Tourist Promotion Board, for example, was accused of publishing falsely high hotel occupancy rates in 1974. Tony Patrick, "The Good Ship of Singapore," *Far Eastern Economic Review*, July 22, 1974, p. 49; *Asia Yearbook* (Hong Kong: Far Eastern Economic Review, 1974), p. 274; "Pleas Fall on Deaf Ears," *Far Eastern Economic Review*, August 9, 1974, p. 36. Still, it is doubtful that the price figures are so wrong as to invalidate the qualitative proposition that Singapore suffered two years of high price inflation flanked by periods of near-stability.

[62] Monetary Authority of Singapore, *Quarterly Bulletin*, September 1973, p. 1; idem, *Quarterly Bulletin*. First Quarter 1974, p. 5; *Asia Yearbook* (Hong Kong: Far Eastern Economic Review, 1977), pp. 277–278.

by 15.0 percent in 1973 and 44.9 percent in 1974, but only mildly thereafter.

The money supply and exchange rate also deserve attention. As table 9 also shows, Singapore experienced two years of exceptionally high monetary growth, which came just before the years of greatest price inflation. In the first quarter of 1973, money expanded at a 36 percent annual rate; in the second quarter, after some liquidity-tightening steps had been taken and with an adjustment made for termination of the currency-interchangeability arrangement with Malaysia, the growth rate was 31 percent.[63] Throughout the 1970s (through 1978, anyway), the growth in the foreign assets of the monetary authorities was consistently much larger than—sometimes several times as large as—the growth in domestic reserve money; the growth in government deposits was partially sterilizing the domestic monetary impact of the growth in foreign assets.[64] These facts, considered along with the push from import prices and the qualitatively similar experiences of many other countries around the same time, suggest that Singapore's inflation of 1973 and 1974 was largely imported from abroad.

The floating of the Singapore dollar late in June 1973 helped reduce the influence of the external sector on monetary growth and reinforced other strands of antiinflation policy, such as government budget surplus, a rise in bank reserve requirements, and a special deposit requirement of 9 percent of banks' net foreign liabilities.[65]

The government continued to restrain wages despite a labor shortage. It recommended through the National Wages Council (an organization composed of representatives of labor, management, and government that substitutes for direct wage bargaining between workers and employers) that wage increases be limited to 9 percent in 1973. To ease the labor shortage, the government allowed and even encouraged the importation of foreign labor, mostly from Malaysia. The Housing Development Board, for example, required that all contractors bidding on its projects in 1973 recruit specified minimum percentages of foreign workers.[66]

---

[63] Monetary Authority of Singapore, *Quarterly Bulletin*, September 1973, p. 1.

[64] International Monetary Fund, *International Financial Statistics Yearbook*, 1979, p. 365.

[65] Monetary Authority of Singapore, *Quarterly Bulletin*, Third Quarter 1973, p. 4; idem, *Quarterly Bulletin*, Fourth Quarter 1973, p. 4; *Asia Yearbook*, 1974, p. 274. From the end of 1972 to mid-1973, the Singapore dollar appreciated 19.5 percent against the U.S. dollar.

[66] *Asia Yearbook*, 1974, p. 274. Evidence on the submissiveness of the labor movement to government influence appears in ibid., pp. 264–266; "Grumbling But Little Action," *Far Eastern Economic Review*, August 9, 1974, pp. 17–18; and

In the first quarter of 1974, the government supplemented the antiinflationary tight-money policy with removal of import duties on certain essential items and with accumulation of government food stocks for the purpose, in the words of the deputy premier, of getting "through the troublesome period ahead without being held ransom by profiteers."[67] Later in 1974 and in 1975, as price inflation abated and as signs of contagion of the world recession appeared, with the creation of new jobs in Singapore falling off, the government shifted its emphasis in monetary and credit policy from a general squeeze to more selective credit controls favoring priority sectors of the economy, including the export sector, and enforced through monitoring of bank lending. Singapore's dual system of domestic and foreign banks was supposedly amenable to this sort of monitoring.

The diversified nature of Singapore's economy partly cushioned its vulnerability to business fluctuations abroad. In the second half of 1974 and in 1975, growth in the services sector offset the decline in manufacturing and external trade.[68] Annual figures of gross domestic product at constant prices exhibit no actual decline, although growth was as small as 4.1 percent between 1974 and 1975. Recession shows up hardly at all in official annual unemployment rates.[69]

Summary and Comments. Singapore's experience rested on untypically favorable circumstances. The rather obvious imported nature of the inflation, followed by partial removal of the mechanism of transmission at fixed exchange rates, helped give the inflation more the character of a one-time shift to a higher price *level* than of an entrenched and continuing process. Its dual character made the banking system relatively amenable to official monitoring. The cooperation practiced between the National Trade Union Congress and the ruling People's Action Party facilitated policies of wage restraint. Being quasi-authoritarian and firmly entrenched, the government was relatively free of short-run political considerations. The character of the government presumably also enabled the public to form expectations of a more consistently and durably noninflationary policy than might otherwise have been followed. In short, Singapore's experience, because of the very contrast that it offers, provides some insight into the problems posed by a long-entrenched inflation. Its experience again illustrates the importance of the political factor.

Stanley S. Bedlington, *Malaysia and Singapore: The Building of New States* (Ithaca: Cornell University Press, 1978), p. 246.

[67] *Asia Yearbook*, 1975, p. 273.

[68] Singapore, Ministry of Finance, *Economic Survey of Singapore*, 1975, p. 1.

[69] Singapore, Ministry of Finance, *Economic Survey of Singapore*, 1977, p. 44.

6

Conclusion

A summary section can and should be brief, especially as summaries or lessons followed the reviews of most of the individual historical episodes. Because these episodes were not chosen by random sampling from the complete universe of monetary history, as well as for other reasons, they cannot actually prove anything. They do offer some support, though, for the concepts set forth in the introductory theoretical section: (1) the momentum of inflation and its catch-up and expectational elements; (2) reasons why this momentum threatens recessionary side effects from an antiinflationary monetary-fiscal policy; (3) reasons why it may be easier and less painful to stop an extreme inflation than a moderate but long-entrenched one; (4) reasons why it may be relatively easy to stop an inflation due to war, importation from abroad, or some similarly clearcut and removable source; and (5) the role of turning expectations around in breaking the momentum of inflation, and the political element that has often apparently conditioned expectations.

The theory and history that we have reviewed suggest that inflation of the intermediate degree and long duration currently being suffered by the United States is particularly difficult to stop. Is the only possible implication one of sheer despair? Must we reach or cross the brink of hyperinflation before restoring monetary stability?

The fact (if it is a fact) that long-lasting inflation never has been stopped in its intermediate stage does not prove that the feat is impossible. Understanding the difficulties, illuminated by historical experience, is prerequisite, though, to figuring out how to overcome them. Historical review of stabilization programs brings to mind policy measures that might be adopted in different circumstances or combined in new ways. Furthermore, frustration in finding examples of success in conditions closely resembling those of the United States today leads naturally into theorizing about new types of stabilization program.

Indexing has sometimes been recommended as an ingredient of a program aimed at gradual rather than quick stabilization. Contracts and schedules extending over some period of time, such as ones concerning loans, rents, taxes, and wage rates, would be denominated in dollars of constant purchasing power as defined with reference to some price index. Carried to an extreme, indexing might even extend to the prices of goods and services not entering into contracts over some span of time. (Whether such comprehensive indexing is an internally consistent idea or, on the contrary, would be parasitical on other prices remaining unindexed is too complicated a question to tackle here.)

Herbert Giersch argues that indexing of loans would help reduce distortions in the structure of prices and production that originate in a flight from money into real assets. With money no longer functioning as a store of value, investors turn to gold, land, houses, and condominium apartments. If the supply of these assets reponds to the rise in their relative prices, then real productive resources are channeled into producing such "concrete gold." Loans with escalator clauses, however, do serve as a store of value and so can help avoid an inflation-induced building boom. The more widely loans with escalator clauses are introduced, the less likely will a stabilization program be to cause a collapse in the construction industry.[1]

Milton Friedman also argues for indexing, particularly of wages, to lessen the side effects of stopping inflation. In the absence of indexing, an initially unexpected tapering off of price inflation would raise *real* wages because nominal wages had been set high enough in the first place or had been scheduled to rise over time to allow for the persistence of inflationary momentum. Employment would accordingly suffer. Indexing would in effect set wages in real terms in the first place and so avoid their excessive rise. For Friedman, indexing is thus a way of hastening the translation of a money-supply deceleration into cost and price deceleration. William Fellner, for one, is skeptical. Instead of assuming that monetary growth will be tapered off, he worries that it will be made to accommodate a worsening inflation. Indexing would facilitate wage-price interaction, steepening the uptrend and tempting the monetary authorities all the more to accommodate this process for fear of otherwise touching off a recession.[2]

---

[1] Giersch in Giersch et al., *Essays On Inflation and Indexation* (Washington, D.C.: American Enterprise Institute, 1974), pp. 7–8.

[2] At least this is how one might interpret the main points of Friedman and

Alexandre Kafka recognizes that indexing may help avoid the textbook inequities and distortions of inflation, including discouragement to saving and discouragement to production in sectors with lagging prices. Indexing proved helpful to Brazilian public finance by helping to maintain the profitability of government enterprises, rationalize the tax system, and facilitate government borrowing on the market. By institutionalizing protection against inflation, indexing may discourage income or price demands made big enough in nominal terms to allow for inflation with a margin to spare; this would facilitate tapering off inflation without causing recession.

On the other hand, Kafka expressed worries similar to Fellner's. Economic developments tending to benefit some sectors at the expense of others tend to be translated by indexing into a general rise in nominal prices and incomes. The more sectors are shielded from the effects of inflation, the fewer are left to absorb them. Indexing creates feedback effects from yesterday's inflation to today's. It means linking some magnitudes to others, which implies either linkage to past events or reliance on estimates of the present or future. Both lags and estimates can result in misleading signals. Attempts to avoid them may bring changes in the formula linking current to past magnitudes or deliberate allowances in estimated magnitudes; judgment thus displaces supposed objectivity. Not only unindexed ragged inflation but also partial indexing may cause distortions in relative prices; so may simultaneous use of two or more indexes constructed by different formulas.[3]

Widespread indexing introduces something other than the ordinary dollar as a unit of accounting, pricing, and wage setting. That other unit is a dollar of constant purchasing power as defined with respect to the specified index. Recognizing this prompts us to consider the idea of alternative money units more explicitly. These might be used in parallel with, or eventually might displace, the inflation-plagued national currency. Possibilities include gold units, foreign currencies, composites of national units defined in such a way as to have stable purchasing power, or even fiat moneys issued by private banks under competitive pressures to keep their units stable in value.[4]

Could a parallel, optional gold standard work? Once gold had

Fellner. Their articles are reprinted in David C. Colander, ed., *Solutions to Inflation* (New York: Harcourt Brace Jovanovich, 1979).

[3] *Essays on Inflation and Indexation*, pp. 71–98.

[4] On the last two possibilities, see Jacques Riboud, *Une Monnaie pour l'Europe: L'Eurostable* (Paris: Éditions de la R.P.P., 1975); *Eurostable*, Bulletin du Centre Jouffroy pour la Réflexion Monétaire, March-April, 1977, and F. A. von Hayek, *Denationalisation of Money*, 2nd ed. (London: Institute of Economic Affairs, 1978).

somehow already come into widespread use as money, it might well be that the nature of the demand for money—a demand for *real* balances—would exert a stabilizing influence on the value of gold. But how could gold attain that position? As long as it remained predominantly a speculative commodity and its value in terms of other goods and services remained unstable for that reason, gold would prove an unsatisfactory money for the people who might otherwise go first in using it as a unit of account and medium of exchange. Although gold, once in general use as money, might well prove more satisfactory than government money, it might well prove to be to almost no one's advantage to take the first steps toward that general use. How to accomplish the transition does seem to be a major problem.

Adoption of competing private moneys, mentioned above, would also seem to give rise to a transition problem. Suppose, setting aside doubts similar to those mentioned for gold, that such moneys could develop into genuine alternatives to dollars. Their expected stability in purchasing power would lead holders to dump dollars to acquire them instead, causing the dollar to depreciate even more sharply in real value than it had been doing. How, then, could competing moneys come into widespread use without further victimizing people holding claims denominated in dollars? Once parallel moneys had somehow come into widespread use and were competing for users even within the same geographical area, as the proposal envisages, would not their holders and prospective holders be sensitive to changing assessments of their issuers' policies and thus of their prospective future purchasing powers? With the cash-balance demands for the rival currencies being so sensitive, would not the exchange rates between them, as well as their purchasing powers, prove quite jumpy? Would not this circumstance defeat the very purpose of the proposal?

This is no place for going into further detail on alternative monetary systems. The existence of such proposals suggests, however, one silver lining to the current inflation problem: It has spurred some original monetary theorizing.

Index

Exports: Argentina, 138; Bolivia, 112; Czechoslovakia, 84; exchange rate and imported inflation, 8; Germany, 63–64, 163; Italy, 105, 107; Japan, 167; Paraguay, 120–22, 126; Switzerland, 142, 154, 156

Federal Council (Switzerland), 148, 154–55
Federal Reserve Bank (Minneapolis), 38
Federal Reserve Bank (New York), 92
Federal Reserve Board, 11, 31
Fellner, William, 176–77
Feltenstein, Andrew, 139
Finland, 41
Foa, Bruno, 106
Foreign exchange, 5; Argentina, 129, 133, 135, 139; Austria, 46, 50–51; Bolivia, 113–15; Colombia, 79; Czechoslovakia, 85; France, 90, 94–95; Germany, 61, 63–64, 158–60; Italy, 104–05; Japan, 168; Paraguay, 120–22; Poland, 70; Russia, 77; Switzerland, 143, 146–50, 152
Foreign workers: France, 95; Singapore, 173; Switzerland, 151, 156, 171; West Germany, 164
France, 47, 84, 170; inflation and stabilization (1920s), 32–33, 43, 85–96
Friedman, Irving S., 42
Friedman, Milton, 176
Frondizi government, 131–32, 134

García Martinez, Carlos, 130, 134
de Gasperi government, 100
Gehrig, Bruno, 145
Geneva protocols: Austria, 49; Hungary, 54
Gerber, Beat, 145
Germany, 47, 51, 67, 70, 84, 170–71; inflation and stabilization efforts (1920s), 4–5, 12–13, 31–32, 43; inflation and stabilization efforts (1970s), 32–34, 157–68. See also East Germany
Giersch, Herbert, 176
GNP. See Gross national product (GNP)
Gold standard: Colombia, 78–79; Czechoslovakia, 80–81; France, 95; Germany, 57–59, 61–62, 64, 66; Great Britain, 85, 90; and indexing, 177–78; Poland, 71
Government Petroleum Corporation (Bolivia), 115
Grabski, Wladyslaw, 68–70, 72
Graft. See Political conditions
Great Britain, 47, 85, 90

Gross national product (GNP): Argentina, 138; Bolivia, 117–18; Germany, 164; Italy, 105–06; Japan, 169–70; Paraguay, 122, 124; Switzerland, 150

Haberler, Gottfried, 15–16, 31
Habits. See Distortion
Havenstein, Rudolf, 13, 56, 59, 67
Hegedüs, Dr. Roland, 53
Helfferich, Karl, 12, 58
Herriot government, 90, 93
Hicks, J. R., 3
Hildebrand, George H., 105, 107
Hoarding. See Distortion
Housing, 128–29
Housing Development Board (Singapore), 173
Hungarian National Bank, 54, 111
Hungary: inflation and stabilization efforts (1920s), 51–55

IAPI. See Instituto Argentino de Promoción del Intercambio (IAPI)
IMF. See International Monetary Fund (IMF)
Imports: Bolivia, 110, 112–13, 118; exchange rate and imported inflation, 8–9; Germany, 63, 163; Japan, 167, 169; Paraguay, 121–22; Singapore, 172–74; Switzerland, 142, 145, 149–50, 156
Indexing, 176–77
Industrial Bank (Argentina), 131
Industrial production. See Production
Instituto Argentino de Promoción del Intercambio (IAPI), 128, 130
Inter-American Development Bank, 124
Inter-Ministerial Committee on Credit and Saving, 100
Interest groups. See Social conditions
Interest rate: distortion, 2, 4, 23; France, 89; Germany, 159, 163–64, 166; Italy, 106; money supply and, 164; social conditions, 31; Switzerland, 142, 144–47, 152–56
International Monetary Fund (IMF), 163; aid to Argentina, 132–33, 137; aid to Bolivia, 112–16; aid to Paraguay, 120–21
Inventories: Italy, 99, 105, 107; Paraguay, 122; stabilization on, effect of, 5
Investment: Argentina, 127, 132; distortion, 5, 23, 38, 65; France, 88; Germany, 165; Italy, 107; Japan, 167; Paraguay, 122; Switzerland, 142–47, 152

Italy, 47; inflation and stabilization efforts (1940s), 33, 98–107, 170

Japan: inflation and stabilization (1970s), 166–71
Johnson, Harry, 7
Kafka, Alexandre, 23, 38, 41, 177
Karasz, Arthur, 111
Kasper, Wolfgang, 166
Kemmerer, Edwin, 71, 112
Kennedy, John, 16

Küng, Emil, 150

Labor unions: cost-of-living index, 3, 16–17, 24–25; France, 96; Germany, 65, 160, 166; Japan, 171; Latin America, 17; US, 17, 96
Latin America: cost-of-living index, 16–17; deficits, 7–9; inflation controls, 34–35; money supply, 7–8; multiple exchange rate, 9–10; state enterprise, 7–8. *See also specific countries*
Latin Monetary Union, 69
League of Nations: and Austria, 47, 51, 53; Geneva protocols, 49, 54; and Hungary, 47, 52–55; and Poland, 69
Lechín Oquendo, Juan, 114, 116
Lenin, Nikolai, 73
Leutwiler, F., 10, 153
Lithuania, 67
Livestock, 138–39. *See also* Agriculture
Loans, domestic: Belgium, 97; Bolivia, 112; France, 87–91; Portugal, 97; Switzerland, 143
Loans, foreign: Austria, 47–50; Italy, 98, 101, 103; Paraguay, 120; Poland, 69
Luther, Hans, 57–59, 66
Lutz, Friedrich A., 99
Lutz, Vera C., 99

Machlup, Fritz, 10
Malaysia, 173
Marshall Plan, 100, 104
Menichella, Donato, 100, 106
Michalski program (Poland), 67–68
Momentum, 1–2
Money supply: Argentina, 128, 130–31, 134, 136–39; Austria, 45–52; and balance of payments, 8; Bolivia, 108–11, 116; Colombia, 78–79; and credit, 8, 24; Czechoslovakia, 81–82; debt, public, 96–97; deficit spending, 7–9; and exchange rate, 34; expectations, 32–33; France, 85; Germany, 12–13,

51, 56–66, 157–58, 160–62, 164, 166; and gold value, 12–13; Hungary, 51, 53, 55; and indexing, 176; inflation, degree of, 1–2, 7–9, 21, 32–33; inflation fallacies, 12–14; and interest rates, 164; Italy, 98–99, 101–03, 105–06; Japan, 167–68, 170; and multiple exchange rates, 9–10; Paraguay, 119–25; Poland, 71; political conditions, 22; price levels, 36, 165; and productivity, 9; real-bills doctrine, 13; rediscounts, 158–59; restraints, 15, 17–21, 36; Russia, 72–73; Singapore, 172–73; and state enterprise, 9; Switzerland, 141–43, 149–50, 152–56; and unemployment, 21; wartime, 14; Yugoslavia, 51. *See also* Currency

National Bank (Austria), 50
National Bank (Belgium), 97
National Development Bank (Paraguay), 124
National Monetary Stabilization Council (Bolivia), 111–13, 115–16, 119
National Mortgage Bank (Argentina), 130–31, 133
National Trade Union Congress (Singapore), 173
National Wages Council (Singapore), 173
Nationalization: Argentina, 130–31; Bolivia, 108, 112
Needs-of-trade doctrine. *See* Real-bills doctrine
Neumann, Manfred J. M., 158
New Economic Policy (Russia), 72
Nixon, Richard, 35

OECD. *See* Organisation for Economic Cooperation and Development (OECD)
Okun, Arthur, 16
OPEC. *See* Organization of Petroleum Exporting Countries (OPEC)
Open-market operations, 143
Organisation for Economic Cooperation and Development (OECD), 150, 162, 169
Organization of Petroleum Exporting Countries (OPEC), 10

Pablo, Juan Carlos de, 39–40, 135, 137
Paraguay: stabilization efforts (1956–1962), 34, 119–26
Paz Estenssoro, Víctor, 119
Pazos, Felipe, 16, 138
Pensions: Austria, 45, 50; Hungary, 53

People's Action Party (Singapore), 174
Perón, Juan, 128–29, 139
Phillips curve, 20–21
Pigou effect, 6
Pilsudski, Jozef, 71–72
Poincaré, Raymond, 10, 88, 93–95
Poland, 51, 74; stabilization efforts (1920s), 67–72
Polish Socialist Party, 71
Polish State Loan Bank, 69
Political conditions: Argentina, 128, 134, 138–40; Austria, 47, 52; Bolivia, 110, 114–15, 118–19; corruption, 110, 118–19; distortion, 4; France, 87–93, 96; Germany, 56–67; Hungary, 53; inflationary, 10–12; inflation restraining, 7, 12, 31; Italy, 100, 103; Japan, 171; money supply, 22; multiple-exchange-rate systems, 9–10; Paraguay, 119, 123, 126; Poland, 67, 70–72; Portugal, 97–98; Singapore, 174; stabilization, gradual, 40; stabilization, quick-fix, 42; Switzerland, 148
Popkin, Joel, 25–26
Portugal: stabilization efforts (1920s), 97–98
Prebisch, Raúl, 129
Price levels: Argentina, 16, 126, 131–40; Austria, 45–46; Bolivia, 109, 110, 112–15, 117–18; Chile, 16; and competition, 28; controls, 34–36; cost-push theory, 25–26; Czechoslovakia, 81, 83–85; deficit, government, 8; distortion, 3–4, 16, 24, 33; expectations, 32; France, 89–91, 95; Germany, 56, 61–62, 157–58, 162–63, 165–66, 170–71; Hungary, 54; and indexing, 176–77; inflation duration, 16–21; Italy, 98–99, 104–07; Japan, 169–71; and money supply, 36, 165; Paraguay, 119–24, 126; Poland, 68, 70–71; and profits, 7, 32; real-bills fallacy, 13; Russia, 74–76; Singapore, 171–74; and social conditions, 3; stabilization efforts, 22–23, 38–44; Switzerland, 141–42, 145, 148, 150, 152–53, 156, 170–71; United States, 33; unresponsive, 25–26; wartime, 14–15. See also Consumer price index; Wholesale price index
Production: Argentina, 128, 131–33, 138; Bolivia, 117–19; and competition, 23; controls, 34–35; Czechoslovakia, 82; distortion, 3, 23, 27; France, 95; Germany, 65, 164; and indexing, 176–77; inflation effect, 2, 7, 33; Italy, 99, 105–07; Japan, 167,

169–70; and labor, 2; money supply effect, 9, 20; Paraguay, 122; Poland, 71; real-bills fallacy, 13; stabilization effects, 22–23, 25–27, 35, 118; Switzerland, 151; and wage rates, 7
Profits, 7, 148
Psychological factors. See Expectations; Political conditions; Social conditions
Public enterprise. See State enterprise

Rabin, Alan, 161
Rašín, Alois, 80–82, 84
Rationing, 73. See also Subsidies
Real-bills doctrine, 13; Czechoslovakia, 81–82; France, 91; Germany, 56; needs of trade, 36–37
Rediscounts, 158–59
Reichsbank (Germany), 13, 56, 58–59, 62–67
Rentenbank (Germany), 58–59, 62, 66
Reparation Commission: Austria, 45, 49; Hungary, 52–54
Reparations, 96; Czechoslovakia, 84; France, 87, 96; Germany, 54, 56–57, 62, 66, 87, 96
Reserves, bank: Argentina, 132–33, 136; and balance of payments, 168; Bolivia, 112; and credit policy, 162; Germany, 66, 158–59, 161–62; Italy, 100–01, 103; Japan, 168; Paraguay, 120–21, 124–25; rediscounts, 158–59; Switzerland, 146–48
Resource allocation: Austria, 51; distortions, 4, 23–24, 38, 51; Germany, 65; Pigou effect, 6
Retail price index. See Consumer price index
Rose, Victor R., 116
Rothschild, Edouard de, 92
Ruhr, 56–57, 62, 66, 84, 87
Rumania, 53
Russia, 67; stabilization efforts (1920s), 72–78

Savings: Argentina, 129–33; distortions, 5–6; Germany, 65; Hungary, 54; and indexing, 177; Italy, 99, 107; Japan, 167; Paraguay, 122, 124; Pigou effect, 6; and stabilization, 65
Schacht, Hjalmar, 10, 59–60, 62–65, 67
Seipel, Monsignor Ignaz, 10, 47, 49
Siles Zuazo, Hernán, 111, 115–16, 119
Singapore: stabilization efforts (1970s), 171–74
Smithsonian Agreement (1971), 147, 157, 160, 170
Smuggling, 110, 112–14

A Note on the Book

The typeface used for the text of this book is
Palatino, designed by Hermann Zapf.
The type was set by
Maryland Linotype Composition Company, of Baltimore.
Thomson-Shore, Inc., of Dexter, Michigan, printed
and bound the book, using Warren's Olde Style paper.
The cover and format were designed by Pat Taylor.
The manuscript was edited by Ann Petty, and
by Anne Gurian of the AEI Publications staff.